EISENHOWER AND CHURCHILL

The Partnership That Saved the World

James C. Humes

FORUM

An Imprint of Prima Publishing

Published by Prima Publishing, Roseville, California. Member of the Crown Publishing Group, a division of Random House, Inc.

Random House, Inc. New York, Toronto, London, Sydney, Auckland

PRIMA PUBLISHING, FORUM, and colophons are trademarks of Random House, Inc., registered with the United States Patent and Trademark Office.

Library of Congress Cataloging-in-Publication Data
Humes, James C.
   Eisenhower and Churchill : the partnership that saved the world / James C. Humes.
   p. cm.
   Includes index.
   ISBN 0-7615-2561-0
   1. World War, 1939–1945—Biography. 2. Eisenhower, Dwight D. (Dwight David), 1890–1969. 3. Churchill, Winston, 1871–1947. 4. Prime Ministers—Great Britain—Biography. 5. Generals—United States—Biography. I. Title.
   D736 .H86   2001
   940.53'092'2—dc21   001040172

01 02 03 04 HH 10 9 8 7 6 5 4 3 2 1
Printed in the United States of America

First Edition

Visit us online at www.primaforum.com

To Henry Luce III,
whose presidency has revived the Society of the Pilgrims,
the oldest Anglo-American organization—a leadership that
would have gladdened the heart of his father
whose two greatest heroes were Churchill and Eisenhower.

CONTENTS

FOREWORD

IN THE TWENTIETH CENTURY, no two men did more than Winston Churchill and Dwight Eisenhower to combat the twin evils of tyranny: fascism and communism. And for the most significant passages of their historic public careers, they worked in partnership, representing different nations and in distinctly different capacities and roles.

In the Second World War, if Churchill was the voice of freedom, Eisenhower provided the implementing hands.

With the vision of an Old Testament prophet, Churchill will forever be known as the first Western statesman to decry the rise of Nazism, and his stirring rhetoric would rally England and the Free World at the precipice of defeat. And after the ultimate victory over Germany, Churchill, in his Iron Curtain speech, became the first Western statesman to warn against the Stalinist threat to Europe. Genius and moral leadership are terms that describe Sir Winston, arguably, the leading man of the century.

Eisenhower's gifts lay not so much in his voice or in an articulated vision but in organizational brilliance and perceptiveness about people. Military strategist and diplomat are terms that describe him. As commander of the combined Allied force in northwest Europe, Eisenhower staged the greatest amphibious landings in military history. As a military diplomat, he forged the most celebrated integrated command in history. And as a naturally gifted politician, Eisenhower would go on to become president of the United States at the height of the cold war struggle for which Churchill had mobilized the sentiments of the Free World.

The relationship between two such different men would be interesting in any context, but it is of special historical interest for several reasons. First, the cause they served together succeeded. Second, that success was completely dependent on cooperative efforts by an international coalition, hence the importance of their working relationship, one that succeeded though the relationship defied easy definitions of protocol and was rarely one of equals. During the war, Eisenhower, as an Allied military commander, was ostensibly subordinate to the British prime minister, though technically he was accountable only to a combined U.S.–British authority over which British influence steadily waned. As the war progressed, as differences of opinion arose, differences stemming from the contrasting outlooks of a military–minded officer and a politically oriented prime minister, the "subordinate" Eisenhower tended to prevail more and more against his "superior" Churchill. But invariably, the clash of views led to consensus and unprecedented Allied effectiveness.

The unevenness in rank continued in 1951, when their earlier collaboration resumed with Churchill's return as prime minister and Truman's designation of Eisenhower to lead the fledgling NATO command. Again, if Churchill's warnings served to galvanize the Free World to action, it was Eisenhower who organized the military and organizational might that consolidated the Atlantic alliance that would prevail in time over the Soviets. When Eisenhower was elected president in 1952, the relationship changed again. Eisenhower became Head of State—equivalent to the King—while Churchill remained Head of Government. More important, an economically bankrupt Britain that was losing its empire was no longer the equal of the United States. Incontestably, the Americans had assumed leadership.

The familiar differences in outlook remained, and despite Eisenhower's formal seniority, the pattern of their personal relationship seems unaffected. The aging statesman, who had invented the word "summit" conference, unsuccessfully pressed Eisenhower at the outset of his presidency to engage the Soviets in discussions, only to get his way eventually. Arguably, it was in the years 1953–1955, Churchill's last as prime minister, Eisenhower's first as president, that the alliance they both cherished became a bipartisan commitment and a geopolitical fact.

In assessing the successful collaboration between these two men, historians may be prone to emphasize impersonal forces that compelled cooperation among the allies. But it would be a mistake to ignore the personal factor. Put simply, Churchill and Eisenhower worked well together because they got along. They did so because Churchill appreciated and esteemed Eisenhower's professional and personal qualities, and Eisenhower knew it. And for his part, Eisenhower revered Churchill as a personal hero, which Churchill doubtlessly knew, enhancing Churchill's esteem for Eisenhower.

Indeed, through the years, the warmth of friendship ever increased by each talk on the phone, by every exchange by letter, or during their personal meetings in Washington, one of which I observed as a child.

The day was Monday, May 4, 1959. As grandchildren of the President, my three sisters and I were permitted to leave school early in nearby Alexandria to greet Sir Winston Churchill, now retired, who had arrived in Washington for several days as Granddad's guest in the White House. Often in those days, the grandchildren had been included in "socials" for prominent foreign visitors. But this one was special, and it will always stand out in my mind, not so much because of Churchill's fame and renown—we had met Queen Elizabeth, Nehru, MacMillan, and Krushchev, to name a few—but because of Granddad's demeanor and conduct. Diminished by age and strokes, Sir Winston had difficulty getting around and he occasionally lapsed into silences when we gathered in the west hall of the White House. But Granddad was completely thrilled to have him anyway. Usually formal with visitors, Granddad completely doted on Sir Winston, physically guiding him around the room, tending to his wants, filling the silences with cheerful stories and reports lest Sir Winston be taxed. At dinner, he startled my mother with an aside: "If only you could have spent five minutes with him in his prime," Granddad whispered.

Their backgrounds could not have been more different—the grandson of an English duke and a small town Kansas boy who grew up on the wrong side of the tracks. And as James Humes emphasizes in this book, they shared many common interests and passions and, in several key ways, had parallel experiences. Perhaps the most important similarity was that both were graduates of military academies. During the Great War and afterwards, both championed the tank and embraced the new doctrines of mobile warfare. Interestingly, both were to be the first heads of government in their respective country to be licensed pilots. In the twenties, they each suffered the loss of a child in the same year. In the thirties, in the prime of life, Churchill and Eisenhower simultaneously endured analogous frustration—of political exile in Churchill's case, of obscurity in Eisenhower's. Both men had powerful premonitions of the coming catastrophe in Europe and of the challenges ahead; having quit the cabinet, Churchill spent most of the decade at his Chartwell estate running a virtual "shadow" government; by early 1938, in the faraway Philippines, restless under the imperious General MacArthur and transfixed by developments a world away in Europe, Eisenhower began priming himself for eventual command duty in the inevitable European war.

And not the least, Eisenhower and Churchill would find relief from stress in painting. It has often been said of Churchill that had he devoted himself to painting, he would have been one of the greatest artists of the century. Eisenhower took up painting during the war, inspired by the example of several British colleagues, including Churchill. As painters, Eisenhower and Churchill were especially adept at landscapes, finding tranquility in quiet hours spent in contemplating the harmony and wonders of the outdoors.

Finally, transcending common interests and passions, Eisenhower and Churchill shared a love of freedom and a hatred of tyranny. Eisenhower's resolve to combat fascism and communism was no less fervent than Churchill's and rooted in a similar appreciation of the peculiar threat posed by twentieth century totalitarianism to the nineteenth century values that shaped both men. Both Churchill and Eisenhower were galvanized to action and to greatness in war, both contributing mightily to the Anglo-American partnership that literally saved the world in their time. Indeed, the world was fortunate to have the wisdom and valor of their leadership, their knack for cooperation, their distinct patriotisms, and their common humanity. Churchill and Eisenhower is a story for the ages—and the story of this book.

—David Eisenhower

ACKNOWLEDGMENTS

WERE IT NOT for my mother, I would not have accepted an English Speaking Union (ESU) scholarship for a year to Stowe School in England. It was the 1952–1953 year in between Hill School and Williams, and in that magic year I danced with the queen and met Winston Churchill. The seventy-eight-year-old prime minister told this eighteen-year-old schoolboy on May 28, 1953, "Study history; in history lie all the secrets of statecraft."

Mother was an Anglophile who would wake me from a nap to hear Winston Churchill speak in 1940. My first long trousers were a copy of an RAF uniform, with miniature wings awarded to my mother for her volunteer work for Bundles for Britain. My daughters inherited the mania. My younger, Rachel, also went to Stowe on an ESU arrangement. The older, Mary, studied "Greats" at Oxford after Harvard. While managing editor of the Harvard *Crimson*, when asked her politics, she replied, "Monarchist."

And were it not for my wife, Dianne, I would never have become friends with the Eisenhower family. She worked in the Eisenhower White House. (She was one of the few who found Governor Sherman Adams, the former governor of New Hampshire, warm and friendly, perhaps because they were both New Englanders.) She first served under her fellow Massachusetts native Max Rabb and then under Robert Gray in the area of appointments. While she was there, we met and became acquainted with Roemer McPhee (who had been friends with my cousin John Humes at Princeton), Ed McCabe, and Gerry Morgan while I was attending George Washington Law School. (In 1961, I clerked at their law firm, Hamel, Morgan, Park, and Saunders, in Washington.) Others we met and saw regularly included Ann Whitman; Mary Jane McCaffery, the social secretary; and Abbott Washburn. Another was Rev. Fred Fox, a former Congregational minister for whom I taught Sunday school while at Williams College. In late 1960 Fox had me write a few ceremonial remarks for an Oval Office presentation by President Eisenhower.

In 1962, while a candidate for the Pennsylvania General Assembly, I was invited to Gettysburg to see General Eisenhower. We discussed Churchill, to whom Eisenhower had just sent a letter, wishing him congratulations on his sixtieth year in the House of Commons. In 1967 I also drafted some remarks for Eisenhower. I was at the time working with then Col. John Eisenhower, who headed an early national citizens committee for Nixon.

Over the years I have kept up my friendship with John Eisenhower. He is a scholar and an intellectual (although he would deny the description). He is also one of the world's finest military historians. His children, David and Susan, have inherited his writing ability. Their mother, Barbara, has been a familiar warm face and friend for thirty-five years!

I was also a guest of Milton Eisenhower for two nights at his home at Johns Hopkins University. He regaled me with stories of his youth with Ike in Abilene. He insisted that Ike was "the most intelligent of all the Eisenhower brothers."

David and Julie Nixon Eisenhower have been both personal and political friends with Dianne and me, sharing our passion for politics and history (and with David and myself, baseball.) David wrote the foreword for my book *The Wit and Wisdom of*

Benjamin Franklin, and Julie wrote the foreword to my autobiography, *Confessions of a White House Ghost Writer: Five Presidents and Other Political Adventures.* Julie's father, President Nixon, for whom I was a one-time White House writer, wrote the introduction to my book *The Wit and Wisdom of Winston Churchill.*

In the half century since I studied at Stowe, I have also made many British friends, including some from the Churchill family. Sir Winston's son Randolph entertained me at a dinner in Blackpool in 1963. (I was then a Pennsylvania legislator on an ESU speaking tour in England and attending the Conservative Party conference at that seaside resort.) Randolph really was an entertaining host and raconteur. I have also many times been the guest of Winston Churchill II, his son, in the House of Commons, at his house, and at his club, Bucks. Winston has inherited the Churchillian flair at the podium and facility with the pen.

I have come to consider as a friend his cousin Edwina Sandys of New York, who has inherited from her grandfather not only his sandy hair and fair complexion but also his artistic flair. She is a prize-winning artist and sculptor. Her sculpture from the ruins of the Berlin Wall now adorns the Churchill Museum at Westminster College in Fulton, Missouri, where I once spoke on the thirty-third anniversary of Churchill's "Iron Curtain" address at that college.

I have twice been the guest of the venerable Grace Hamblin, once a Churchill secretary, who now lives at Westerham, Kent (near Churchill's home, Chartwell). A statue of Sir Winston stands outside her cottage. She is a fascinating source of anecdotes about Churchill and his working habits and private pleasures. I was referred to Grace Hamblin by Anthony Montague-Browne, private parliamentary servant (PPS) to Sir Winston for a score of years until Churchill's death. A fellow Old Stoic, he arranged for me to meet Lady Churchill in 1966 at a formal dinner honoring her husband, who had died the year before.

My wife and I were also the household guests of Lord and Lady Avon in 1970. The former Anthony Eden was then the leader of the Conservative Party in the House of Lords. His wife, Clarissa, was Churchill's niece. In that visit I learned much about Churchill's wartime tenure as prime minister.

Her brother John Spencer Churchill (another artist, as well as raconteur) was our guest twice in our house in Washington. He was full of stories about his grandmother Lady Randolph. Through John Churchill, I met the late Kay Halle, a friend of the Churchill family who authored books on Churchill and his son, Randolph. When I lived in Philadelphia and visited Washington, I was often a guest at her home at Dent Place in Georgetown. She was the key figure in organizing the honorary U.S. citizenship granted Sir Winston in 1963. She had been a frequent guest at Chartwell both during the 1930s and later after World War II. I also dined in a small group with former Prime Minister Harold Macmillan (later Earl of Stockton) twice, once in 1966 at a small table at the Beefsteak Club in London and again at the Smithsonian Institution, where he spoke in 1981.

In 1960 I met in Washington, as a delegate to the Young Political Leaders of NATO conference, the Hon. James Dugdale (now the second Baron Crathorne). We, the two "Jamies," have been friends for over forty years. His father, Sir Thomas Dugdale, was a PPS to Prime Minister Stanley Baldwin and later a minister in Churchill's second cabinet. He hosted us at Crathorne Hall in Yorkshire on two occasions. His son Jamie Crathorne, a godson of Lord Mountbatten, now heads the Arts Committee in the House of Lords. Lord Crathorne wrote the introduction to my biography *Citizen Shakespeare*. He is a frequent lecturer and writer on art and has spoken at the Metropolitan Museum on "The Palace of Westminster."

Other English friends include Commander and Baroness Byford. Hazel's father was Sir Cyril Osborne, who served in the House of Commons during the Churchill era for many years as a Conservative from Leicestershire. Hazel is now the "shadow minister" in charge of agricultural matters for the Conservative Party in the House of Lords.

Lord Cope, who once served in the Thatcher and Major governments, is a principal leader of the Conservative opposition party in the House of Lords. John and Djemila Cope encouraged me to write this book some years ago.

I should also mention Sir Alec Douglas-Home, once prime minister and twice foreign secretary. His mother, the Countess of Home, gave a reception for us when my wife and I were married in Scotland in 1957. He was our host once at a luncheon in Carlton Gardens when he was foreign secretary and again in the House of Lords a year before he died. (I am distant kin, being a member of the Hume clan.) Home, as former Prime Minister Edward Heath told me, was "next to Churchill the greatest prime minister in terms of character, integrity, and principle in this century." His sister-in-law, Felicity Douglas-Home, continues to be a warm friend whom we see in Scotland.

And let me particularly thank Dan Holt at the Eisenhower Library in Abilene and his archivist, Jim Leyerzapf, who sent me materials, as well as assisted me in the two days I spent there.

While serving on the Executive Committee of the Pilgrims, the premier organization devoted to Anglo-American relations, I had the good fortune of making friends with Herbert Brownell, perhaps President Eisenhower's finest appointment and certainly one of the greatest U.S. attorney generals in history. I learned much from him about the maneuverings to draft, nominate, and elect General Eisenhower; I have also spoken several times with a fellow Pilgrim, Dr. Grayson Kirk, who succeeded General Eisenhower as president of Columbia. Furthermore, no one helps more to keep Churchill's memory alive than Richard Langworth, C.B.E., president of the International

Churchill Society. That society's regular publication, *The Finest Hour*, has been a continual resource.

I also want to mention my frequent visits and lunches with former Gov. Harold Stassen, Sen. Hugh Scott, and former Gov. Jim Duff. I used to lunch often with Stassen at our Union League Club. Scott and I were allied in Pennsylvania politics from 1956 until his retirement in 1976. An erudite and wily politician, Scott was like a Medici prince who could spend the morning inspecting his *objets d'art* and the afternoon plotting to destroy a political rival. Duff, who gave our family a dog that we named for him, hosted us on several occasions at his farm near Harrisburg.

Of course, no book on Churchill is possible without referring to my friend Sir Martin Gilbert, the historian and author of the most monumental biography on Churchill ever written.

In a list of friends, I want to thank Dr. Jarvis Ryals, who accompanied me on my trip in 2000 to London, where I saw Winston Churchill II, Grace Hamblin, former Prime Minister Heath, and others. Jarvis and Mary Jo established me as Ryals Professor of Language and Leadership at the University of Southern Colorado. I also wish to thank Bob Rawlings, publisher of the *Pueblo Chieftain*, who encourages my op-ed articles on Churchill and Eisenhower. (Mamie Eisenhower once lived in Pueblo.) I am grateful to Dick Eisenbeis, my friend from childhood, whose efforts helped bring me to USC to teach and write; to West Pointer and neighbor Col. Al Hughes; and to Gen. Charlie West, who runs "The Ends of the Earth," the oldest Anglo-American military society, of which I am president. I also include Gerry Dumont of Lansdowne Resort, who has for seven years hosted dinners celebrating Churchill.

Another who pressed me to write this book is former Congressman John LeBoutillier. He and his mother, Pamela, are cousins of the Duke of Marlborough. Another who encouraged me is my son-in-law Cecil Quillen, the husband of Mary and father of Caroline and James. Cecil, a Phi Beta Kappa from Harvard, is the best-read student of presidential history of my acquaintance.

For typing assistance, I thank Debra McLean. I am grateful to the capable Katie Gomez. In particular, I am appreciative of Carol Prichard Toponce for her proofreading, advice, and last-minute help.

Finally, Patricia Waldygo, my copy editor, did wonders in straightening out my pronoun references and reversing my passive voice, among other improvements.

ST. PAUL'S CATHEDRAL, LONDON, 1965

Here was a champion of freedom.

— DWIGHT DAVID EISENHOWER

THE *LONDON TIMES* editorialized on January 12, 1965, "No one can predict when the end will come but death is now certain." Two days before, Churchill had suffered a massive stroke and then had slipped into a coma days later. But the date of his death had been prophesied much earlier. Churchill himself had said on at least three occasions that he would die on the day his father, Lord Randolph, had died. And so he did. Sir Winston Churchill died on the morning of January 24, 1965. The doctor determined the time as 8 A.M.—seventy years from the day and the minute of his father's death in 1895.

From the time Churchill had returned to his home at 28 Hyde Park Gate from King George V Hospital in September 1964, it had been a gentle decline for the venerable warrior. On November 30, he celebrated his ninetieth birthday. His wife gave him a small golden heart engraved with the figure 90. Before lunch, Lady Churchill gathered the nursing staff in his bedroom for a glass of champagne. After lunch, he appeared in a photograph from the window in his 28 Hyde Park Gate, London, townhouse. He was a slumped and feeble figure in a chair, with his limp hand raised in a "V"-fingered salute. Among the 70,000 greetings was a letter from his friend and fellow leader in war and peace General Eisenhower:

> On this your Ninetieth Anniversary I take particular pleasure in sending you felicitations. Our long and warm friendship is a source of great pride to me and I only wish that occasionally we could again have the opportunity to visit together.
>
> Mamie joins me in these sentiments and in sending to Clementine our affectionate greetings.
>
> Happy Birthday and may the years to come be filled with all good things.
>
> *Ike*

Another note came from Mexico City. A little girl had designed her own birthday card with birds and flowers. She had addressed the card, "To the greatest Man in the world." Without a stamp, it arrived at the Churchill address.

The family members who gathered at Churchill's London house knew it would be the last birthday celebration. In December Sir John "Jock" Colville dropped by to pay a visit to his former chief. Colville had been private secretary to Churchill in both of his tenures as prime minister. Colville, who had also served Neville Chamberlain in that capacity, had not been at first an admirer of Churchill, but over the years Colville's initial distrust had turned to esteem and reverence.

Colville approached the seated Churchill. "Sir Winston," he said. Churchill showed no recognition of his former aide.

Lady Churchill interrupted: "Winston, you remember Jock." Still there was no response. Colville chatted with Lady Churchill as minutes passed.

Then Churchill spoke: "It's been a grand journey—well worth taking," and then with a pause he added, "once!"

Days later—just before the last stroke—he muttered to his son-in-law Christopher Soames, "I am tired of it all." These were his last recorded words. On January 10 he suffered that massive stroke and slipped into a coma. The vigil for his death had begun.

On the other side of the Atlantic Ocean, in Palm Springs, California, General Eisenhower received word of Churchill's stroke on January 11. He knew immediately that this was the end for his friend, the old warrior. Death, he estimated, might take place around the time of President Johnson's inauguration. That did not particularly concern Eisenhower, since he had no plans to attend the ceremony. Lyndon Johnson had won the election in his own right the previous November, in a landslide defeat of Sen. Barry Goldwater. Eisenhower had given nominal support to the Republican candidate in a hopeless cause. He felt no animus toward Lyndon Johnson. In fact, he was far better disposed toward Johnson than he had been toward Johnson's predecessor, John Kennedy. Kennedy's campaign invention of the "missile gap" particularly infuriated the old general, who felt he had forgotten more about defense than Senator Kennedy had ever known.

Eisenhower, who had been born in Denison, Texas, had enjoyed a cordial relationship with Sen. Lyndon Johnson, when he was the Senate majority leader during Eisenhower's presidency. (It was the first time in history that the president, Senate majority leader, and speaker of the House [Sam Rayburn] were all natives of the same state.)

In Palm Springs, Ike drafted a contingency letter for the English Speaking Union to send out from its New York office when Churchill's death came. General Eisenhower was the chairman of the organization in the United States (Prince Philip still heads its counterpart in the United Kingdom).

Lady Churchill:

My heartfelt sympathy to you and the whole British nation over Sir Winston's death, which is a heavy blow to all Americans and to me. Not only did I serve with him in the struggle for freedom in the last war but as Chairman of the English Speaking Union I have also been privileged to work with him for the preservation of the spiritual unity between our peoples which he did so much to establish and strengthen.

Winston Spencer Churchill will be sorely missed by people of all races and countries but particularly those who have been inspired by his famous statement: "I am an English Speaking Union."

With profound admiration and affection.

Dwight D. Eisenhower
Chairman
English Speaking Union

Eisenhower had been given a courtesy invitation to attend the inaugural festivities on January 21, but the president had not called or written to him with a personal invitation. Eisenhower considered it President Johnson's day in the sun and felt no obligation to attend unless the president so requested. And so Eisenhower stayed in southern California, his wife's favorite winter escape. He knew he would have to start clearing his calendar for a trip to the state funeral in London. Churchill had revealed, when last visiting Washington in 1959, his elaborate plans for his memorial service. He had called it "Operation Hope."

Eisenhower knew it would be a pageant the likes of which had not been seen since the death of Queen Victoria. The state funeral for Churchill would be a magnificent orchestrated ritual and spectacle, held at St. Paul's Cathedral. When the announcement of Churchill's death was read to the world, it was midnight in Palm Springs. Eisenhower heard it on the news the next morning and read the *Los Angeles Times*, whose front pages were covered with stories relating to Churchill's death and life.

President Johnson's statement that he would not attend the services in London surprised Eisenhower. Eisenhower would have gone if he had been in Johnson's place. It was an opportunity for the president to meet other world leaders, such as President Charles de Gaulle of France, Prime Minister Harold Wilson of Britain, Prime Minister Pierre Trudeau of Canada, and others. Face-to-face meetings with presidents and prime ministers, Eisenhower had found, were invaluable when in future days they had to talk on the telephone to iron out differences.

Eisenhower was also taken aback when President Johnson did not include him in the official delegation to represent the United States. Eisenhower had no quarrel with the selection of Vice President Hubert Humphrey or Chief Justice Earl Warren. They both held offices that were nominally second to that of the presidency in prestige. But President Johnson was not limited to only two for a delegation.

Despite the lack of presidential sanction, Eisenhower decided to go anyway, even if he had to sit in the back pew. He owed it to Churchill and his family. He also owed it to himself. When he informed the White House, a military jet was put at his disposal. Eisenhower would first have to stop in Gettysburg to pick up the right clothes. He planned to deliver a short eulogy if a proper time and occasion arose for it. Kevin McCann, his former speechwriter, was included in the Eisenhower contingent, along with his military aide Col. Robert Schultz and his personal aide Sergeant John Moaney. The president's official representatives, Chief Justice Warren and the newly inaugurated Vice President Humphrey, would be lodged at the new London Hilton on Piccadilly Street. Eisenhower opted for his old World War II haunts, the Dorchester hotel, where he always stayed in London. In fact, he had been there just the past

August, when he had last seen Churchill, who had been recovering from an earlier stroke in King George V hospital.

Colonel Schultz coordinated all the travel details with the White House. A military transport would pick up the general in Palm Springs and take him to Washington. After a day in Gettysburg, he would then take the same plane from Andrews Air Force Base to London.

On these two trips, memories of Churchill flooded his mind. Eisenhower first had met Churchill in December 1941, right after Pearl Harbor. The British prime minister had come to Washington with his top military advisers to discuss the war with their U.S. counterparts. During that visit, Churchill addressed the joint session of Congress ("If my father had been American and my mother English instead of the other way around, I might have gotten here on my own") and spent Christmas with the Roosevelts at the White House.

Churchill was no stranger to Major General Eisenhower. He had followed Churchill's career since World War I. Those U.S. army planners who saw the tank as the decisive weapon in the next war knew Churchill as the politician who fathered the tank against entrenched opposition. Eisenhower had headed one of the first tank schools in the U.S. Army.

As Eisenhower reflected on their first meeting, he recalled wryly that Churchill had suffered from no lack of confidence. Churchill had only one idea on how to win the war—his idea. Even though his military career had not advanced beyond the rank of major, Churchill propounded the details of military strategy like a field marshal.

The two men could not have had more different backgrounds. Churchill was born in a palace—Blenheim—the estate of the ninth duke of Marlborough. Eisenhower was born in Denison, Texas, in a rented shack. Eisenhower's grandfather had no title, unless you counted "pastor" because he was a Mennonite preacher.

Yet despite the contrast between the palace-born Englishman and the prairie-bred American, there was much in common. Both had fathers who had failed. Lord Randolph mounted a meteoric career, becoming the youngest chancellor of the Exchequer in history, until it crashed in disgrace. David Eisenhower had asked for the equivalent of his inheritance of the farm and invested in a business that went bankrupt.

Despite their cold and unresponsive fathers, both sons revered their fathers. Eisenhower had renamed the presidential retreat of Shangri-La as Camp David, after David Eisenhower, and Churchill had adopted the trademark polka-dot bowtie of Lord Randolph and wore every day on his vest the gold timepiece and chain that belonged to his father.

Both suffered setbacks in getting into military school. Churchill had to take his exams three times before qualifying for Sandhurst. Eisenhower's first choice was Annapolis. A year later he made it into West Point.

World War I was not a happy time for either man. The disaster at Dardanelles was a blight on the Churchill reputation. For Eisenhower, never getting to go to France and see battle was almost as traumatic.

The year 1921 was a time of heartbreak for both men. Eisenhower's first child, Dwight David ("Icky"), died in January, as did Churchill's daughter Marigold in August. Both leaders in the 1930s sought out the U.S. financier Bernard Baruch for advice and counsel: Eisenhower for Baruch's ideas on industrial mobilization in time of war and Churchill for prudent investments for his book earnings.

The next decade contained years of frustration and discontent for both. "Back-bencher" Churchill was a voice in the wilderness—a latter-day Cassandra whose predictions of Nazi arms build-up fell on deaf ears—while Eisenhower chafed as the imperious General MacArthur's top aide, first in Washington and then in the Philippines.

Over their mutually shared choice of poison—Scotch and soda—Eisenhower and Churchill discussed their common interests and experiences. Both were early advocates of air power. Eisenhower told Churchill that he was the first president to have a pilot's license. He had earned one in the Philippines. Churchill was also the first prime minister to have flown a plane. As secretary of state for munitions in 1917, he flew to France every day to examine where supplies were needed and then reported back.

Each of them was called on to put down a massive protest and riot. Churchill in 1910 had to put down a Welsh miners' strike. Eisenhower, as chief of staff for General MacArthur, devised the Army's plan to handle with minimal injury the Bonus March in 1932 by World War I veterans.

In the beginning, the relationship between the two men was uneven in rank and often inharmonious in views. Churchill's domineering superiority riled Eisenhower. He thought of how his hero Washington must have felt when the Redcoat General Braddock had forced his views down the throats of what he considered those ill-bred colonials.

Not until much later did Eisenhower come to realize that Churchill's style was to dominate. He did it to British generals as well as to Americans. It was his way of eliciting views. Unlike MacArthur, however, Churchill relished and respected anyone who stood up to him, and he dismissed those whom he could roll over. He had contempt for what some British call "terminal colonels"—staff types whose mode of operation is to "kiss ass" and "cover their ass." If Churchill ever had the notion that Eisenhower, who had no battlefield experience, might fall into that category, he was soon disabused of it.

It was true that the British prime minister and the younger U.S. general had contrasting temperaments and styles. Churchill, by his command of language and forceful personality, would thrust his views on an audience. Eisenhower tried to insinuate his recommendations as his listener's idea. Churchill was confrontational, while Eisenhower was more collegial. Both did not suffer fools gladly, but Eisenhower knew how to mask his contempt. Churchill had the nature of an autocrat; Eisenhower was a born diplomat. And finally, both were men of considerable egos. Churchill paraded his, but Eisenhower repressed his.

Despite their initial suspicions of each other, mutual respect grew, followed by affection. What was at first adversarial grew more accommodating.

It was Churchill, Eisenhower told friends, who directed him toward oil painting as an avocation. Eisenhower once painted a portrait of Churchill, but the prime minister, who was the superior artist, did not reciprocate, saying, "I only paint pictures of landscapes, Ike, because a tree doesn't complain that I have done injustice."

Another escape they shared was a mutual fictional hero, C. S. Forester's Captain Horatio Hornblower, about whom they read during the war years.

When Eisenhower was elected president in 1952, a year after Churchill returned to 10 Downing Street as prime minister, their relationship had a new dimension. Now Eisenhower, as chief of state, outranked Churchill as head of government. More significantly, the wartime partnership of equal powers no longer was in effect. The older man was now the junior power in the "special relationship."

But the friendship was nevertheless on an equal basis. Eisenhower was no longer a military commander but commander in chief. As president, he had come even more to appreciate the lonely burden of leadership. He found that he could unburden himself to Churchill. They could easily share their ideas and hopes, which had not been possible in wartime London.

When President Eisenhower suffered his massive heart attack in August 1955, his mind again turned to Churchill, who two years earlier had been stricken by a cerebral hemorrhage. For over two months Churchill had been virtually incapacitated as prime minister.

Churchill had left 10 Downing Street that year of 1955, but in May 1959 Churchill—still, however, a member of Parliament—had visited Eisenhower as a private citizen. Eisenhower himself had experienced a slight cerebral incident two years earlier in November 1957. The pressures of office, the tolling efforts of stress on the body, and the afflictions it engendered were ordeals they both had endured.

Both Winston Churchill and Dwight Eisenhower harbored contempt for their successors. In 1959 they had the occasion to compare notes. Anthony Eden and John Kennedy were glamorous figures whose style exceeded substance, and both men had committed their nations to dubious military adventures—Suez and the Bay of Pigs. Both operations had ended in failure. In Prime Minister Eden's invasion of Suez and President Kennedy's Bay of Pigs in Cuba, each leader had attempted to impute the sanction of his prestigious predecessor. As a result, Churchill dismissed Eden as a "preening popinjay," whose failure to secure U.S. approval doomed his mission's success. Eisenhower privately railed at the inexperienced Kennedy for attempting the Cuban invasion "on the cheap."

On the air military transport to London, Eisenhower jotted down notes on a lined yellow tablet for his brief remarks at the Churchill memorial services. Eisenhower lacked neither talent nor experience in writing. True, he was no Churchill, for whom mastery of the English language was his staircase to power and leadership. Churchill never called on the talents of a speechwriter and won a Nobel Prize for Literature, for his speeches and histories. Yet Major Eisenhower had first caught the attention of General Pershing for his battlefield guidebook. In addition, General MacArthur had hand-picked Eisenhower as his chief of staff in Washington partly for

Eisenhower's writing skills. Later, Eisenhower drafted most of MacArthur's speeches in the Philippines. After the war, Eisenhower's bestselling *Crusade in Europe* was written without a ghost writer. But his efforts as a speechmaker dimmed any appreciation of his skills as a speechwriter. As president, he read texts prepared by writers, including the gifted Emry Hughes, a former *Time/Life* correspondent. Eisenhower's dry and halting delivery failed to do justice to the text. Yet if he was no Churchill in eloquence, he knew how to write an essay, as his diaries and field reports prove. After all, his scores in history, like those earned by Churchill at Harrow and Sandhurst, only exceeded his grades in English at Abilene High School and West Point.

In his first draft for the Churchill eulogy, Eisenhower began almost on a note of defensive pique:

> As the world pays its tribute to the giant who now passes from among us, I have no charter to speak for my countrymen[,] indeed only for myself.

It was a veiled rebuke to Lyndon Johnson, who had not appointed him to the delegation. In his redraft Eisenhower had second thoughts. His second draft majestically opened,

> Upon this mighty Thames, a great avenue of history, moves at this moment the mortal remains of Sir Winston Churchill. He was a great maker of history, the record closes, and we can almost hear him with the poet say:

> *Sunset and evening star and one clear call for me!* . . .
> *Twilight and evening bell,*
> *And after that the dark,*
> *And may there be no sadness of farewell*
> *When I embark.*

The Tennyson verse, which both Churchill and Eisenhower could recite from heart, was apt. And then Eisenhower improved his original opener with these lines:

As I, like all other free men, pause to pay a personal tribute to the giant who now passes from among us, I have no charter to speak for my countrymen—only for myself. But, if in memory, we journey back two decades to the time when America and Britain stood shoulder to shoulder in global conflict against tyranny, then I can presume—with propriety, I think—to act as spokesman for the millions of Americans who served with me and their British comrades during three years of war in this sector of the earth.

Eisenhower then thought of the opening title page of the five-volume *History of World War II* that Churchill had sent him, inscribed,

In War: Resolution
In Defeat; Defiance
In Victory; Magnanimity
In Peace; Good Will

With this as an inspiration Eisenhower wrote,

To those men Winston Churchill was Britain—he was the embodiment of British defiance to threat, her courage in adversity, her calmness in danger, her moderation in success. Among the Allies his name was spoken with respect, admiration, and affection. Although they loved to chuckle at his foibles, they knew he was a staunch friend. They felt his inspirational leadership. They counted him a fighter in their ranks.

The second draft changed little in the next paragraphs, except for a tightening of the sentence structure and pruning of some words:

The loyalty that the fighting forces of many nations here serving gave to him during that war was no less strong, no less freely given, than he had, in such full measure, from his own countrymen.

An American, I was one of those Allies. During those dramatic months, I was privileged to meet, to talk, to plan, and to work with him for common goals. Out of that association an abiding—and to me precious—friendship was forged; it withstood the trials and frictions inescapable among men of strong convictions, living in the atmosphere of war.

The war ended, our friendship flowered in the later and more subtle tests imposed by international politics. Then, each of us, holding high official posts in his own nation, strove together so to concert the strength of our two peoples that liberty might be preserved among men and the security of the free world wholly sustained.

Through a career during which personal victories alternated with defeats, glittering praise with bitter criticism, intense public activity with periods of semiretirement, Winston Churchill lived out his four score and ten years.

With no thought of the length of the time he might be permitted on earth, he was concerned only with the quality of the service he could render to his nation and to humanity. Though he had no fear of death, he coveted always the opportunity to continue that service.

The old soldier in Eisenhower emerged as he penned the next line:

At this moment, as our hearts stand at attention, we say our affectionate, though sad, goodbye to the leader to whom the entire body of free men owes so much.

Eisenhower—like Churchill—believed that every speech should resonate with a clear theme, like a dominant chord in a Beethoven symphony. For Eisenhower, this chord was the uniqueness of Churchill. His first draft ended a bit flat with "Here was a man." In the next draft he found his phrase, "champion of freedom":

In the coming years, many in countless words will strive to interpret the motives, describe the accomplishments, and extol the virtues of Winston Churchill—soldier, statesman, and citizen—that two great countries were proud to claim as their own. Among all the things so written or spoken, there will ring out through the entire century one incontestable refrain: Here was a champion of freedom.

Ann Whitman, Eisenhower's secretary, who after eight years in the White House had followed the general to Gettysburg, typed it up. Whitman, who had worked for Thomas Dewey in Albany before going to Washington, once told me she had a harder time reading Eisenhower's cramped handwriting than the neat script of the precise New York governor.

At the Dorchester Hotel in London, Eisenhower dictated a coda to the now typed draft, and signed his name at the end of it:

May God grant that we—and the generations who will remember him—heed the lessons he taught us: in his deeds, in his words, in his life.

May we carry on his work until no nation lies in captivity;
no man is denied opportunity for fulfillment.
And now, to you Sir Winston—my old friend—farewell!

Dwight D. Eisenhower

At the service at St. Paul's Cathedral on January 30, the general wore a dark gray three-piece suit. As protection against the bitter winds that swept across London that black, somber day, Eisenhower had on his dark topcoat and a Homburg hat atop his balding head as he mounted the cathedral steps to be ushered to his seat. Eisenhower sat with the fifteen heads of state, next to Chief Justice Warren and Vice President Humphrey.

Over the cathedral, Hurricane and Spitfire fighter planes soared in a "V" formation, piloted by those who twenty-five years ago had won the Battle of Britain. Eisenhower left his pew at the crypt to speak before the formal service began. His ruddy complexion was even pinker from the brisk winds outside. It lit up the dome of his head almost like a halo. He pulled out his clear-rimmed glasses and read his remarks in a measured voice. It only cracked with the final line ". . . my old friend—farewell!"

For Eisenhower, the closing of the services was the most poignant. Churchill had told him in May 1959 at Gettysburg something of his "Operation Hope," the plans for his funeral. Churchill said that the service would end with a hymn, for which his American mother had taught him the words. The anthem was also Eisenhower's favorite: "The Battle Hymn of the Republic."

Beside Eisenhower sat President de Gaulle of France, King Olaf of Norway, King Baudouin of Belgium, and Queen Juliana of the Netherlands—heads of state, whose countries' freedom had been redeemed by the warrior lying in state before them.

Their eyes surely misted with memory and gratitude as they sang out the words in the anthem: "He sounded forth the trumpet that shall never call retreat. . . . / His will goes marching on."

CHAPTER I

BLENHEIM PALACE

At Blenheim I took two very important decisions: to be born and to marry. I am content with the decision I took in both occasions.

WINSTON CHURCHILL

IT WAS ONLY by a coincidence of destiny that Winston Churchill was born in Blenheim Palace, the estate of the duke of Marlborough. Lord Randolph and Lady Churchill had planned to have their first child in London, where the best doctors were available. The townhouse they had chosen, 48 Charles Street in Berkley Square, would become available for occupation the second week of December. Lord Randolph's responsibilities in the House of Commons, to which he had been recently elected, required a city base. Randolph had been elected on February 4 and married on April 15 in Paris—a simple ceremony at the British Embassy there.

Although the passions of those two headstrong lovers had made the birth of their first son "premature," it was not expected to be quite that "'premature." In fact, it happened so suddenly that the mother didn't even have time to get to the bedroom. Winston's unexpected arrival in a coatroom of Blenheim Palace on November 30, 1874, was such a surprise that baby linens had to be borrowed from the wife of a nearby attorney. Perhaps the birth was induced by Lady Randolph's taking a bumpy carriage ride and then dancing at the Palace's St. Andrew's Eve Ball in the hours before the sudden delivery. Whatever the cause of Winston's unexpected entrance into the world, the place of birth in the home of one of England's greatest heroes must have shaped and colored the young Churchill's mind.

Dreams of glory were the escape of the lonely boy's life. His father, busy with parliamentary duties, had no time for him. His mother was more concerned by what she would wear to the fashionable parties in her smart London set, whose focal point was Queen Victoria's son and heir, the prince of Wales. The only real affection Churchill felt in his early years was for his nanny, Mrs. Everest, whom he called "woomany" for "woman." Today a photograph of Mrs. Everest occupies a niche of honor in Churchill's bedroom at Chartwell.

The solitary boy had no friends to romp with (his brother John was five years younger). He spent hours playing with his toy soldier collection. In the nursery he could pretend he was a king or, even better, the first duke of Marlborough, the captain-general John Churchill, who defeated the French on the German battlefield of Blenheim.

His maneuvering of miniature soldiers far surpassed those of the typical child. He organized wars; the metal battalions were pushed into formation. Peas and pebbles caused great casualties, forts were stormed, cavalries charged, bridges were destroyed. On one of those few occasions when he had a playmate, his cousin Clara Sheridan, he built a small log fort with an actual ditch for a moat and a drawbridge. But Sheridan wrote that she dissolved in tears and fled the fort when he began to throw rocks in an all-too-real storming of "the castle."

Winston Churchill's only son, Randolph, later wrote about his grandparents' treatment of his father. Winston's parents' neglect and lack of interest in him were remarkable even by the standard of late Victorian days. His letters to his mother teem with pathetic requests for letters and school visits. Lord Randolph was an ambitious politician whose whole interest was absorbed in politics, and Lady Randolph was caught up in the world of fashionable dinner parties.

The irony is that but for a snub, Lord Randolph might never have concentrated on a political career. He did so after social banishment by Edward, the Prince of Wales. Randolph's older brother, the Marlborough heir, had bedded the Countess Aylesford, who had been an inamorata of Prince Edward. This happened when Edward and the earl of Aylesford were on a state visit to India. An irate Edward, on hearing of the affair, persuaded the earl to bring divorce proceedings against his wife, with Lord Randolph's brother, the marquis of Blandford, being named co-respondent. Lord Randolph countered by threatening to leak to the press Edward's letters to his former mistress. Edward then let it be known that he would not set foot in any house that would invite Lord Randolph. In a London that took its cue from the sportive prince, Lord Randolph and his wife, Jennie, became pariahs.

The rebuff triggered the change in Lord Randolph from a social gadfly to a maverick politician. Excluded from the great homes of England, Lord Randolph decided to win recognition in the House of Commons.

If Lord Randolph had not chosen a career of politics, it is doubtful that his son would have made parliamentary fame his obsessive goal. To become a member of Parliament was a way of connecting with a father who had spent almost no time with him. Success in the House of Commons would also redeem his father's failure.

At first Lord Randolph was triumphant. He was one of the youngest chancellors of the Exchequer in history. Unlike his son, Lord Randolph could speak eloquently without any preparation. But his splendor was like a comet—flashing for a time in the sky, then crashing to the earth. His meteoric career was cut short by physical collapse and then early death, caused by what we know now to be syphilis. The only way Churchill could learn more about the father he never really knew was to read his speeches and his public papers. When a public figure of a father dies young, the orphaned son's tendency is to idolize and emulate the father to a far greater extent than when a longer life brings out the inherent masculine rivalry between two generations.

Lord Randolph's social exile turned his diversions to politics, and his membership in Parliament now qualified him to be selected as parliamentary assistant to the viceroy of Ireland. Lady Randolph, fretful and restless as a young beautiful bride with an empty calendar, encouraged her husband to take the job under his father, the duke of Marlborough. The viceroy of Ireland, ensconced in the royal castle of Dublin, was a deputy monarch.

Winston's first memory of his mother was of her standing in a receiving line, welcoming visitors to a state banquet or ball.

She stood on one side to the left of the entrance . . . a dark, lithe figure standing somewhat apart, and appearing to be another texture to those around her, radiant, translucent, and intense. A diamond star in her hair[,] her favorite ornament, its luster dimmed by the flashing glory of her eyes.

As he added later,

My mother seemed to me a fairy princess; a radiant being possessed of limited riches and power. She shone for me like the evening star. I loved her dearly but at a distance.

The remoteness of his parents spelled loneliness for the child. At first glance Winston, as a boy, seemed the Hollywood stereotype of the "poor little rich boy."

But the irony was that his parents were not really rich—at least, not by the standards of their social set. Lord Randolph, as the younger brother of the duke—under the British rule of primogeniture—was not an heir. Lord and Lady Randolph's spending tastes always exceeded the former's allowance. In those days, membership in Parliament was a gentleman's profession and received no stipend.

Nevertheless, Lord and Lady Randolph scraped enough money together to send Winston off at age seven to St. George's, a boarding school in Ascot near Windsor Castle.

Although it was not rare for upper-class parents to ship their children off to boarding school at such an early age, it is inexcusable that Lord and Lady Randolph knew so little about this dreadful school and its perverted headmaster. The Rev. H. W. Sneyd-Kynnersley had a name that suggested the Dickensian horrors that Victorian masters inflicted on their charges. Sneyd-Kynnersley seemed to be a psychopath who merged a bent for sodomy with sadism. His mistreatment of his students was only exceeded by his bootlicking obsequiousness to their parents.

At one point Sneyd-Kynnersley forced Churchill to run in a circle around a chair at full tilt for hours, until he collapsed in dizziness. A visitor, noticing the red-haired youth, asked the headmaster, "Who on earth is that?"

Sneyd-Kynnersley answered, "Why that's young Churchill, that's the only way we can keep him restrained."

But that sort of punishment, along with the almost daily floggings, did not subdue the Churchill spirit. In fact, Winston took revenge by finding the headmaster's straw hat and stomping it to pieces. Churchill's wretched career at St. George's was predicted by his first Latin lesson on opening day, when he was told to memorize the declension of the word *table*. Winston was puzzled by the vocative case.

"It means," said the master, "O table! You would use it in addressing a table or invoking a table."

"But I never speak at a table," replied the confused Winston.

"If you are impertinent, you will be punished, and punished, let me tell you, very severely," was the stern reprimand.

His parents did not notice the school's oppression of the child. Lord Randolph now was England's most talked-about and caricatured politician; he and his wife were again caught up in the social swirl. The attitude of the Prince of Wales, as Benjamin Disraeli had predicted, had thawed, and Randolph's career surged. Queen Victoria, Prince Edward's mother, had signaled the change by inviting Lord and Lady Randolph to Windsor.

Winston's parents may not have been concerned about the child, but his nanny, Mrs. Everest, was. She, no doubt, saw the bruises from birching and recommended a change. So, after two years at St. George's in Ascot, Winston was enrolled at Brighton, a school run by two genteel spinsters; the treatment was kind but the academic standard soft. Even with a less rigorous regimen, young Winston almost died from an attack of double pneumonia—possibly a delayed reaction to his abusive ordeal at St. George's. His lungs soon regained their strength, yet he remained heartsick. Winston yearned for any parental display of interest. At age ten he began avidly following newspaper accounts of the father he didn't really know. School for Winston was a prison term until vacations. One Christmas holiday he was left at the school for three weeks—despite his pleas—with hardly enough allowance to buy sweets. The only things that continually stirred his interest in the classroom were poetic readings or theatrical recitations. In letters to his mother, Churchill wrote that he enjoyed learning a poem by Sir Walter Scott, "Edinburgh After Flodden," and later Milton's "Paradise Lost." Even more fun were the plays the school put on, such as Gilbert and Sullivan's *The Mikado*, which Winston beseeched his mother to attend. His favorite gift as a child, besides his burgeoning tin soldier collection, was a toy theater that one of his two American aunts gave him, which, as he wrote to his mother, was a "source of unparalleled amusement."

The happiest moments of his Brighton years were his acting leads. He played the title role in *Robin Hood* and later had principal roles in dramas by Aristophanes and Molière. Perhaps the highlight of his three years at Brighton was his appearance as Dick Dowlas in Colman's play *The Heir at Law*. As the school's best actor, he was given the leading role in this 1808 melodrama. He brought down the house with his continued misreading of the line "I will send my carriage." Instead of "carriage," he said "carrot," which, as it was the color of his flaming hair, triggered gales of laughter. He was not so successful in his planned production of *Aladdin*, which, despite S.O.S. messages to home for more props, proved too ambitious for the school's capability.

Theater became the outlet for his pent-up frustrations. It was an avenue for his imagination and an escape from his lonely exile. In the world of make-believe, he could be that important personage he evidently was not in the eyes of his parents. Winston could, however, gain esteem in his own eyes. In acting, a lack of inhibition was an asset, and when Winston combined that with his exceptional memory, he found a talent that far exceeded that of his classmates.

In 1888, the twelve-year-old Winston was shipped off to Harrow. It was an odd choice because Eton was the family school that Lord Randolph, like generations before him, had attended. Eton was the premier school for the British elite.

The prime minister's son, Randolph, later wrote, "It seems strange that the twelve-year-old boy did not know that his father had been to Eton." Winston's son added that his father, in contrast, had taken him to inspect both institutions, and he had selected Eton. Winston's weak lungs were the reason given by Lady Randolph, Winston's mother. The school is located on the Harrow-on-the-Hill in London (old Harrovians affectionately refer to the school as "The Hill"). The higher-situated Harrow was chosen over Eton, which was situated in the wet swamps of the Thames Valley and was no place for Winston's frail constitution.

In retrospect, weakness of lungs was an unlikely assessment for someone who would become the twentieth century's greatest orator.

Lady Randolph also entertained the idea of sending him to a boarding school in her native land. She applied to St. Paul's in Concord, New Hampshire. But such a wet and wintry site hardly made sense if a cold climate would endanger Winston's frail health. Winston, however, was turned down by St. Paul's for insufficient grades at school. They did add in the rejection letter that her son displayed "a flair in English."

Winston loved English as much as he detested Latin and Greek. His failure in the classical tongues made him repeat his form. But his command of English grammar was such that he was asked to take over the English class and teach his classmates. For diagramming sentences, he developed the use of colors for parts of speech. Blue for the subject, red for the verb, yellow for an adjective, orange for an adverb, and green for a preposition.

Harrow, however, was not a happy experience for Churchill, who later wrote, "This intolerable school makes a somber gray pattern upon the chart of my journey. It was an unending spell of worries that was uncheered by frustration; a time of discomfort and purposeless mutiny."

At Harrow School, Winston did not win any prizes for his behavior and comportment. After a host of infractions, young Churchill was issued an order to report to the headmaster's office. When the thirteen-year-old Churchill entered the study, Dr. J. E. C. Welldon unfolded his six-foot frame from his chair and stared down at his subordinate student. With his hands folded behind his back, Welldon intoned, "Young man, I have grave reasons to be displeased with your conduct."

The boy Churchill looked up and replied, with equal solemnity, "And similarly I have grave reasons to be displeased with your conduct."

Besides acting, Winston's other escape from the bleak regimen of school was athletics. Team sports such as rugby, field hockey, and cricket did not interest him. He relished the spotlight of the solitary challenge in sporting pursuits such as swimming and fencing.

Churchill loved the newly constructed pool at Harrow. At fifteen, he was beating his elders of sixteen and seventeen in school meets. When he left Harrow, he held the best time in the free-style races.

Fencing appealed to his romantic notions of a cavalier. He imagined himself dueling against one of Cromwell's Roundheads for King Charles or sword-fighting French officers in Marlborough's army (actually, it was a French author who stirred most of his fancies—Dumas in *The Three Musketeers* and *The Count of Monte Cristo*). Churchill became Harrow's top fencer and earned its fencing cup.

In March 1882 he begged his father to come see him competing at the Public Schools Fencing Championship. His father, however, preferred the competition at the Ascot: "It is the races I must go to." None of his family saw Winston win the title of public school champion. The *Harrovian* wrote, "His success was chiefly due to his daring and dashing attack, which took his opponent by surprise."

At the time of the fencing championship he was studying hard for the Sandhurst entrance examination. He failed. Of the 693 candidates, he was 390th. Yet he was 18th in the history part of the exam.

In history he received the top grade for a paper predicting the first global war. In it, he foresaw a war fought in trenches with automatic stationary guns like machine guns. The autocratic adversary, however, was not czarist Russia but the Kaiser's Germany.

Churchill had the makings of a soldier. He enrolled in the army class at Harrow and also joined the school cadet force at

Harrow. He mastered the use of the Maritime-Henry rifle, the one used by the army.

Churchill, however, dreamed of carrying not a general's baton but a parliamentarian's dispatch case. His father's house was the House of Commons. That would be his own stage for his role as orator.

In his first year, 1888, he competed for the school prize for reciting a thousand lines of Shakespeare. He came close and wrote his father, "I was rather astonished as I beat some twenty boys who were much older than I."

The next year he tried again. This time it was a thousand lines from Macaulay's poem *The Lays of Ancient Rome*. The day before the event he found out that the required number of lines was actually twelve hundred. He stayed up all night in the bathroom to memorize the additional quotations. Some of the lines he recited were

> *Then none were for a party,*
> *Then all were for the state,*
> *Then the great man helped the poor,*
> *And the poor man loved the great.*
> *The lands were fairly portioned,*
> *And the Huns were fairly sold,*
> *The Britons were like brothers,*
> *In the brave days of old.*

In the rolls of Harrow today one can read "W. S. Churchill P." The "P" was for prize. It was Churchill's only scholastic honor at Harrow. Again, his parents did not attend Speech Day to see him win the prize.

Winston desperately wanted to make his father proud of him. He thought that somehow an accomplishment might break through the forlorn shell Lord Randolph had become. Lord

BLENHEIM PALACE • 27

Randolph at thirty-seven had been one of the youngest chancellors of the Exchequer in history—a position at 11 Downing Street, the second most powerful job in the government. But by the time Winston had entered Harrow, Lord Randolph had descended further into disgrace. In a reckless, self-destructive move, he had tried to topple his party's prime minister, Lord Salisbury, with the idea of replacing him. Because of this, he had been dismissed from office. It had been a mad action that might be explained by the disease that would hasten his death. The effects of syphilis ravage the brain.

While Winston was at Harrow, Lord Randolph—in his friend Lord Rosebery's words—was dying by inches. If in his decline Lord Randolph had few friends, his fiercest defender was his son. Winston's ambition was to redeem his father's reputation.

The first step was to be accepted at Sandhurst. That was his only chance for further education. He couldn't qualify for a university. If he failed to enter Sandhurst, he would have to go into some dreary London company as a stockbroker. His mother had talked to her friend Lord Rothschild about finding a slot for her son.

Once again, he took the Sandhurst exam. Again he failed. An applicant was only allowed to take the exam three times.

In studying for the exam, Churchill decided to concentrate on the geography question that amounted to one-fifth of the total grade. He snipped out maps of the British dominions from an atlas, dumped them into a top hat, and figured he had time to study only one. Putting his hand over his eyes, he shuffled them around and then picked one out. It was New Zealand.

He traced and retraced the North and South Islands, which constitute the empire dominion. On examination day, the sergeant major who was giving the exam wrote out on the blackboard, "Question #1 (20 points): Draw a map of New Zealand."

As Churchill told it later, "It was like breaking the bank at Monte Carlo. I drew both islands, put in the key cities and river. Then I added the parks, the libraries, and even the tram lines, I got the full twenty points and squeaked into Sandhurst with a sixty!"

CHAPTER 2

ABILENE

Abilene folk believed in education and its value.

DWIGHT DAVID EISENHOWER

IT WAS NOT David Eisenhower's plan to have his son Dwight David or any son born in Texas. The Eisenhowers were Kansans, but David's life had not turned out the way he had hoped. His aspiration was to become a successful merchant. He hated the field drudgery of his father's farm. Most of all, he wanted to escape his father's overseeing eye.

Jacob Eisenhower was a commanding figure in the Riverside Brethren community. The pastor of this Mennonite sect was a charismatic figure. His sermons in the German dialect of the Amish and Mennonites or even in his accented English thundered in eloquence. A full beard complemented his flashing eyes. One stern glance from Pastor Eisenhower could paralyze an errant member of his flock.

Jacob's son David, although tall and muscular, was daunted by his father's presence. The result was a shyness unleavened by any warmth.

When David asked for his inheritance, his father gave him 160 acres out of the Eisenhower farm and two thousand dollars in cash. David then mortgaged the farm to his brother-in-law and with the capital bought a general store in Hope, Kansas, a valley twenty miles south of Abilene.

In future years David Eisenhower would tell his grown sons the story of how he woke up one day to find his partner gone, along with most of the inventory. All that was left was a mountain of debts. The tale, which was repeated by Eisenhower's biographers, is far from accurate. Milton Good, the partner, did not disappear. Jacob Eisenhower, with the help of family money, had bought him out. The two men, the taciturn Eisenhower and the ebullient Good, were temperamental opposites. Good immersed himself in community affairs, and the introverted Eisenhower thought his partner far too generous in his subscription to civic projects. In the late 1880s a recession blighted rural Kansas and the Eisenhower and Good general store foundered. Certainly, David Eisenhower's pinched personality did little to help arrest the slide of customers. The humiliation of bankruptcy would hang on him like a shroud the rest of his life.

David Eisenhower could only find a job working for a railroad in Denison, Texas, at ten dollars a week. The family had to live in a small rented shack set by the railroad tracks. For David Eisenhower, who in his one year at Lane College in Compton, Kansas, had once dreamed of a professional career as a civil engineer, it was a wrenching comedown.

David Dwight Eisenhower was born in this frame shack on October 14, 1890. Because his father was also David, he was called Dwight (later he reversed the names, to Dwight David).

But Eisenhower's first substantial memories were of Abilene. By then, his father had moved back to Kansas. The River Brethren had built the Belle Springs creamery in Abilene, and David—always adept with farm machinery—was given the task of running the boiler engine for the operation. When David Eisenhower arrived at the Abilene rail station, he had twenty-four dollars in his pocket. His family moved into a small farmhouse flat until 1898, when the aging Jacob Eisenhower bought his son a spacious house on the condition that David and Ida Eisenhower would take care of him in his declining years.

To seven-year-old Dwight it must have seemed a mansion. It boasted a basement, two stories, and an attic. Behind the house was a barn, with a hayloft and stalls for animals.

Not until the Eisenhower boys (five of them—one died in infancy) went to school did they discover the only drawback of the house. It was on the wrong side of the tracks—the south side. A half century later two venerable old maid sisters, the owners of Abilene's only real mansion, the Seelye House, were asked if the Eisenhowers had ever been entertained at their home. "Goodness, no," they replied, "they were from the south side."

The social stigma bothered David more than it did his boys. It was a continuous reminder of his business failure and the collapse of his aspirations for prosperity and prestige. The stigma soured his life and made his relationship with his sons stiff.

David Eisenhower was a believer in the biblical axiom "Spare the rod and spoil the child." Lord Randolph Churchill may have had only five real conversations with his son Winston, but Dwight had at least five whippings by his father. Once David beat Dwight's one-year-older brother, Edgar, so hard that a tearful Dwight begged his father to stop, saying not even a dog should receive such a thrashing.

David's anger was not confined to his family. In a fit of rage he once seized the son of a neighbor boy and administered a solid spanking. The boy's father filed a complaint with the police, and David was arrested and put in the Abilene City jail. He was released only after paying a fine.

Yet like Winston Churchill's, Dwight Eisenhower's memories were only reverential. When David Eisenhower died in 1942, Dwight wrote of his father's "commanding presence," that he owed much to his father's "integrity, training and discipline." Dwight wrote in his diary, "I'm proud he was my father. ... I loved my dad."

David Eisenhower did implant at least two iron beliefs in his son's character: an antipathy to debt and the ambition to get out of Abilene. He didn't want his sons to suffer his own fate. Actually, the beating he had given Edgar was after discovering that his son was truant at school. Edgar had been working a part-time job without his father's knowledge.

The family was poor, and Dwight grew up thrifty. Later, in the shopping boom of the postwar years, Eisenhower said of his purchasing forays as a youngster, "You've heard of the guy who squeezed the penny so hard, the eagle screamed! Well, that was me!" But whereas Winston Churchill, growing up in London, thought he was rich, Dwight Eisenhower in Abilene didn't know he was poor. Even if hand-me-downs and patches on patches were the usual features of the boy's trousers, no one ever went hungry. Most of all—notwithstanding the dour David—the Eisenhower home was a happy one. The reason was Ida Stover Eisenhower.

Her eyes would sparkle merrily as she played the piano in the front parlor. In contrast to her tight-lipped husband, she had full and generous lips that suggested her unstinting affection. Her smile, which she bequeathed to her famous son, was as wide as Kansas. Ida Eisenhower was no beauty, yet an Abilene woman once told me, "When I was a young girl, Mrs. Eisenhower would stop me in the street and ask me how I was doing in school and what I was planning to do in the summer. She made herself pretty. She was so interested in what you were saying that she shined like the morning sun."

It has been written that many of our presidents had strong mothers but fathers who were either dead or less than successful, as if the mother had transferred her aspirations and hopes to the son. In this century Franklin Roosevelt, Harry Truman,

Richard Nixon, Ronald Reagan, and Bill Clinton all fit this pattern. Ida Eisenhower was such a mother. Not that Dwight Eisenhower was singled out, by any means—years later, when Ida Eisenhower was asked if she was proud of General Eisenhower, she answered, "I am proud of all my sons."

Having five brothers allowed little room for egocentricity. Egos were often bruised, and fights resulted. Once when relatives visited, Edgar and Dwight were bloodying each other in a yard fight. "Aren't you going to stop it?" one of the aunts asked.

Ida replied, "They've got to get it out of their system. You can't keep healthy boys from scrapping." The Eisenhower boys were known in their neighborhood as scrappers, but they were a solid front against the outside. They adopted the motto from Dumas's *Three Musketeers*, "One for all and all for one."

Wild Bill Hickock had once been a town marshal in Abilene, but, of course, by the time the Eisenhower boys were born, cowboy shootouts were long in the past. Yet their tales were still the stuff of a boy's imagination. In town lore one of the most talked-about fights in Abilene since Wild West days was the Eisenhower-Merrifield scrap.

Northsider Wesley Merrifield had taunted Southsider Ike. The fight lasted more than an hour; Abileners said later it was the toughest kid fight they had ever seen. Both boys had bloody noses, wet lips, and battered ears.

At last Wesley gasped, "Ike, I can't lick you!"

Ike replied, "And I can't lick you!"

Dwight Eisenhower did not suffer from a lack of playmates or companions, either inside or outside his house. In fact, the hours of solitude that Winston Churchill endured as a boy, Dwight Eisenhower might have occasionally envied.

High school for "Little Ike" was a happy time. The husky youth was called that not for his size but because his brother Edgar, one year older, was nicknamed Big Ike. Edgar had dropped back to his brother's class because he had failed algebra.

In his biography of Eisenhower, Stephen Ambrose wrote, "Ike's interests in high school were sports, studies, work and girls in that order."

Ike's daydreams in school were about triumph in the playing fields, not the battlefields. Years later in the Rose Garden, President Eisenhower talked to some champion Little Leaguers.

"Boys, have you ever skinny-dipped?"

The youngsters nodded.

"Well, these two boys about the end of the summer were drying themselves off, and the light-haired boy said to the dark-haired boy, 'What do you want to be when you grow up?' The dark-haired boy said, 'President of the United States.' And then he asked his friend, 'What do you want to be?' And he answered, 'Pitcher for the New York Yankees.'"

And then Eisenhower added, "Well, that's America. You can dream to be anything you want no matter your color, religion or how poor you are.

"By the way, the boy who wanted to become president became president all right, president of Abilene creamery. As for the other boy, that was me."

Baseball and football were the center of his life. At about 150 pounds in his teens he was well coordinated and quick in foot. A big grin would wreathe his face when he banged out a single to drive in a run or sacked the other team's star halfback for a loss.

Yet Joe Howe, the local newspaper editor, wrote, "Ike had self-assurance but never in my contact with him did he ever show any conceit." A braggart had no audience with Ike.

In baseball and football Ike was the spark plug that cheered each batter as he came up to bat or yelled his encouragement after a football huddle. He was quick to praise others but could be hard on himself. In a postcard to a boy he wrote, "They [the Kansas freshman team] beat us the other day 7-3. I made a terrible error."

Besides being modest, Ike was a fanatic about fair play. He would dress down a football teammate who had clipped an opponent. One Saturday, Abilene team members discovered that the visiting team playing against them had a black footballer. Each Abilene player refused to play in the line opposite the black, who was a center. Although Ike usually played end, he played center for the first time that day.

In sports Ike first discovered his ability as a leader and organizer. The players needed football and baseball gear and uniforms, as well as bats, and the school did not provide balls. So Ike founded the Abilene High School Athletic Association. He charged dues of twenty-five cents a month, canvassed livery stables for leather to be used as shoulder pads, and corresponded with other schools to make a schedule.

In his year-end report for the yearbook he wrote, "We improved the condition of the Association by drawing up a constitution which makes the organization a permanent one and each year it will be a question of electing new officers." It was typical of Ike that he wrote "we" and that the constitution was good enough to be operating forty years later.

Dwight relished the challenge of solving problems. He was an innate tactician. Perhaps that was why he earlier became fascinated with military history. He became so engrossed in it that he neglected his household chores and schoolwork. His mother had to take his history books away from him and lock them in a closet. But Dwight found the key to the closet in her desk and, whenever his mother went grocery shopping in town, would grab the books and read them until just before his mother's return.

Before attending high school, he had already studied the accounts of Greek and Roman battles. Not that he dreamed of one day walking in the footsteps of Alexander or Caesar. Rather, his passion for sports carried over into contests in the field of battle. He had a curiosity to find out who attacked whom, and where and when. And on what flank. And by what maneuver.

At high school he devoured United States and European history. He so excelled that his teachers began to assign him reports on a particular battle or general. His hero in junior high was Hannibal; in high school it became George Washington, who remained Ike's idol the rest of his life. To any new listener he could find, he expounded on the treacheries of the Conway Cabal (Conway had tried to persuade the Continental Congress to remove General Washington from the command of the Continental Army).

In the 1909 high school yearbook, called *The Helianthus* (Greek for "sunflower," the Kansas state flower), Cecilia Curry wrote the class prophecy for each of the classmates. One was to be president of the United States. It was Edgar Eisenhower. As for Dwight, he would end up as a professor of history at Yale.

Only slightly less than his mastery of history was Dwight's proficiency in English. If sports were his escape outside the house, reading was his recreation inside. At least, that partially explains his A-plus or A grades in that subject. Years later Eisenhower told his friends that he had also been helped by the daily family reading of the Bible at home: each of the boys took turns reading passages of Scripture. After tackling such names as Golgotha or Nebuchadnezzar, Ike had no problem reciting any words.

In fact, Dwight was picked to play the comic role of Gobbo in *The Merchant of Venice*. As the blundering clown, he stole the show from the leads playing Portia and Shylock. The Abilene paper reported,

> Dwight Eisenhower as Gobbo won plenty of applause and deserved it. He was the best amateur humorous character seen in the Abilene stage in this generation and gave an impression that many professionals fail to reach.

Work was Dwight's third priority, a means to an end. Picking apples and corn or scything barley and wheat earned him the money to buy football gear and new clothes, as well as an occasional ice cream treat.

One woman told an interviewer that first-year high school classes were held in the municipal hall, on top of which was the fire alarm. When it jarringly sounded, most boys ran to see the fire, but Little Ike left to buy an ice cream cone for his girl of the moment.

The next year everyone moved to the new high school, which had a gymnasium that could be used for school dances. Another witness later commented that Dwight was an awkward dancer, but his rugged frame and big smile more than compensated for that deficiency.

Only one shadow ever darkened this happy pastorale, reminiscent of a Norman Rockwell portrait of turn-of-the-century life in the heart of America. That was Dwight's freshman year, when he fell and scraped his knee. Infection set in, and the next day he collapsed into delirium on the parlor sofa. A local doctor was summoned, but despite his application of carbolic acid around Dwight's leg, the poison spread toward the boy's abdomen. Dwight slipped into a coma. A specialist was called in from Topeka. The two doctors agreed that only an amputation would save Dwight's life.

Dwight might have suffered the same fate as the character played by Ronald Reagan in *King's Row* if not for his brother Edgar. Dwight came out of his coma for a moment to hear his parents discussing the amputation, and he piped up, "You are never going to cut off my leg!" The doctors told him the alternative was death.

By this time the infection had moved to his groin, and his moments of consciousness were few. In one of them Dwight said, "Ed, they are talking about taking my leg off. I want you to see they do not do it, because I'd rather die than lose my leg." Edgar raised his right hand in a pledge to stop the doctor. He then slept on the floor at the threshold to Dwight's bedroom so that the doctor could not get through the door while his brother was asleep.

Doctor Conkling muttered dark curses that Edgar was going to "murder" his brother, but Edgar remained resolute. At the end of the second week the poison started to ebb and the fever cooled. Dwight was now fully conscious. But the two-month convalescence forced Dwight to repeat his freshman year. Dwight always credited his recovery to the prayers of his parents but no less than to his brother's pledge.

Another friendship in his senior year shaped Dwight's life. Everett "Swede" Hazlett, son of a prominent Abilene physician, was Dwight's first pal who did not like sports. In fact, Swede hated contact sports and was bullied for being a sissy. Once Dwight had to face off Swede's tormentors with his fists.

Dwight was drawn to Swede Hazlett because he had read lots of books and visited many places. Doctor Hazlett had sent his son to a military academy in Wisconsin for the last two years of his high school, and the boy had traveled with his parents to big cities such as New York. Swede had the ambition and intelligence to match Dwight's.

Swede Hazlett wanted to see the world, and the U.S. Naval Academy at Annapolis, Maryland, would be his ticket to do so. While the two boys worked at the creamery in the summer, Swede sold Dwight on going to Annapolis with him. Until Hazlett convinced him otherwise, Dwight had intended to follow his brother Edgar to the University of Michigan. Edgar wanted to study law. But the boys' father, who had hated lawyers ever since his bankruptcy, refused to pay the tuition. So Edgar and Dwight agreed to pool their job money to finance Edgar's tuition.

Dwight wanted to go to Michigan because its football team had Fielding "Hurry-Up" Yost, America's most famous football coach. But Hazlett persuaded Dwight that Annapolis had great football teams, and, furthermore, it was free.

Swede procured an appointment to Annapolis from the local congressman, who had been one of his father's patients. But when Dwight approached the representative, the man said he had filled all his vacancies and told the youth to turn to Sen. Joseph Bristow.

With all his characteristic directness, Dwight launched a campaign for an appointment. He called on Abilene's leading bankers, merchants, and newspaper editors to write to Senator Bristow. The letters, as well as his own, went unanswered. In September 1910 he read an announcement in the local paper for competitive exams for the service academies, to be held in Topeka. Dwight took second place.

He chose Annapolis but, unfortunately, because of his leg injury, was too old at twenty to qualify. Yet he was not too old for West Point, and it would be for history's and the army's gain. In June 1911 he boarded the train for West Point.

CHAPTER 3

SANDHURST

At Sandhurst I had a new start.

WINSTON CHURCHILL

FOR CHURCHILL, SANDHURST was more than a military school; it was the start of manhood. The words of the Bible might have rung in his ears as he entered Sandhurst: "When I was a child, I spoke as a child, I thought as a child, I understood as a child, but when I became a man I put away childish things." A sense of purpose was beginning to replace the attitude of capricious dissent. Perhaps the influence of the stern and Spartan academy had its effect. But of greater impact was Winston's realization that failure at Sandhurst would spell the end to any dreams of glory. His father had cut short his own brilliant political career by an impulsive and headstrong resignation on principle and was now a shadowy figure declining under the ravages of his debilitating disease. Winston sensed that he would soon have to make it on his own. He was eighteen and becoming a man. In Victorian England, young men started to earn their living in their teens. Even today in Britain, where a college education is the exception, not the rule, eighteen is the age at which most men begin their lives as adults. Winston was still at school but now possessed a maturity in the way he applied himself to the courses at hand. Courses such as tactics, fortification, topography, and military law commanded his full attention. He learned how to blow up bridges, construct breastworks, and make contoured maps. He studied major battles of great wars, and the one he found most fascinating was the conflict at Gettysburg in the American Civil War.

At Sandhurst, Churchill began to assemble his first library. He ordered Henley's *Operation of War*, Prince Kraft's *Letters on Infantry*, and Maine's *Infantry Fire Tactics*. He did not have to purchase these books as part of his curriculum; he did it out of interest and ambition. He saw his father dying and told his classmates, "We Churchills are a frail-stemmed lot." He thought that he, too, would die young. So if he were to be a success, he had to prepare right now, beginning at Sandhurst.

His newly found seriousness of purpose had its results. Winston finished 20th in a class of 130. If this wasn't the brilliance of a Douglas MacArthur or Robert E. Lee, both of whom finished first at West Point, it was better than Omar Bradley and Dwight Eisenhower, who in a class of 160 were 44th and 61st. Such comparative rankings may be meaningless, but the contrast to Churchill's record at Harrow is significant. He had moved from the bottom ranks there into the upper at Sandhurst. The often-delinquent schoolboy had become a diligent cadet. What he had learned was the secret of Napoleon, whose maxim he later often quoted: *"L'art est de fixer les objets longtemps sans etre fatigue"* (The ability to concentrate for a long time without tiring). He thus acquired the ability to throw himself into an unfamiliar field or subject and master its essentials. His experience at Sandhurst did not make him a general, but it did make him a generalist, the sine qua non of any great leader. Churchill's son, Randolph, describing Winston's Sandhurst years, wrote,

He had to fight every inch of his road through life; nothing came easily to him, not even oratory and writing, in which he was later to excel. To achieve success, he had to develop that intense power of concentration, which, as it grew, was to serve him and his fellow countrymen so well.

Churchill's sudden maturing was aided by his father's early decline and death. A couple of years after Lord Randolph died, Winston wrote, "Solitary trees, if they grow at all, grow strong; and a boy deprived of a father's care often develops, if he escapes the peril of youth, an independence and vigor of thought which may restore in after life the heavy loss of early days."

The year 1895 made Winston feel very solitary indeed. On January 24 his father, who for months had been a pitiful spectacle, finally passed away. On Lord Randolph's death Winston became the man of the house, with a mother to console and a younger brother to supervise.

And other deaths that year removed from his life old, familiar sources of strength and stability. His grandmother Jerome, of whom Winston was a special favorite, died in April. Most important was the death in July of Mrs. Everest, his old nanny, who was more than his surrogate mother. She was, excepting only his wife, the one person in his life who gave him the most unconditional love. At Harrow, to the surprise and gibes of his classmates, he had invited his old nanny down and walked hand in hand with her across the campus, showing her the sights. A classmate wrote years later that it was one of the greatest acts of courage and compassion he had ever seen. For years before her death, his nanny had been in retirement, where her days were brightened by letters from her beloved Winston. He was the only Churchill to attend her funeral. Even though he had only an officer's pay, a meager 120 pounds a year, on leaving Sandhurst he made an arrangement with a florist for the constant upkeep of her grave. To the end of his life Winston kept her picture on his desk at Chartwell.

When he left Sandhurst, he knew what he wanted to do with his life. It was not soldiering. In August a speech by his cousin, the duke of Marlborough, eulogizing Lord Randolph, prompted this passage in a letter from Winston to his mother:

> It is a fine game to play—the game of politics—and it's well worth waiting for a good hand before really plunging.
>
> At any rate, four years of healthy and pleasant existence, combined with both responsibility and discipline can do no harm to me, but rather good. The more I see of soldiering the more I like it, but the more I feel convinced that it is not my métier.

Yet at the same time, Winston realized that the narrowness of his Sandhurst education had not prepared him for political life. His had been the specialized training of a military officer. There were gigantic gaps in his knowledge, wide spaces of ignorance that had to be filled fast. When he was stationed at his first post with the Queen's Own Hussars at Aldershot in Hampshire, his mother had suggested that he make himself an expert on "the supply of horses." Churchill demurred, writing his mother,

> No—my dearest Mamma—I think something more literary and less material would be the sort of mental medicine I need. . . . You see—all my life—I have had a purely technical education. As a result my mind has never received that polish, which for instance Oxford or Cambridge gives.
>
> I am going to read Gibbon's *Decline and Fall of the Roman Empire* and Lecky's *[History of] European Morals*. These will be tasks more agreeable than the mere piling up of statistics.

It is clear that his mother was no longer "the remote but dazzling figure." The young widowed Lady Randolph still scintillated, but now she employed her radiance to help promote her son, just as she had his father. In a man's world, her son now succeeded his father as a focus for her own ambitious dreams. She was, after all, not only an American in the midst of the British aristocracy but also a widow without the base of her husband's position or the security of a large inheritance. Her only asset was her unfading beauty and her will to use it. According to one count, the number of her male companions amounted to almost two hundred. But she was selective—she only chose those who were able to advance her economically and socially. Although vain and self-centered, Jennie had a shrewdness that belied a seemingly brittle shallowness.

Her primary object for her maneuvering was her son, who, himself, was not an unstriking figure. The youngest lieutenant in the service of Victoria, Winston was, if not tall, lithe and supple. His head, if too large for his body, fit Plutarch's conception of the look of leadership. A pug nose, large blue eyes, and a pink-and-white skin that would make any girl envious set off the head. A shock of reddish-gold hair just about matched the braid on his Hussar uniform.

But in 1895 this newly turned-out Hussar cavalryman found himself all dressed up with no place to go. There was no field on which to make a name. Hardly a cloud dotted the horizons of the Empire. The last war Britain had fought was in the Crimean Peninsula in 1854. The only place any fighting was now going on was in Cuba, and one could scarcely call a minor rebellion a war. Yet it promised more excitement than the round of parties with which young officers filled their two-month vacations. So Winston went, but only after his mother obligingly scraped up some extra pounds out of her limited income to pay for his passage.

On his twenty-first birthday, November 30, 1895, Winston experienced a singular entry into manhood. A barrage of gunfire opened up on the cavalry contingent with which he was traveling. A bullet that passed inches from his head killed the horse immediately behind him. Although his stint as a military observer with the Spanish army gave him his first taste of gunfire, perhaps his more significant initiation was his first venture as a journalist. The editor of the *Daily Graphic*, for whom Randolph Churchill had once written a few articles, engaged Winston to write a series of dispatches at five pounds apiece.

For an untrained eye, young Churchill was prescient. He sensed the paradox that would describe almost every revolution in the following century. As he put it, "I liked the rebellion, but not the rebels." In other words, although he thought the cause was just and would soon prevail, he had little faith in the movement's leadership, which he thought might manipulate the people to its own ends. "Though the Spanish administration is bad," he wrote, "a Cuban government would be worse, equally corrupt, more capricious and far less stable. Under such a government revolutions would be periodic, property insecure, equity unknown."

Winston might have observed only three days of the Cuban conflict, but he picked up some habits that would last a lifetime. The first was his taste for Havana cigars and the second his discovery that the Spanish siesta, taken at midday with clothes removed, could add at least three or more productive hours to one's day at night.

When Churchill returned, he soon learned that his unit of the Fourth Hussars had been called to India. Most of his fellow officers welcomed the assignment to this subcontinent, where Kiplingian life spelled one continuous round of polo parties.

Garrison life centered on equestrian sport, which called for the brave and daring horsemanship that would produce a superb cavalryman. Drills and reviews were just routines that marked the hours before the daily five o'clock match. Evening mess at 8:30 and the hours that followed in the cool night were opportunities for officers to rehash the day's game.

But Churchill had to play with a strapped shoulder. When he had arrived at Bombay Harbor, he had reached out his hand for a ring at the dock and the boat had surged. The result was a dislocated shoulder. As he wrote later, "I had sustained an injury which was to last me my life. It was to cripple me at polo and prevent me from ever playing tennis."

Churchill loved playing polo but was soon bored talking about it. His mind was elsewhere, reaching for the mental stimulation that was absent in the banalities of bungalow chatter that dwelt only on the flesh, be it equine or feminine. The idea of thirteen or fourteen more years of this Indian tour of army duty was unbearable. It would be a virtual prison sentence for the few remaining years of what he felt sure would be his short lifespan. How could he ever pick up his father's fallen political banner? How could he be worthy if his father's mantle plagued him? He had not been an Oxford scholar and, with his inadequacies in Greek and Latin, never could be.

The only answer was for Churchill to educate himself. He would use the three or four hours in the torrid midday, when his fellow officers played cards, to read what he would have studied at Oxford or Cambridge. To his mother, he sent urgent letters asking for books. The first to arrive was Edward Gibbon's *Decline and Fall of the Roman Empire*, which his mother said had been his father's favorite and which he had already begun reading at Aldershot. Then came Macaulay's various histories, which he had heard were easy reading and afforded an accessible overview of British institutional and political history. He followed up those with philosophers both ancient and modern, Plato and Aristotle, together with Darwin and Lecky.

As if he were at a university, Churchill gave himself daily assignments such as reading twenty pages of Gibbon, along with fifty of Macaulay. His motive was more than just simulating an academic atmosphere. He found that he could absorb more if he alternated his readings among several authors. On Sunday he would test himself by writing essays on what he had learned the previous week. At the same time, he asked his mother to send him copies, beginning with his birthdate of 1874, of the *Annual Register* (the parliamentary equivalent of the *Congressional*

Record). As an intellectual exercise, he would not read the debates until he had first read the bill in question and mastered its implications. Thus he would record his own views on a bill, such as the purchase of Suez Canal shares, before reading the debated pro and con. In this way he assessed the logic of his own views. He became his own university.

Churchill's regimen of studies comprised more than history and politics. For biology he read Darwin. In the realm of philosophy, he added the German Schopenhauer to the Greeks Plato and Aristotle. In economics he added Thomas Malthus and Adam Smith to his studies. Soon he came to look forward more to his midday lessons than to his late-afternoon polo. What had started as a discipline became a diversion. As soon as he arrived back in his bungalow, he would get out his books, pour some brandy and soda, light up a cigar, and read away.

Churchill remained undaunted in his course. He was considered a bit odd, but he had always accepted eccentricity as the badge of his individuality. At Harrow his impertinence had made him an outsider; now his intellectualism did. The difference was that in India, Churchill commanded some grudging respect. There, he obviously was not the typical officer in the queen's service. He had little interest in gossip or women. He had more important conquests to make. What he wanted was the world, or at least to make his mark on the world. To do that he had to understand the world, the forces that shaped it and moved it. If he was going to have his place in the world, he had first to learn where he stood in the scheme of things. With this growing realization, Churchill grew mentally as well as physically into manhood.

CHAPTER 4

WEST POINT

From the first day of West Point I often asked myself, What am I doing here?

DWIGHT DAVID EISENHOWER

FOR DWIGHT EISENHOWER, West Point was sports. The education the school offered was a chief benefit but certainly not a priority. All across the half-a-continent train ride from Kansas to New York, Eisenhower daydreamed about feats on the West Point diamond or gridiron.

He had no idea what awaited him. At Abilene High he stood out as one of the best athletes and students. Suddenly, he was "Mr. Dumbjohn"—the lowest of the low, a plebe consigned to Beast Barracks.

For the first time his smile was not an asset but an affront to upperclassmen. He took the haranguing in stride:

"Get your shoulders back!"

"Suck in that stomach!"

"More yet. Still more!"

"Come on, hold your head up!"

"Drag in that chin!"

His relaxed and easygoing nature seemed to challenge his tormentors. They sensed that they aroused in Eisenhower no anxiety or awe.

Churchill at Sandhurst had changed from unmanageable schoolboy to model cadet, but in Eisenhower's case the reverse was closer to the truth. Eisenhower's conduct in high school was without blemish. At West Point that changed.

One time, because of a messy room, a cadet corporal barked at Eisenhower and his roommate, "Appear at my room in full dress coat" (the full dress coat is a cutaway with long tails in the back and tailored to end straight across the waist in the front). So Dwight and his mate marched into the corporal's room at the appointed time in their dress coats and no stitch of clothing below the waist.

Another incident that drew a raft of demerits was Ike's style of dancing. One of the few recreation times at the Point was the Saturday night "Feed Hop," which was a late snack outing where young women were invited. Even decorous ballroom dancing was allowed, on the school's hardwood floor.

The dress code for young ladies in the decade before the Roaring Twenties demanded skirts that covered their ankles and gloves that sheathed their hands. Dwight's technique was to swing his favorite partner so fast that the skirts would reveal the ankles, if not sometimes the knees. The father of Dwight's girl at the time was not amused—and he was an instructor at the academy. Dwight was sternly reprimanded, but the un-daunted Dwight continued to flaunt his dancing style, earning even more demerits.

Curiously, in Abilene Dwight had never smoked a cigarette, not even to experiment as a lark behind the barn with some of his friends. But at West Point, because it was forbidden, he started rolling his own Bull Durhams. Caught by an officer, Eisenhower took his punishment but would not stop smoking. He said later, "I looked with distaste at those who were haunted by fear of de-merits and low grades." In World War II, when he heard that a classmate had been promoted to general, he exclaimed, "How did he do it, he always was afraid to break a regulation!"

Sports were Dwight's escape from the tyrannical regimen of regulations. Yet in baseball Dwight had to conform to the coach's ways if he was to make the team.

In Abilene Dwight was known defensively as a center-fielder with a strong arm and fair speed. But at the plate he choked up the bat to spray his hits, like Wee Willie ("Hit 'em where they ain't") Keeler, to all fields. In fact, the summer before he left for the Academy, he was a good-enough hitter to be picked up by the pros. In the Kansas State League he played under the name Charlie Wilson to earn some extra cash. It was a risk, because if he had been found out, it would have jeopardized his ever playing at the college level.

The West Point coach took one look at Dwight's husky shoulders and thought he was underusing his power. Even though this was still the pre–Babe Ruth days of the "dead ball," Dwight was told he had to change his batting style if he was ever to play for the West Point nine. Dwight should adopt a more open swing and hit for more distance.

In football as well, Dwight immediately caught the eye of the coach after the first practice game against Navy, for his hard tackles. Afterward, he was doing the required postgame laps around the field, when he heard the cry "Eisenhower." It was the head coach.

"Where did you get the pants?" They were torn at his ankles.

"From the manager, sir," was Eisenhower's reply.

"Look at the shoes. Can't you get anything better than that?" asked the coach.

"I'm only wearing what I was issued."

Dwight raced to the dressing room, as he wrote later, "high as a kite." He had made the varsity.

Eisenhower is famous for his legendary smile, but on the football field it was a snarl. As a tackle he was still light at 174 pounds, but he made up for it with his ferocity. Once an opposing freshman complained to the referee. The referee was puzzled.

"Did he slug you or rough you up?"

"No," yelled the freshman, "but he's going to!"

His big chance came when Army's star halfback was injured before the first game. To replace him, Dwight was switched from tackle to halfback, and he led Army to victory in that first game. The next game was against Rutgers. Again he starred.

A *New York Times* reporter came out to the Point to write a feature story on halfback Dwight Eisenhower. Under a picture of Eisenhower punting, with his right leg high, the article concluded, "Eisenhower is one of the most promising halfbacks in the East."

Halfback Eisenhower was enjoying his moments of glory. The game the following week would put him against the most famous football player, if not the greatest athlete, in history, Jim Thorpe. In the 1912 Olympics at Stockholm, Thorpe had raked in the gold—he won running, jumping, and throwing feats and, in addition, the decathlon and pentathlon. The Carlisle Indians' Thorpe lived up to his all-time great billing. By the first half he had run for two touchdowns, one for ninety-five yards, passed for another, and drop-kicked three field goals while in the middle of a run.

Eisenhower and a fellow defense halfback decided to high-low Thorpe to take him out of the game. The next play Ike hit Thorpe high on the one side, while his teammate tackled him at the ankles. Thorpe got up real slowly, to Dwight's satisfaction. The next play Thorpe stared right at them from the huddle and then proceeded to run right through the two of them for a touchdown. Thorpe routed Army 27-6.

The following week against Tufts was the next-to-last game of the season. In the first quarter Dwight felt his ankle twist as he went down after rushing through the line. The ankle swelled, and he spent two days in the hospital under ice packs, hoping he would recuperate for the big game against Navy. He was released and returned to regular assignments. On Thursday he was in cavalry hall, where cadets were jumping off and onto galloping horses. After one jump off, his knee crumbled. He had torn his cartilage and tendons. The doctors put his leg in a cast. He would never play football or baseball again.

Although the riding incident was the real cause of Dwight's misfortune, the Tufts team took perverse pride in insisting that its tackle in the game with West Point was responsible. Later Eisenhower joked, "Tufts must have had a hundred men playing that day, because that's about how many would come up to me and say, 'Ike, I wish I hadn't hit you so hard in that tackle.'"

One might think that the end of his athletic career would cause Eisenhower now to concentrate on academics. But Eisenhower descended into a tailspin of despondency. His grades, which had never been particularly high, sank even lower. He only emerged from his depression the next fall when he was asked to coach the junior varsity team. Coaching brought out his best talents: his organizational ability and his skill at drawing the best out of his players.

Eisenhower's enthusiasm energized his players. His passion for the game was so contagious that the head football coach asked him to be West Point's first cheerleader. It would give Eisenhower his first experience as a public speaker. The night before the game, Eisenhower would address the entire Corps of Cadets.

For some reason Eisenhower, who had enjoyed acting in high school, never liked speaking before audiences. But he was excited by a challenge. He wrote and rewrote his talk and then rehearsed it, and he found his spirits lifted by the cheers that followed. After all, he did know how to write. His best grades at West Point were in English, for his succinct essays.

In mathematics he did not fare as well, perhaps because he was a lazy student. On one occasion he barely escaped disgrace. A problem in integral calculus was assigned to his class of twelve. Because the odds were great that he would never be called, he didn't study. He was called, however. With his good memory, Ike remembered the answer to the problem from a month earlier when an instructor worked out the solution, but he forgot the route to the solution. In a cold sweat he tried various ways until, just before the bell, he found one that worked.

It was not the method the instructor had used before, and he accused Eisenhower of making up figures to fit the answer. In short, Eisenhower was accused of being a cheat. Just then, the head of the math department walked in and made Eisenhower go through the solution again. The head pronounced Eisenhower's analysis superior to the one the instructor had used. Despite this, the instructor gave Eisenhower a C for the course.

Eisenhower's mediocre grades at the academy did not bode well for a bright future in the Army. His knee injury was even more of a liability. In 1915 the entire U.S. Army totaled 120,000. The graduating class at West Point more than supplied the demand for second lieutenants. Some of those low in class standing, such as Eisenhower, were awarded the second-class status of "additional second lieutenants," but West Pointers with injuries were looked at with disfavor. The War Department had sent down orders not to accept those whose physical impairment might cost the army in the matter of future disability pensions.

Curiously, Eisenhower was resigned to his fate. He saw his future in Argentina, not in the army. On the desk in his cubicle lay brochures on the South American nation. World War I had started in Europe that year, but it was a war toward which President Wilson had proclaimed firm U.S. neutrality. Argentina interested Eisenhower for three reasons: It was not in Europe; next to the United States it was the fastest-growing country in the world, promising great business opportunities; and, finally, it offered an adventure in another continent.

The colonel in charge of his assignment told Eisenhower that if he applied for service in the Coast Artillery, he would receive a commission. Eisenhower replied, "I do not want a commission in the Coast Artillery." (In those days the Coast Artillery was not quite considered the regular army. It was a dead-end assignment.) The colonel was taken aback by Eisenhower's curt answer. Some days later, to his surprise, Eisenhower was called back.

"Mr. Eisenhower," the colonel said, "if you will not submit any requests for mounted service [cavalry] on your preference card, I will recommend to the Academic Board that you be commissioned."

So when the time came for him to submit his preference card, Eisenhower put down *Infantry* first, *Infantry* second, and *Infantry* third.

Eisenhower had drifted into West Point and drifted out of it. He had obtained the free education he wanted but was uncertain what he wanted to do next. He accepted his commission in the infantry primarily because he had no better offer.

CHAPTER 5

THE HOUSE OF COMMONS

I am a child of the House of Commons.

WINSTON CHURCHILL

FOR CHURCHILL, the Royal Army was not his mission but a means. It was to be his path to Parliament. His first public speech was in 1894. It was not, however, a maiden address. In fact, it was a speech in support of unvirginal pursuits. The Women's Entertainment Protection League had mounted a campaign to remove the solicitation by "ladies of the evening" at the music halls. At the insistence of this blue-nose lobby, the Empire Theater had erected canvas partitions to prevent streetwalkers from catching the eyes of young blades imbibing at the theater's bar. During breaks between the variety skits, cadets at Sandhurst used to chat up the "ladies of the evening," who were parading their wares. The partitions now screened the young cadets from such temptation.

Churchill launched a crusade against such comstockery. Along with some like-minded officers, Churchill bought tickets to a performance at the Empire. Then, during an intermission, he sounded the signal for assault. "Charge the barricades," he roared. The canvas was ripped down, and Churchill mounted the stage against "the prowling prudes" who would deny Londoners of their civil liberties. His final presentation closed with the words "Gentlemen, you have seen us pull down the barricades.

See that you pull down those who are responsible for them at the coming election."

His second venture into the public arena was more serious. On his first home leave from India he dropped in at the Conservative Party's headquarters in London and allowed that he was considering a political career. To his astonishment, he was asked to speak at a local Tory Party function. The occasion was a meeting of the Primrose League in Bath. It was a women's group founded by his father to promote the memory of Benjamin Disraeli (primrose had been the Conservative Party prime minister's favorite flower).

Churchill wrote draft after draft of this twenty-minute address. He worked up a catchy line to capsulize his talk: "England would gain far more from the rising tide of Tory Democracy than the dried up drainpipe of Radicalism." He was raising aloft the creed of Lord Randolph. But who would hear about it except the fifty or so women assembled at Bath? To correct that, he took a step rare in the age before electronic media. He sent a copy of his speech to the *Morning Post*. The paper, bemused by the bravado of the late Lord Randolph's boy, sent a reporter down from London to cover it. By chance, Churchill met the reporter on the train and talked his ear off.

The correspondent wrote, "In years he is a boy . . . but in intention, in deliberate plan, adaptation of means to end, he is already a man. . . . Mr. Churchill is a man with ambitions fixed."

To stay in the army would stymie those aspirations. Yet he couldn't just quit his military career. Parliament paid no salary, and he had no independent means of support. He confided his plan to his mother: In military service he would seek adventure, find glory, and write about it. For how many soldiers could put subject and predicate together?

While stationed in Bangalore, India, Churchill volunteered during his Christmas vacation leave for a "search and seizure" mission five hundred miles north of the Afghan border. Pathan tribesmen from their ridge position wiped out his detachment. Churchill soon found himself all alone and pinned down by their continuing fire.

Later, in 1900, Churchill told American audiences that it was like a scene from a "Wild West" movie: "pistol in hand surrounded by Indians." He recounted how he stood off his pursuers and eventually escaped. When he returned to Bangalore, he wrote down notes on his first military adventure. "I found that there is nothing more exhilarating than to be shot at without result." (It was a line that President Reagan quoted in the hospital to his doctors when a would-be assassin shot him some eight decades later.)

The upshot of this escapade was Churchill's first book, *Malakand Field Force*. It was a bestseller. Among the fascinated readers was Edward, Prince of Wales, who wrote, "My dear Winston, I cannot resist writing a few lines to congratulate you on the success of your book! . . . Everybody is reading it, and I only hear it spoken of with praise."

While on leave, Churchill called at 10 Downing Street, the prime minister's residence, to give Lord Salisbury a signed copy of *Malakand Field Force*. The prime minister, perhaps feeling sorry for how he had dismissed the young lieutenant's father, asked, "Is there anything I can do for you?"

"There is a staff position," Churchill replied, "with Lord Kitchener in the Sudan." Salisbury accommodated him. Little did Churchill imagine that he would participate in the Royal Army's last cavalry charge.

At Omdurman, while attached to the Twenty-first Lancers, Churchill on dawn patrol was the first to sight the assembled mass of almost 40,000 riflemen and swordsmen, whose suicidal religious fervor gave rise to their nickname "the Whirling Dervishes." They combined the fervor of a latter-day Khomeni with the ferocity of the *banzai* charging Japanese at Iwo Jima.

Churchill and his fellow Lancers broke through the Arab phalanx not once but twice. Officers on either side of him were sliced to death by Dervish scimitars. But Churchill survived to write another hit book about his Nile adventure, *The River War.*

Now he had enough capital to resign his commission and stand for Parliament in Oldham, located in the heart of industrial Lancashire. It was a four-man race for two open seats that had been held by Liberals. He came a close third.

Undaunted, Churchill signed up with the *London Daily Mail* as war correspondent, to cover the newly breaking war in South Africa against rebelling Boers. At Capetown he found that as a civilian he was barred from boarding the troop train to the front, but, undeterred, Churchill hid under the seats. A little later, an ambush by the Boer Army derailed the train. Braving gunfire, Churchill organized the moving of a train car off the track to free the engine. In the effort, he soon found himself surrounded by Boer horsemen and was taken to prison.

Weeks later, he vaulted over the prison wall and hopped a freight train. After two days without food Churchill clambered off the train. Only one habitation remained in sight. He approached the house and knocked. A big burly man appeared. Churchill said haltingly, "I'm a Dutch clergyman."

The owner replied, "If you're a Dutch pastor, I'm the German Kaiser. You're Winston Churchill, and there's a prize on your head dead or alive—and lucky for you this is the only English house within twenty miles."

His host hid Churchill in the cellar for a week, where the only company was a pack of beady-eyed rats. His benefactor then hid Churchill in a cotton bale and loaded him on a train for Salisbury.

He arrived to find himself a minor celebrity. A London musical even sang this ditty.

You've heard of Winston Churchill
This is all I need to say
He's the latest and the greatest
Correspondent of the day.

Now he had material for two books—one on his escape and another on the war.

This time when he contested for a seat at Oldham, he won handily. His new stardom won him an offer to do a speaking tour of the United States. Major Pond, who headed the world's first lecture bureau in New York, signed him up. Pond at that time was also the agent for Oscar Wilde and Mark Twain.

Churchill was lionized by his U.S. audiences, mostly groups of women who eyed the bachelor grandson of a duke as a prospective son-in-law. He also saw Gov. Theodore Roosevelt in Albany while visiting with some of his Jerome cousins. Churchill was impressed with Roosevelt, now the vice president elect. The feeling was not reciprocated. As Roosevelt's daughter, Alice Roosevelt Longworth, told me, "They were too much alike. Father was like the former debutante looking at the prettiest of this year's season."

In Washington, Churchill went to the White House to meet President William McKinley. This time the rapport was mutual. The president's broad face and impassive presence reminded Churchill of his own grandfather, the duke of Marlborough. McKinley in turn warmed to the young hero and new member of Parliament.

One Washingtonian who was not so impressed was a young woman with an hourglass figure and honeyed accent. When Churchill told her of meeting the Republican president, she replied coolly that her family consisted of southern Democrats who had opposed the Republican policy of Reconstruction.

"Mr. Churchill," she said, "you see before you a rebel who has not been 'reconstructed.'"

"Miss," he replied with a deep bow that surveyed her décolletage, "Reconstruction in your case would be blasphemous."

His American trip was suddenly interrupted by news of Queen Victoria's death on January 22, 1901. By the British constitution, Parliament would have to convene to hear the address of the new monarch, Edward VII.

Weeks later Churchill delivered his maiden address in Parliament, which dealt with his experience in the Boer War. He closed with this allusion to his father:

> I cannot sit down without saying how very grateful I am for the kindness and patience, with which the House has heard me, which has been extended to me. I well know, not on my own account but of a certain splendid memory which many honorable members still preserve.

Months later the first-year parliamentarian dared to do the unthinkable. He attacked the policy of his own party's government. The secretary of state for war, Brodrick, had proposed a full-scale reform of the army, which would in essence make Britain, like the Kaiser's Germany, a military nation. Churchill, with clairvoyance beyond his twenty-seven years, saw that the proposal would end Britain's reliance on its navy and thus alter the whole course of her future foreign policy.

"The Navy is our strong suit," he argued. "Why should we sacrifice a game in which we are sure to win to play a game we are bound to lose?"

For an address Churchill wore his customary polka-dot blue tie, which had been Lord Randolph's trademark. He invoked memories of his father by fingering the gold watch that had once been Lord Randolph's. In that first year in the House, Churchill also attempted a mustache. His father had had a black

THE HOUSE OF COMMONS • 63

bushy one, but, unfortunately, Churchill's sandy hair was unequal to the task. A young woman who disapproved of Churchill's dissenting views encountered him at a dinner party.

"Winston," she scolded, "I approve of neither your new politics or new mustache."

"Madam," replied Churchill, "you are not likely to come in contact with either."

Churchill shaved off the mustache soon afterward. He also moved out of his father's shadow. A new father figure was pulling him from the Conservative Party toward the Liberal.

Bourke Cockran had a tall presence and commanding voice. Cockran was one of the very few people in his life whom Churchill never lectured but instead listened to. Churchill wrote later, "Bourke's conversation exceeded anything I have ever heard."

But Cockran's views clashed with those of the Conservative Party. An Irishman who had immigrated to New York, he was an anti-imperialist who championed the Boer cause and free trade.

His mother, who knew Cockran from Paris, had written a letter of introduction to him for her son when Winston visited the United States on his way to Cuba. As the foremost trial lawyer of the New York bar, Cockran had developed firm beliefs on the art of speaking. One dominant theme he stressed was that "one strong reason was better than two or three and then all the facts should be amassed behind that reason. . . . And after one convinces the mind, one should capture the heart with an emotional ending."

Churchill expanded on Cockran's rules in unpublished notes for speaking, called "The Scaffolding of Rhetoric." Churchill had been fortunate to have this tutor in speech. President William Howard Taft wrote in his diary, "Congressman Cockran is the greatest orator using the English language today." Cockran later pushed Franklin Roosevelt back into politics after he had been stricken with polio in 1921. A dying

Cockran told Roosevelt that he should deliver the nominating speech for Governor Alfred Smith in place of himself at the 1924 Democratic Convention. Roosevelt did and electrified the delegates with a speech that ended with "I give to you the happy warrior, Al Smith."

Without the persuasive influence of Cockran, it is hard to imagine Churchill's switch to the Liberal Party in 1904. He did this just in time to reap the fruit of the Liberal Party's massive victory the next year. He was rewarded with the post of under-secretary of state for the colonies.

Churchill now hitched his star to the most brilliant orator of the Commons, David Lloyd George, the firebrand reformer from Wales. The two of them moved the Liberal Party to the left, championing pensions and unemployment insurance.

In a speech that differentiated the new Liberal policies from socialism, Churchill said in Glasgow, in what was later described as the "safety net" speech, "We do not want to pull down the structure of science and civilization—but to spread a net on the abyss."

In 1908, when David Lloyd George left the presidency of the Board of Trade to become the chancellor of the Exchequer, Churchill took his place. The promotion meant that Churchill had to stand for reelection.

In one of his most brilliant addresses, he again compared liberalism with socialism in a speech in Dundee, Scotland, the constituency he hoped to serve. "Socialism seeks to pull down wealth; Liberalism seeks to raise up poverty. Socialism assails the preeminence of the individual. Liberalism exalts the man. Socialism attacks capitalism; Liberalism attacks monopoly."

One person whose favorable comment Churchill sought was not in politics. She was Clementine Hozier. He had met this granddaughter of a Scottish earl at a dinner party. An elegant young woman with classical features, she looked like a queen, Churchill told friends later. Before dinner, Churchill scouted out the table to see where she would be seated. Then he switched his card with the man who was supposed to be positioned next to Miss Hozier.

Clementine was asked later, "Did you find him good looking?" and she replied, "Men may be attracted to what they see but women by what they hear."

Clementine came from a family with strong Liberal Party convictions, and she herself was interested in issues such as working conditions. She earned a living as a teacher. Clementine, like Winston, came from a family that was aristocratic but not affluent. It was a love match.

A half century later in the United States, Churchill was asked to pick his greatest speech. He replied,

> My greatest address was delivered to an audience of one. I was at Blenheim Palace in 1908 walking with Miss Clementine Hozier. Suddenly the clouds opened up and we escaped from the downpour to a gazebo. And there I asked for her hand. It must have been my greatest speech because she accepted.

Liberal Party minister Churchill won the heart of Clementine but was soon to lose the affection of many workers who had rallied to his and Lloyd George's plans.

In 1910 Churchill, now Home Secretary, had to quell a riot of Welsh miners in 1910 by dispatching troops. Then months later, in what was called "the Siege of Sydney Street," Churchill, in top hat and cape, took over on-the-scene direction, shouting orders for Bobbies to encircle and capture armed revolutionaries. Criticized by the left for his ruthless efficiency in crushing the revolt, he said, "I do not claim to be neutral between the fire and the fire brigade."

The heads of the Liberal Party decided it was time to move Churchill away from the arena of domestic policy. In September 1912 Churchill was enjoying an afternoon at Prime Minister

Asquith's summer home in Scotland. At the end of the weekend he hauled Asquith's daughter away from the afternoon tea.

"Will you come with me?" he asked breathlessly.

"You don't want tea?"

"I don't want tea. I don't want anything. Your father has just offered me the Admiralty."

CHAPTER 6

FORT SAM HOUSTON

*I lived the life of a hermit and I could not indulge in any kind of
spending.*

DWIGHT DAVID EISENHOWER

IF WINSTON CHURCHILL was a young man in a hurry who
knew exactly where he wanted to go, Dwight Eisenhower was
not. He was in the army—perhaps for life. He entertained no
fantasies of receiving a general's star. Unlike Churchill, he was
never a romantic. He was a realist.

Yet his experiences at West Point could not help but foster
the belief that he was, if in a small way, part of a splendid tradition. At the academy Eisenhower knew which rooms Grant,
Lee, or Sherman had once occupied. Now he was part of that
history.

Later Eisenhower wrote that his most poignant day at the
Point was the first one:

> The day has been one of confusion and a heroic brand of
> rapid adjustment. But when we raised our right hands and re-
> peated the official oath, there was no confusion. A feeling
> came over me that the expression "The United States of
> America" would now and henceforth mean something differ-
> ent than it had before. From here on it would be the nation I
> would be serving, not myself.

Eisenhower had been one of the oldest of his graduating class. If his maturity, however, made him disdainful of the academy's many senseless rules and regulations, it also made him more disciplined in carrying out real responsibilities. He did not know where the army career would lead him, but for the present he would be the best junior officer at Fort Sam Houston.

Eisenhower had never expected to be assigned to Texas. He had asked for the Philippines. It was not considered a good post but was far away in the Pacific. The reason he had originally applied to the Naval Academy was to see the world.

For that reason Eisenhower went to the tailors at the academy and put down his savings for the khaki uniforms he would need for field service and the tropical white for dress occasions. He had no doubts about his destination, for he was the only one in his graduating class to ask for the Philippines.

To his debt and dismay, Second Lieutenant Eisenhower found himself sent to a fort in Texas. It was a time when Pancho Villa, the Mexican-Indian guerrilla, was battling to topple President Carranza of Mexico, whose administration Woodrow Wilson had recognized and vowed to support.

Camp life at Fort Sam Houston in San Antonio would require dress uniforms of blue, including another big dress (frock) coat for ceremonial occasions. Lieutenant Eisenhower had to borrow on his future monthly salaries to swing the cost. For the young bachelor officer, this financial straitjacket spelled no entertainment funds for the fair sex.

On October 3, 1915, Eisenhower was officer of the day and looked it—a handsome specimen of a young man, with his calf-length boots and his campaign hat cockily a-tilt on his large, golden head. About five o'clock he strode out of his bachelor quarters with a big black Colt pistol strapped to his side. Across the street Leonard "Gee" Gerow, perhaps his best friend on the base, was sipping cold grape juice, along with some civilians dressed in their Sunday worship finest. Ike had recently told Gee that he was swearing off women.

"Hey, Ike, come over here!" Earlier, Gee had just described Ike to his listeners—"He's a big good-looking guy who hates women." This only whetted the interest of the young ladies present—one of whom was Mamie Geneva Doud of Denver (her name at christening was Mary, but she was never called that). When Ike sauntered over, Mamie whispered to her friend, "He's a bruiser," which in the argot of the day meant "a hunk."

After some small talk, Ike said, "I've got to go, I have to inspect the guard." As he started to leave, he asked Mamie, "You wouldn't want to walk out with me?"

Mamie smiled and said, "No, I have a gentlemen friend picking me up at eight."

Eisenhower replied, "I could have you back in plenty of time." She agreed.

As they passed one of the barracks, Ike noticed some soldiers changing clothes. "Don't look, Miss Doud, the boys aren't too careful about pulling down the shades." Mamie's response was to peer at the windows more closely. As she did, Ike roared with laughter, "Now, isn't it just like a woman?" Eisenhower told Gee later that he found Mamie to be "saucy," which may have been the pre–World War I word for "sexy."

Mamie had to struggle to keep pace with Ike on his rounds because she was wearing her new high, beige boots. They were tightly laced and were killing her feet. But Mamie masked her discomfort with a smile and a patter of questions about his work. Mamie was feisty, fashionable, and feminine. She could even be a bit flirty. That was the style of woman Eisenhower liked. Four decades later at the White House, women knew not to appear in front of the president wearing pants and no lipstick.

The pert Mamie had caught Ike's fancy, and he mapped out a siege. The Douds kept a winter house in San Antonio, Texas, in addition to their main one in Denver. In San Antonio Eisenhower was a frequent caller.

John Sheldon Doud was a contrast to Eisenhower's father. Doud had graduated with high honors in math from the prestigious University of Chicago. Doud's own father, a speculative businessman, had gone through several fortunes and had wound up broke. Mamie's father not only repaired the family's finances but also made a fortune in the meat-packing business—enough so that he could retire at forty.

John Doud was an indulgent father who wanted the best for his three daughters. He had arranged for them to become Denver debutantes. Mamie had had her coming-out party the previous fall. Like her sisters, Mamie had no shortage of suitors. The affection among the sisters and their laughter at each other were contagious.

Ike hung around their home in San Antonio, even when Mamie's gentlemen friends came calling. He was still there when they brought her home. Ike was there to stake a claim and make his presence felt. He was falling for Mamie but was also fond of the whole Doud family.

It was not surprising that the Doud women, mother and daughters, were charmed by the husky blond lieutenant with the big smile, but so was Mr. Doud. In a house filled only with women, Doud now had another man to talk to. Both had an interest in sports and history. John Doud was a Civil War buff, and the two of them rehashed the battles of Gettysburg and Chickamaugua and Grant's siege at Vicksburg.

For Eisenhower, John Sheldon Doud was the father he had never really had. (Mamie and Ike's surviving son would be named after him.) Doud was a well-read paternal figure who shared with the younger man all his passions and opinions.

Eisenhower pressed on with his pursuit of Mamie. Courting would have been costly to his limited budget. But Eisenhower, who was already displaying his logistical ingenuity, came up with a solution. Saturday night was a ride downtown on the nickel jitney (it had prescribed routes, like a tram), then a dinner at the Original, a Mexican cantina by the river of some fifty-cent tacos and frijoles, and afterward to the vaudeville house at the Orpheus for another dollar. This date once a week may have strained but did not break his budget.

On Valentine's Day, 1916, Ike gave Mamie a miniature of his West Point ring. They were engaged—pending the approval of Mr. Doud.

The father was not enthusiastic. He liked Eisenhower but not his financial prospects. The standard of living provided by an Army officer's salary was not what he envisioned for his daughter. He acceded, however, on the condition that they would have to wait until November for the marriage, when Mamie would be twenty.

Eisenhower then had an idea that would have improved his finances. From his boyhood in 1903, when the Wright brothers made their experimental flight, and onward, Eisenhower had been fascinated with airplanes. The Army Signal Corps, the forerunner of the Army Air Corps, had openings in Fort Sam Houston. As an aviator, his salary would increase by 50 percent (presumably a stipend for risk). So Eisenhower figured he could fill his routine base life with a little adventure and fatten his pocketbook at the same time.

Poppa Doud exploded when he heard that notion. It was one thing for his daughter to want nice things—it was another for her to become a widow. Mamie agreed. She gave Ike the ultimatum: "Choose flying or me."

A week after the engagement was sealed, Pancho Villa invaded New Mexico. While General Pershing was chasing down Villa in vain, Lieutenant Eisenhower was just as futilely seeking orders to be posted to duty in Mexico. It was the last time that Eisenhower would be denied the chance for battlefield experience.

Instead of being posted with "Black Jack" Pershing, Eisenhower was sent to a nearby border camp in Austin, Texas, under "Fighting Dan" Moriarty of the Illinois Infantry. Yet like so many turns of fate in Eisenhower's career, what seemed like a frown by Dame Fortune was actually a smile.

Col. Dan Moriarty, who commanded a regiment of Irish toughs from the streets of Chicago, preferred battle to bookwork. So did his men. Rarely was the report filed by the officer of the day missing an account of a brawl or disturbance.

Eisenhower, whose reputation as a taskmaster football coach at West Point had preceded him, was brought in as an instructor to this unruly regiment. Moriarty, however, soon realized that the young captain had a penchant for paperwork. As Eisenhower noted, "I wrote all of his orders, prepared reports and other official papers for signature and became the power behind the throne."

Eisenhower later called his "chief of staff" experience in 1916 "the most valuable" in his early career. It was also the year he married. For that, he wangled a ten-day leave. He and Mamie were off to Denver by train, which cost $250 (all he had for train fare and a honeymoon). He managed to persuade a San Antonio jewelry storeowner to let him have a wedding ring on credit.

Later Eisenhower wrote, "With a new ring, new debts, ten days and high hopes, I began my journey."

After a wedding in a Denver Presbyterian Church and a honeymoon weekend at a nearby mountain resort in El Dorado Springs, the couple went to Abilene briefly to meet Eisenhower's family and then headed back to San Antonio.

Back at Fort Sam Houston the newlyweds lived in their three-room quarters on post. For the first time in her life Mamie had to manage without the services of a maid or a generous allowance (although Poppa did send a check to buy some furniture).

Mamie did not complain. She had been trained at Miss Walcott's, a finishing school in Denver, to be a wife. There she had honed her talents for entertaining, and at Sam Houston she did that, with a great deal of dash and only a few dollars. In fact, the Eisenhower home was dubbed "Club Eisenhower" by fellow officers and their wives. Mamie had a knack for making a house warm and the conversation lively. She held birthday dinners for bachelor officers, and the finishing school alumna also smoothed Ike's rough edges. Although he had been by nature shy with women, he learned under Mamie's tutelage to ask questions and draw a woman out.

A month later Ike was assigned to a new post at Camp Wilson near Austin, Texas. Mamie said, "You are not going to leave me so soon after we've been married?"

"There is one thing you must understand," Ike replied, "—my country comes first and always will; you come second in my life."

Ike set off for Camp Wilson on April 1, 1916. The next day President Woodrow Wilson declared war on Germany. While at Camp Wilson, Ike almost made Mamie an early widow. The newly captained Eisenhower, like one of his heroes, Ulysses S. Grant, had been appointed regimental supply officer. One afternoon, during a thunderstorm and while standing beneath some trees, Captain Eisenhower lectured to his men about makeshift supplies or "field expedients." He was so involved in his talk, he didn't notice he had backed up against a telephone wire caught in the branches. Lightning struck, and Eisenhower was "flattened." It took several minutes for him to regain consciousness.

Not only could Mamie have become a widow, but also their expected child would have been an orphan. At that point, Eisenhower purchased his first life insurance policy.

The baby, christened Doud Dwight but nicknamed "Icky," was born in September 1916. Poppa Doud was so elated with his grandson that he relented and began giving Mamie an allowance.

But the joy of fatherhood did not ease Eisenhower's frustration at being grounded in Texas while America was at war. He pestered the War Department with requests for overseas duty. All were turned down. He was sent instead to Fort Leavenworth, Kansas. At this time, the commandant called him "on the carpet" because of his frequent requests for transfers and added a stern reprimand of his own.

"Sir," replied a scarlet Eisenhower with clenched lips, "I have only asked to be allowed to go to battle and this offense— if it is an offense—was committed before I came under your jurisdiction. If there is punishment to be given out, it should be given by the War Department and not by you, with all due respect, Sir!"

The greatest conflict in history, called the Great War, was taking place. The United States was now in World War I, but Eisenhower was not.

CHAPTER 7

THE ADMIRALTY

Guard them well, admirals and captains, hardy tars and tall marines; guard them well and guard them true.

WINSTON CHURCHILL

CHURCHILL SAW THE Royal Navy as the first bastion of defense for the British Empire. That might seem odd for a Sandhurst-trained soldier, but Churchill knew that Britain was by geography an island nation and that its command of the seas had led to its far-flung empire. As First Lord of the Admiralty in 1911, he was like a captain being given his first ship.

Winston happily threw himself into the task of making the empire seaworthy against any challenge or attack. Overboard went old shibboleths on naval usage and precedent. Seniority, which Churchill almost equated with senility, was shoved aside. For first sea lord he chose Prince Louis of Battenberg, whose one special claim to prominence was that he had married Queen Victoria's granddaughter.

Because of Battenberg's German accent, veterans resented this career sailor in the Royal Navy. (Battenberg's family later flourished under his son Admiral Lord Mountbatten and his grandson Prince Philip, who married Queen Elizabeth.) As naval chief Churchill appointed the young and dashing Rear Adm. David Beatty, who had startled the stuffy world of the

Royal Navy high command by taking as a bride a young American heiress to the Marshall Field department store in Chicago.

Superannuated admirals were not the only ones to be scrapped. Churchill wanted to replace the thirteen-inch guns with the longer-range fifteen-inch ones, which had greater power and speed. He proposed sacrificing the battle-plate armor of the old "dreadnoughts" for a lighter cruiser squadron. Finally, to make the whole navy faster cruising, Churchill recommended that the fleet be converted from coal to oil, thus adding maneuverability by allowing ships to be fueled at sea. He also launched a new light search-and-seizure vessel, for which he coined the name "destroyer."

One admiral, enraged by Churchill's reforms, spluttered to him at an Admiralty meeting, "Aren't you mindful of the traditions of the Royal Navy?"

"Tradition!" roared Churchill. "Tradition! I tell you what the tradition of the Royal Navy is—rum, sodomy, and the lash."

When a former admiral, Lord Charles Beresford, accused Churchill on the House of Commons floor of wrecking the navy, Churchill scathingly replied, "Charles Beresford can best be described as one of those orators who, before they get up, do not know what they are saying, and when they have sat down, do not know what they have said."

Churchill even established the first air force in 1912—the Royal Naval Air Services—a precursor of the Royal Flying Corps in World War I (later the Royal Air Force in World War II). Because of his efforts, England became the first country to equip a plane with a machine gun and then the first to have a plane drop a bomb. Interestingly, he also coined the term *seaplane*.

To raise money for his innovations, Churchill had to convince not only admirals but also his fellow members in the Liberal Party. The reforms cost money—appropriations, which pared down the amounts allocated to social welfare projects.

Lloyd George complained to him, "Winston, you've become a water creature. You think we all live in the sea, and all your thoughts are devoted to sea life, fishes and other aquatic creatures. You forget that most of us live on land."

To the critics of his defense spending, Churchill gave this ringing answer at Glasgow, the seat of the nation's shipbuilding industry:

> The purposes of British naval power are essentially defensive. We have no thoughts, and we have never had any thoughts, of aggression. There is, however, this difference between the British naval power and the naval power of Germany. The British Navy is to us a necessity, and from some points of view the German Navy is to them more in the nature of a luxury. Our naval power involves British existence. It is existence to us; it is expansion to them.

If the pacifists in England were temporarily silenced, the militarists in Germany flared up. Kaiser Wilhelm ranted, "Why should a big fleet be a luxury to us and only a necessity to them?"

Churchill countered by quickly proposing to Germany a year of no shipbuilding for both nations. "A naval holiday," was Churchill's phrase, headlined in the newspaper, "to put a blank page into the book of mutual understanding."

When the Kaiser did not reply, Churchill's counsel in favor of a stronger Royal Navy began taking hold in the court of public opinion. With this leverage, after a threat to resign, he won a compromise from the Cabinet members: They would go along with his increased budget request of 1913 but would return to the previous level in 1914. (Of course, after the cataclysmic events of that year, no such restriction was ever imposed.)

Ever since his days at Harrow, when he had predicted a "world war" with civilian armies, trenches, and machine guns,

Churchill had manifested a prophetic gift. In 1905 he foresaw the creation of the state of Israel and in 1908, the eight-hour day. (One could also say that his choosing "New Zealand" as the geographical area to study for the Sandhurst exam showed psychic ability.) But his most incredible forecast to the War Department was just before he took over the Admiralty: "The decisive military operations will be those between France and Germany."

He then predicted that Germany would attack France through Belgium, a neutral country. "The balance of probability is that by the twentieth day the French armies will be driven from the line of the Meuse [River] and will be falling back on Paris and the south." The same memorandum foretold the exact day that the German army would reach its farthest penetration point, where the two armies would entrench themselves.

The army staff called the document "ridiculous and fantastic," yet in three years it all happened just as Churchill predicted. He gave the twentieth day of the German offensive as the day on which the French armies would be driven from the Meuse River and then forecast that the German army would be fully extended by the fortieth day on all fronts. That is exactly what occurred. Germany lost the Battle of the Marne on the forty-first day.

What gave Churchill the vision that older and more experienced leaders in the War Office and the Admiralty lacked? Churchill gave the clue when he later modestly described the document in his book *The World Crisis* as "an attempt to pierce the future; to conjure up in the mind a vast imaginary situation; to balance the incalculable; to weigh the imponderable." It is what today's CEOs describe as an "out of the box" mindset. The key to his gift of prophecy was his imagination—an uninhibited mind that was not afraid of making mistakes. Like a Columbus, he could array the facts, sift the possibilities, and with a full calculation of the odds ride his conclusion far into the horizons of the future. Where the military and bureaucratic mind, confronted by an image of contingencies, would opt for the immediate and safer present, Churchill weighed each imponderable, gauged the outcome, and proceeded to the next step. Casting aside the less probable "ifs," he invaded the veiled future until the course had been resolved. Such a conclusion, unencumbered by qualifications or conditions, became, under the force of Churchill's words and the power of his description, not just a prediction but also a revelation.

After Belgium was invaded, Prime Minister Asquith declared war on the Central Power (Germany) on August 4, 1914. That evening the First Lord of the Admiralty took the chancellor of the Exchequer for dinner at the Savoy Hotel. Lloyd George was glum. Future plans for the welfare state would have to be shelved. But Churchill was glowing. Weeks earlier, he had ordered full mobilization of the fleet without waiting for approval by Asquith. The Royal Navy was at sea, safe away from any harbor strikes by German U-boats, bragged Churchill. Because of Churchill's preemptive dispatching of the ships to the high seas, there was never any chance for another "Pearl Harbor." On a curious note, as the two future prime ministers talked that night at the Savoy, a third was listening; Ho Chi Minh, future leader of Vietnam, was their waiter that evening.

Churchill's success cowed his critics in the War Department and the Foreign Office. Never shy about offering advice, he now peppered other departments with memoranda. One idea was "the land ship"—an armored car with treads that could roll past machine-gun fire and over barbed wire, to destroy trench battlements. The army named it "Winston's Folly." Eventually, it was called "a tank" because that's how the top-secret new armored mobile vehicles were referred to in the naval factories, to mislead spies.

This is not to say that Churchill was an inventor. He had hardly a schoolboy's knowledge of physics, with a disdain for what he called the "infernal combustion engine." He was, however, inventive. The inventiveness, like his gift for prophecy, came from an imagination coupled with single-minded concentration—no barrier could stop his flow of thought. Any impossibility might be wrought into a possibility. If the war was stalemated by barbed wire and trench warfare, why couldn't an armored car with movable tracks be designed?

Churchill was a prime example of "the Alexander syndrome"—the conquer-the-world attitude of youth that brooks no limits to ambitions. Even though Churchill had turned forty, he still entertained "the impossible" dreams of youth. His boyish enthusiasm made itself felt in speeches across the British Isles—exhorting office staff to keep the long working hours, rallying banquet audiences with his eloquence, cheerleading workers at shipyards, and christening new ships.

Some temperance groups called on Churchill to discontinue the Royal Navy's practice of christening ships by breaking a bottle of champagne across the bow.

"But Madam," replied Churchill to their spokeswoman, "the hallowed custom of the Royal Navy is indeed a splendid example of temperance. The ship takes its first sip of wine and then proceeds on water ever after."

Churchill always had a lot of the irrepressible boy inside of the man. This was displayed in his role in "the Antwerp Circus." Churchill's fledgling air force, in a daringly innovative bombing raid, had just destroyed some German Zeppelin sheds and damaged a North Sea submarine base. So the army called on him to undertake another maneuver. To divert the German army from moving on Dunkirk, the important French harbor on the North Sea, Churchill was asked to stage a diversionary charade in the Belgian port of Antwerp.

Unlike the army that seeks to do much by stealth, Churchill, in the not inaptly named Circus, was asked to do little and parade much. To ask Churchill to draw attention to himself was like ordering a little boy to put on his first cowboy costume. The uniform he actually arrived in was that of elder brother of Trinity House, a ceremonial costume that made him look more like Bonaparte than Buffalo Bill. In Antwerp, atop an armored car in a gold-braided uniform and a crested plumed helmet, he led some red London buses carrying Royal Marines. At home the British public laughed at his antics, but in Antwerp the Belgians cheered as Churchill in his bizarre outfit strode through the lobby of his hotel headquarters to assume command.

Finding no Belgian defenses, Churchill took the army, navy, and civil defenses in his hands. For three days he was virtually the Belgian chief of staff. From Antwerp, he orchestrated darting forays behind German lines. Although the Circus actually fulfilled its mission by buying time, Antwerp finally fell. But as King Albert of Belgium later said, "Because of Churchill, the Germans never took Dunkirk." The French seaport was saved for British ships, yet Churchill's enemies in England saw the Circus as more fiasco than feat. To them, it displayed Winston's flamboyance at its worst.

The next time the army called on Churchill for a mission, there were no elements of cowboy. Only unrelieved tragedy could describe the Dardanelles episode. The Dardanelles are narrow straits that are the gateway to Constantinople (now Istanbul). Ever since conflict had broken out, Churchill had argued for a combined land-and-sea invasion of the Ottoman Empire (Turkey) that would knock the "sick man of Europe" out of the war and thus shorten the conflict by enabling Russia to attack Germany on its eastern front.

Then, on New Year's Day in 1915, Lord Kitchener, the British commander in chief, whose face—an English version of Uncle Sam—is remembered on "We Want You" posters, approached Churchill. It was Kitchener who had suggested the Circus at Antwerp. Now he wanted Churchill to send a flotilla to bombard the Dardanelles. Churchill agreed, if and only if it was to be a joint military and naval action. His tragedy was allowing this original resolution to be undermined. With the support of the prime minister and cabinet, a sea attack alone was authorized, but cannon power from the ships was not enough to subdue the Gallipoli peninsula, which led to Constantinople. Kitchener delayed because he could not spare any of his troops from the French trenches. Only when the Anzacs (Australians and New Zealanders) arrived did the invasion take place. By then the Turks had been reinforced by the Germans, who placed mounted machine guns on the hills. Thousands of British soldiers, including the poet Rupert Brooke, died on the stark Aegean coast.

It was a classic case of "too little and too late," and the scapegoat was the First Lord of the Admiralty. As he was dismissed, Lord Kitchener said to him, "No one can take one thing from you, Winston. You had the fleet ready in 1914."

But the Dardanelles disaster—even more than his defeat in 1945—was the traumatic event of his life. Political cartoons heaped ignominy on him. One showed a little boy Churchill playing by tossing matches of soldiers on a bonfire.

The defeat impelled the Liberal prime minister to bring in the Conservatives in a wartime coalition. Arthur Balfour, head of the Conservative Party, was made foreign secretary. Implicit in the dealings between the two parties was that Churchill, who was reviled by Conservatives as a turncoat, would be made the scapegoat. Neither Asquith nor Kitchener, who should have incurred the blame, was touched by a word of criticism by the Conservatives. They targeted only Churchill, whose political ambitions were now buried with the soldiers in the sands of Gallipoli.

Although military historians now confirm that a successful invasion of Turkey might have ended the war, Churchill bore the brunt of this failure the rest of his life. At the heaviest of costs, he did take away one lesson about leadership: Never plan a military operation in which you share control.

While waiting for his commission, Churchill repaired to the French seacoast for sun and solace. The "black dog"—the phrase he gave to his fits of melancholy—had overwhelmed him.

He told his daughter Sarah that the brutality of the ouster made him feel as if he were a sea beast fished up from the depths or a diver too suddenly hoisted, whose veins threatened to burst from the fall in pressure. "At a moment when every fiber of my being was inflamed to action, I was forced to remain a spectator of the tragedy."

One day on the beach, while in despair, he picked up a box of his children's watercolors and experimented with them. The next day he bought an expensive set of oils and was contemplating the canvas when a voice behind him said, "Painting? Well, what are you hesitating about?" It was Lady Lavery, the wife of Sir John Lavery, who had recently completed Winston's portrait. "Let me have a brush," she said, "a big one." And with that, she slashed the canvas with bold and furious strokes. As Churchill wrote later in *Painting as a Pastime*,

> Anyone could see that it could not hit back. No evil fate avenged the jaunty violence. The canvas grinned in helplessness before me. The spell was broken. The sickly inhibitions rolled away. I seized the largest brush and fell upon my victim with berserk fury. I have never felt any awe of a canvas since.

Finally, he received his assignment to the front. In July 1916 his base of operations was in a Belgian trench. Fifty feet away in a German trench was Corp. Adolph Hitler.

Later, in a French trench, the finger of fate would rescue Churchill. A summons for Churchill to appear at headquarters was delivered to his trench. Churchill resisted: "I have to finish my inspection of the trench defenses."

The bearer of the message from the commanding general insisted, "This is an order, Major."

Only then did Churchill testily agree to leave his post. Minutes after his departure, a bomb obliterated the very spot in the dugout where Churchill had been standing.

As Churchill later observed, "A hand had been stretched out to move me in the nick of time from a fatal spot."

CHAPTER 8

CAMP COLT, GETTYSBURG

I missed the boat in the war we had been told would end all wars.

DWIGHT DAVID EISENHOWER

IF BEING RELEGATED to the sidelines as a spectator frustrated Churchill, he was at least a soldier in the trenches. That was just where Eisenhower wanted to be.

Eisenhower waited impatiently for the next assignment, which he was sure had to be France. Even if he would land there after almost every one else in his class, it would be better than not arriving at all.

But it was not to be. The next posting was to Camp Colt in Gettysburg. He was angry, though he should have regarded the assignment as an accolade: his task at Camp Colt was to prepare a tank battalion for combat readiness so that it could be shipped overseas.

The airplane might have been the glamour weapon in 1918, but visionary planners in the army at that time believed the tank was the weapon of the future. Eisenhower was promised that when the training was complete, he would command a tank battalion in France. Eisenhower wrote later of his fascination for this new miracle machine: "Juggernauts of combat, titanic in bulk (even though snails in speed), . . . rolling effortless over wire entanglements and trenches, demolishing gun-nests with their fire and terrorizing the foe into quick and abject surrender."

There was one major problem. Camp Colt had no tanks with which to train. Eisenhower foresaw a deteriorating morale among the soldiers, who had nothing to do but the usual routine of basic drills. One of Eisenhower's paramount skills as an officer, however, was his ability to devise inventive solutions to practical problems. "Field expedients" was a favorite subject of his, and he would list to his men the innovations and substitutes that creative captains in past battles had devised as replacements in shortages. Now Eisenhower had to find challenging work for his men, to prevent, as he wrote, "the dry rot of tedious idleness."

Tanks used guns or small-caliber cannons. Why not, Eisenhower thought, requisition similar weapons that are used on ships? A call to the navy department got him his guns (but not the ammunition), and he put his men to work assembling and disassembling the parts until they could do it blindfolded.

When the shells arrived, Eisenhower ordered the guns to be mounted on truck trailers or flatbed trucks. Right on the Big Round Top, the fabled ridge in the Battle of Gettysburg, he had his men shooting from moving trucks at all kinds of mobile targets.

In addition, Eisenhower set up two "schools"—one a motor repair school with instructors, at a big garage. To it, he had brought secondhand motors of all kinds so that his men could become master mechanics.

Another was a telegraph school. Eisenhower knew from history that too many battles had been lost because of misunderstood messages. Therefore, many of his men were taught Morse code. As Eisenhower wrote later, "A first-rate telegrapher might prove himself worth more than a company of riflemen."

Eisenhower was always seeking ways to improve the training. He issued memos that asked for suggestions and ideas. One lieutenant told him that he ran a model camp. In the midst of the man's praise, Ike cut him off: "For God's sake, get out and find something wrong with it. It can't be as good as you say it is. Either you're not being frank or you're as big a fool as I am."

Eisenhower had an art for getting the best out of an officer. For one thing, he was a listener, and he would hear out his men's ideas and problems. The enlisted men presented greater difficulties. The problem was booze. One hotelkeeper in Gettysburg, against Eisenhower's request, was selling liquor under the table to soldiers. Eisenhower called on the man, and he promised not to continue. Weeks later, the hotel was selling liquor again. This time Eisenhower had the hotel surrounded by guards, which kept not only soldiers out but most civilians too.

The hotel owner telephoned his congressman, and the two of them demanded Major Eisenhower's presence at the hotel.

Eisenhower stood his ground. The armed guard would stay. The congressman threatened, "I can go to the War Department. I have connections. If you're going to be so damn stubborn, I can have you replaced."

"Congressman," Eisenhower fired back, "You do exactly that." The congressman was disconcerted

"Nothing would please me more," explained Eisenhower, "to be taken out of this job. I want to go overseas. Maybe if you write I can get there."

The politician did go to the War Department to complain, but the outcome was not what either the congressman or Eisenhower wanted: a letter from the assistant secretary of war, commending Eisenhower for his diligence in looking after the best interests of his men.

Another time a congressman tried to go over Eisenhower's head was when the latter disciplined a lieutenant who had been caught cheating at a poker game.

Eisenhower brought the officer in and confronted him with his marked-card deck. Then Eisenhower asked, "Would you rather resign for the good of the Army or would you like to be tried by court-martial?"

The officer resigned. Three days later the congressman from the officer's district came storming in, accompanied by the lieutenant's father. The meeting ended as the politician raged at Eisenhower, shouting that he was "acting pretty arbitrary for a Major."

"I am acting," replied Eisenhower, "as an Army officer protecting my command."

The experience only fortified the minimal esteem Eisenhower had for politicians. It was a resentment he would continue to harbor and try to hide.

Eisenhower, however, did little to mask his frustration at being bottled up stateside while "the war to end all wars" was being staged in another continent. To vent his frustration, Eisenhower furthered his studies on the Battle of Gettysburg. After all, he was based in Gettysburg. So he decided he would review the various orders while standing in the exact position the various colonels and generals had been. Sometimes he took Mamie along and bent her ear about the various movements of this Confederate brigade or that Union regiment. Later Mamie wryly commented to another officer's wife, "Ike knew every rock on that battlefield." The woman did not know whether it was meant as praise or protest.

Ike's mood turned from frustration to fear when the Spanish flu epidemic struck. By quickly enacting strict hygiene measures, he was able to keep the death toll to only two of his soldiers. That percentage was the lowest of any base or camp in the United States.

Afterward, he was informed that he would be made a full colonel if he would give up his plans for overseas service. Eisenhower would not yield. He wanted action.

The superior did not grant Eisenhower his request but recommended a promotion: not colonel, but lieutenant colonel. In

October 1918, on his twenty-eighth birthday, Eisenhower became one of the youngest lieutenant colonels in the army.

A week later Ike came home brandishing an order.
"Mamie, I've made it!" he proclaimed. "My orders for France
have come!"

"It's grand, Ike," Mamie dutifully replied. "I'm truly happy.
When do you go?"

He let her read the War Department's order. "You will
proceed to Camp Dix, New Jersey, for embarkation on November 18."

Late on November 10, the newspapers announced the
armistice: hostilities would conclude on November 11 at eleven
o'clock—5:00 A.M. in Gettysburg. When Eisenhower went to
his desk at seven the next morning, the guns were already silent.

To one of his West Point classmates, Capt. Norman Randolph, he stated, "I suppose we'll spend the rest of our lives ex-
plaining why we didn't get into this war." And then he
exclaimed, "By God, from now on I'm cutting myself a swath
that will make up for this."

CHAPTER 9

THE WAR DEPARTMENT

Politics is like riding a horse. If you are knocked off, you must brush yourself off and remount.

WINSTON CHURCHILL

TO WITNESS EVERY DAY the mindless massacre of young men enraged Churchill. In the trenches Major Churchill could see at firsthand "the disaster of sending armies to chew barbed wire in France and Flanders." He was sickened by the daily attrition of trench combat snuffing out the young manhood of Britain. Those in charge of the war, thought Churchill, should be held accountable for the senseless sacrifice of men without any target realized or objective gained. (Of course, Churchill's critics had vilified him for what they thought was similar recklessness in the Dardanelles.)

Shortly after the United States entered the war in April 1917, however, a parliamentary report on the Dardanelles was issued: Churchill was exonerated. An emboldened Churchill now drafted his critique of the war and delivered it to a secret session of the House of Commons. He bluntly told the members to wage no more costly offensives but to conserve their troops' strength for that moment when, with the arrival of America's vast numbers, one last massive thrust could be mounted.

Churchill envisioned that such an attack would be empowered by the "tank," which he had developed earlier and which the army had thus far disdained.

Quietly, he sounded out his old constituency chairman in Dundee, Scotland, for a parliamentary seat. Word of his maneuvering made Prime Minister David Lloyd George nervous. He did not look forward to a tart-tongued Churchill second-guessing the conduct of the war from the back benches.

Anyway, as the United States was now in the war, the half-American Churchill, figured Lloyd George, might be able to expedite armament supplies from the United States. To his reluctant colleagues, Lloyd George managed to sell the idea of putting Churchill in the Cabinet. His argument was a variation of the Arab proverb—better the camel inside the tent pissing out than outside the tent pissing in.

Churchill was appointed secretary of state for munitions, where his organizational talents could be harnessed for coordinating the logistical demands of the soon-to-be-landing Americans. He proved so helpful that General Pershing awarded him the Distinguished Service Cross, the only Englishman so honored (and a medal that was later awarded to Eisenhower).

In that role Churchill was persuasive in deploying forty-eight tanks, a move that was decisive in the Battle of Thiepval. In addition to his munitions duties, Churchill arranged for himself to become the air force minister of the first air force that any government in the world had ever installed.

Commandeering a plane for himself, Churchill flew almost every morning over the English Channel from England to France, to track down shortages in ammunition, weaponry, and medical supplies. Then he returned in time to give his report to the House of Commons in the evenings. In the days before the word *commuting* had been coined, Churchill flew his own daily shuttle to France, as a faster and more accurate method than waiting for telegrams.

His wife, Clementine, took a dim view of this commuting. When Churchill's biplane crashed one afternoon in an East London airfield, the aviator-goggled Churchill managed to climb out of the cockpit unscathed. A threat from his wife stopped any further flying: "Either Clementine or the aero-plane."

In his eighteen months as war minister, perhaps Churchill's greatest contribution was his voice. In that final era before radio, no head of government—not even such a dynamic orator as the white-maned Lloyd George—could by himself inspire his countrymen. The prime minister's orations were confined to the House of Commons, except for the occasional address to a London banquet. The burden thus fell on Churchill, who proved as eloquent as he was ubiquitous.

Churchill launched his return to office by a speech to constituents in Dundee. Referring to Woodrow Wilson's recent call for a League of Nations, Churchill reminded his Scottish listeners, "We are the heart, the center of the League of Nations. If we fail, all fail. If we break, all break."

For a war-weary nation, Churchill inspired a renewed vigor. The next July 4, at an Anglo-American dinner, Churchill sounded the note that would be the closing theme of the war:

Germany must be beaten; Germany must know she is beaten; Germany must feel she is beaten. Her defeat must be expressed in terms and facts which will for all time deter others from emulating her crimes and will safeguard us against their repetition.

Then he closed with this final appeal:

No compromise with the main purpose, no peace till victory, no pact with unrepentant wrong.

The popular press picked up the battle cry "No peace till victory." Lord Beaverbrook told Churchill it was his greatest speech and had it printed in pamphlet form and distributed in America. The ring of such resolute words served to dispel the lingering "doubts of 'defeatism,'" a word that Churchill coined, borrowing from the French language to describe the noxious pessimism of war critics.

Churchill's morale-lifting speeches around the country at bond rallies, ship launchings, factory sites, and civic dinners were in a sense a dress rehearsal for his sublime contributions a little more than twenty years later. The ending of the war brought forth words worthy of his World War II finest. In a peroration that borrowed from his mentor Bourke Cockran, Abraham Lincoln, and the prophet Isaiah, he closed thus:

> Five years of concerted effort by all classes like what we have given in the war, but without its tragedies, would create an abundance and prosperity in this land, aye, throughout, the world, such as has never yet been known or dreamt of. Five years of faction, of bickering, of class jealousies and party in utter and universal privation.
>
> The choice is in our hands. Like the Israelites of old, blessing and cursing is set before us. Today we can have the greatest failure or the greatest triumph—as we choose. There is enough for all. The earth is a generous mother. Never, never did science offer such fair gifts to man. Never did their knowledge and science stand so high. Repair the waste. Rebuild the ruins. Heal the wounds. Crown the victors. Comfort the broken and broken-hearted. There is the battle we have now to fight. There is the victory we have now to win. Let us go forward together.

Armistice Day found Churchill ambivalent. The carnage had ceased, but he feared the future. The punitive policies toward Germany disturbed him: "I have always been against the pacifists during the quarrel and against the Jingoists at the close."

To Churchill, the League of Nations was a weak vessel—even more so without the United States. Churchill was dismissive of President Wilson: "Peace and goodwill among all nations abroad but no truck with Republicans at home." About the president's role at Versailles he later wrote, "If Wilson had been either simply an idealist or a caucus politician, he might have succeeded. His attempt to run the two in double harness was the cause of his undoing."

Lenin's Russian Revolution also worried Churchill. "Bolshevism," he said, "is not a policy but a disease." He envisioned the horror that the contagion of communism would spread across the world. His pleas for the British as well as the Americans to assist the White armies against Lenin in Russia went unheeded.

The outspoken Churchill was a loose cannon in the Cabinet. So David Lloyd George decided to channel Churchill's energies in a post that would send him out of London: Secretary of State for the Colonies.

Specifically, he was charged to bring peace to Ireland and the Middle East.

"David," Churchill reportedly replied, "a settlement in Ireland and the Holy Land! I am supposed to do in a year what all of the prophets, saints and diplomats have failed to do for centuries."

In part, Lloyd George picked Churchill because he, more than anyone else, had shouldered the burden of combating Northern Ireland defiance in those uneasy moments before World War I when he was home secretary. This time, however, the threat of sedition came from the Catholic south. The Irish Republican Army, whose soldiers were then less like terrorists and more like troops, as the name suggests, was conducting a full-scale civil war. The Churchill strategy for peace was far from pacific. It combined the threat of force and the flash of rhetoric with fair and even generous terms. That had been his policy for the Boer War, and even at the close of the just-finished war with Germany, Churchill was one of the few English who stood against the revanche demands of "Hang the Kaiser" crowd.

At the end of the war, however, Dublin was rebelling against "home rule" status. The Irish wanted total independence. As Colonial Secretary, Churchill met with Michael Collins, the Irish representative who had led an uprising in 1916.

The defiant Collins told Churchill in their first meeting, "You hunted me day and night. You put a price on my head." Then Churchill said, "Wait a minute, you're not the only one," and showed a framed copy of the reward offered by the Boers for his recapture. "At least you got a good price, £5000. Look at me, £25 dead or alive. How would you like that?"

The relationship between the old soldiers ripened into one of mutual respect. Churchill and Lloyd George handed Collins and the other leaders the stark choice of dominion (like Canada and Australia) or war. They reluctantly agreed to dominion status and to leaving Ulster as part of Britain. Collins knew the wrath he would incur by signing the pact; Collins said, "I expect soon to be killed." He was right. Before his assassination, he wrote one last message: "Tell Winston we could never have done it without him."

Churchill, as Colonial Secretary, now had the task of presenting the Irish treaty to the House of Commons: "For generations we have been wandering and floundering in the Irish bog; but at least we think that in the Treaty we have set our feet upon a pathway, which has already become a causeway—narrow, but firm and far-reaching." Moved by Churchill's eloquence, enough Conservatives joined to ratify the treaty. Churchill the peacemaker is not a role his biographers emphasize, but it is noteworthy that Churchill, at the Colonial Office, was instrumental in securing settlement not only in Ireland but also in the Middle East—two areas where so many statesmen have failed.

To resolve postwar Arab demands in the wake of the defeat of Turkish rule, Churchill called a Cairo conference, with his friend Lawrence of Arabia as chief adviser. Fearful for the Jews' tenuous hold on Palestine, Churchill maneuvered to place on the Middle East thrones of Iraq and Jordan two of the Feisal family, whose moderation would check the more fanatical factions of Arab anti-Zionism.

By this, Churchill wanted to ensure the continuing promise of the Balfour Declaration, particularly for fleeing Jewish refugees from Russia. At one point he proclaimed in the House of Commons, "It is hard enough in all conscience to make a new Zion, but if, over the portals of the new Jerusalem, you are going to inscribe the legend 'No Israelite need apply,' then I hope the House will permit me to confine my attention exclusively to Irish matters." The peace gains in Palestine and in Ireland were not without their price. The Irish treaty particularly shattered much of the Conservative Party members' support for Lloyd George's Liberal coalition. When his government fell, a new election was held.

On the day of the British general election in 1922, Churchill was convalescing in a Dundee hospital from an appendicitis operation. The attack had stopped his campaigning short. In addition to this handicap, his party had been badly split by defections to the Conservatives by Liberals opposed to Lloyd George. When the returns came in, Churchill was in a hospital, listening on a new contraption called the "wireless." He shook his head sadly at the reports of the landslide defeat and murmured to the nurse, "All of a sudden, I find myself without a party, without a ministry, and without a seat, and even . . . without an appendix."

Despite his diplomatic triumphs, the past twelve months had constituted a milestone in his life more mournful than any other since 1895, when both his father and his nanny, Mrs. Everest, had died. In June 1921, his mother, Lady Randolph, died at age sixty-seven from complications resulting from amputation of an infected ankle. Churchill wrote, "She had the gift of eternal youth and never before have I felt this more, in these weeks of cruel pain."

Two months later his youngest child, Marigold, died at age three from a strep throat infection. The loss racked him with despair. (His other children, in order, were Diana, Randolph, and Sarah. Another child, Mary, would be born in 1922.)

Churchill was now middle-aged. Not only private sorrows but also the public memory of Gallipoli had darkened his soul. His frame bore the grief of an anguished father, mourning son, and discredited minister, whose former reputation, despite subsequent Cabinet accomplishments, had not been redeemed. Although in his prime, he found himself a political has-been at the end of his odyssey in the Liberal Party, which he had so brightly begun as a ministerial boy wonder.

CHAPTER 10

———

CAMP GAILLARD, PANAMA

Life with General Conner was a graduate school in military affairs and the humanities.

DWIGHT DAVID EISENHOWER

PRESIDENT EISENHOWER was the father of the interstate highway. One of his administration's most enduring accomplishments was the federal limited-access highway system that crosses the United States, both north and south. The seed of that plan began its germination in 1919.

While at Camp Meade in Maryland, Eisenhower heard that the army was planning to send a truck convoy across America. He immediately applied for an assignment, recommending his assistant at Meade, Major Sereno Brett, a highly decorated veteran from the recent war, as his deputy.

For Eisenhower, the opportunity came at a low time in his fortunes. In the wake of the army demobilization came demotions. Lieutenant Colonel Eisenhower would soon be knocked down to captain. With that salary, he would be looking forward to a decade or more of, in his own words, "stretching dollars and merging dimes." He even considered quitting the army and accepting a job of helping to run a business in Indiana.

The proposed transcontinental expedition jolted him from his doldrums. Just south of the White House grounds, ceremonies were staged for Zero Milestone. There was a dedication and speeches by Secretary of War Newton Baker and the Army Chief of Staff, Gen. Peyton March. The convoy would go north to Gettysburg and then west on U.S. 30, on the old Lincoln Highway (the first to span the nation from New York City to San Francisco). The caravan was a motley America on wheels—all kinds of trucks, vans, staff cars, motorcycles, ambulances, trucks, tractors, and a small Renault "Whippet" tank latched to a flatbed trailer.

This "truck-train," as Eisenhower called it, would cover about 3,200 miles at an average of 6 miles an hour. Almost 3.5 million Americans would witness and welcome the caravan as it wended its way through the towns of the United States.

Ike, the career officer who had never been assigned abroad, became one of the few soldiers who would ever traverse the full continental sweep of his own country. His conclusion was that the richest country in the world had the worst roads.

Years later as a general he would ask soldiers, "Where are you from?" And he would astonish them: they would give the name of their little hometown, and he would remark, "Oh, you have the big Methodist church with no steeple right in the center of town" or "You have that statue in the square to 'Tippecanoe,' General William Henry Harrison."

Few generals could ever claim to have visited as many states and communities as Eisenhower. It was an experience that would serve him well when he ran for president in 1952. Thirty-three years before, as a visiting lieutenant colonel, he had been invited to speak to Rotary Clubs, chambers of commerce, and church groups. It was their introduction to the U.S. Army, but it was Eisenhower's introduction to America.

If the transcontinental trek was educational, it was also enjoyable. Such a crossing, with its numerous minor accidents, engine failures, flat tires, car breakdowns, and detours, was wearying on morale, but Eisenhower knew how to lift spirits by setting up a caper or pulling a prank.

Once, while riding a reconnaissance car across the plains of Nebraska, Eisenhower and Major Brett sighted a jackrabbit. Eisenhower, who had a .22 rifle with him, shot it from about a hundred yards away. Then they had this idea. They propped up the dead rabbit on a bush.

The next day they took two officers, who hailed from the East and had little knowledge of hunting, for a ride to do some shooting.

"Do you see that jackrabbit?" Brett asked the eastern officers. It was early evening and the rabbit just about impossible to make out at 150 yards, but they said they thought they could see its outline.

"Well, Ike here," said Brett, "is one of the finest pistol shots I have ever known, and I saw a lot of marksmen in the war."

Ike immediately pulled out his .45 pistol and fired. "You got him," said Brett. The two officers with Eisenhower and Brett drove over to the bush, and there was the dead rabbit. The officers marveled that Ike must have been as good if not better than his fellow Abilene quick-on-the-draw gunman Wild Bill Hickock, to whom Sereno Brett had told them Ike was related.

One of these easterners, a New Yorker who had never been west of the Appalachians, listened intently one night as some Wyoming locals, whom Eisenhower and Brett had briefed the night before, warned of possible Indian raids. It was proposed to set up a guard for the convoy. The next night the New Yorker was given the sentry duty for the after-midnight shift. During his shift, Ike and Sereno Brett staged a series of Indian war whoops. The guard fired shots, with the intention of scaring them away and arousing the camp to possible action. The scare worked all too well: the conscientious officer fired off a telegram to Washington to alert the War Department of possible Indian insurrections in Wyoming.

When Eisenhower returned to Camp Meade in Maryland, Colonel Rockenbach told him he was to coach the camp's football team. Meade was still the home of the Tank Corps. While he could be preparing to fight the wars of the future with tomorrow's weapon, he was coaching a football team. It would do nothing for his career advancement.

Eisenhower, however, saw in coaching football an army laboratory for studying methods for improving morale and teamwork. A good coach, like a good officer, knew his men and did not always go by the book. He relied instead on intelligence and imagination. For example, there was the situation in his battalion where two men despised each other. Eisenhower ordered them to wash all the windows in the barracks—one working on the inside and the other on the outside. At first they glared and sneered at each other, but after awhile one of them couldn't keep back a chuckle. It triggered a smile on the other side of the window. The scowls turned to funny faces. By the end of the day they were friends.

Life was happy for the Eisenhowers until just before Christmas of 1920. At that time they learned that Icky, the four-year-old who was the focus of their life, had contracted scarlet fever. Little Icky, dressed in complete army uniform with his overseas cap, had become a kind of mascot at Camp Meade.

By Christmas Day the child was too sick to open his presents, and on January 2, 1921, he was dead. "It was the greatest disappointment and disaster of my life," wrote Eisenhower. "I was on the edge of a breakdown."

To keep his sanity, he had to set his mind on something else. He chose the science and theory of tank warfare. For this he had an apt study mate: Col. George Patton.

By family and personality, Patton was Eisenhower's opposite. Patrician and rich in background—flamboyant and volatile in temperament. But they both liked playing poker, shooting pistols, and riding horses. They also shared a religion—belief in the tank. And like true believers in any faith, the two wanted to convert others to the tenets of their creed. The tank promised future deliverance of victory to battle troops.

At Meade, Patton commanded a battalion of French-made Renault tanks and Eisenhower headed a unit of U.S.–built Mark VII medium-range tanks. One day they tested whether the medium tank could pull two of the light Renault tanks up a slope with a cable. The cable ripped, whipping past inches from their faces, slicing off brush and saplings like a machete. Patton asked, "Were you as scared as I was?"

Ike answered, "George, we were certainly not more than five or six inches from sudden death!"

Both wrote papers on tanks for the *Infantry Journal*, which urged the establishment of an independent tank unit free from the three-mph snail pace of the infantry. Eisenhower stressed the tank's mobility and its ability to smash through barbed wire.

"The tank," commented Eisenhower, "was an appendage to troops in the last war." In the next war, he predicted, it would be the vanguard.

That the tank should be the spearhead for attack in future battles rattled the head-in-the-sand thinking of the War Department. It was seditious thinking to the status quo. Eisenhower was warned that he would face a court martial if he continued to publish or propound his views.

One general *had* taken an interest in Eisenhower's views. Fox Conner had been serving as Pershing's chief of staff in Washington. Black Jack had returned from the war planning to run for president, as Grant had done. He had fallen flat on his face. So he just bided his time in Washington until 1921, when he was slated to be Chief of Staff of the Army.

Conner used some of that slack time to search out in Washington men he had heard about who might possess the potential to become generals. At a lunch with Eisenhower and Patton, Conner scouted out their thinking on tanks.

Conner already knew Patton. The more equable and even-voiced Eisenhower caught his interest. For his part, Eisenhower was entranced. Conner was not tall, but his demeanor and poise commanded deference. His eyes and voice signaled intelligence. When Pershing became head of the army in the fall of 1921, Conner went to head Camp Gaillard in Panama. He asked for Eisenhower to be his chief executive officer.

For his first out-of-the-country assignment, Panama was hardly paradise. The almost daily tropical rain leaked through the roof of the Eisenhower house.

In the first week, both rats and bats terrorized Mamie. Once a bat hovered over her bed. "Kill it, Ike!" Mamie screamed.

Ike grinned, "I can't do it, honey, It's against the law here to shoot it."

"Law or no law, kill the bloody bat!" So Ike in his green pajamas unsheathed his gilded ceremonial sword from its scabbard. He looked like a samurai warrior as he sliced the air in a minuet of steps until he finally stabbed the flying rodent.

The lush-jungled Panama had its beauty, but for Ike its blessing was not in its physical surroundings but in its mental environment. When the Conners invited the Eisenhowers for dinner that first week, Ike witnessed the first real library in a home. Conner had hundreds of books placed by region, by history, biographies by subject, and novels by authors. That first evening he handed Ike a novel to take home: *The Adventures of Brigadier Gerard*, a fictional account of Napoleonic warfare. Like any great teacher, Conner hooked his student first with an entertaining and exciting lesson.

Soon his studies escalated into more challenging works: the classics of military warfare, such as von Clausewitz's *On War* and the memoirs of generals Grant and Sherman. A month later he graduated to more philosophical works—Plato and Aristotle of ancient Greece, followed by Cicero and Tacitus of Rome. Eisenhower would spend a day in the field drilling the infantry and then come home. After dinner with Mamie, he would read and take notes until two in the morning. The next day he would rise at six and repeat the routine.

Sometimes, over campfires in the field, Conner debated with the twenty-year-younger Eisenhower on the strategy and tactics of Gettysburg. Steele's *Campaigns* was their bible and reference book.

Principal among Conner's firmest convictions was that another world war loomed in the not-too-distant future. The harsh handling of Germany in the Treaty of Versailles had sown the seeds of that next war. Conner told him that the next conflict would not be his but Eisenhower's war. Eisenhower would be ready.

Conner had recommended him for Fort Leavenworth. The army's Command and General Staff School was the seminary for future generals. Eisenhower observed later that some truth lies in the old adage "It's not *what* you know, but *who* you know. Had I been denied the fortune of knowing Fox Conner, my career might have been radically different. Because I *did* know him, I did go to Leavenworth."

Before going to Leavenworth, Ike and Mamie stopped in Abilene, Kansas. One night Ike went out with some high school classmates for a game of poker. At midnight a "steaming" Mamie waited with Ike's mother, with whom relations were not always easy.

"I'm going to call him," said Mamie.

"Better not," Ida Eisenhower warned. "Ike would not appreciate that."

"But I would!" Mamie grabbed the phone. "You come back here right now," she yelled at Ike.

"I can't, I'm behind—I'm losing. You don't understand the strategy of poker."

Mamie yelled, "I don't want to hear it. You come back right now," and hung up.

Two hours later Ike returned with a hundred dollars in his pocket. But the winnings did little to mollify Mamie.

In August 1925, determined to graduate first in the class, Eisenhower arrived at Leavenworth, which was located not far from the Missouri border.

At Fort Leavenworth Ike found that he would have to compete with his old friend from Houston, "Gee" Gerow. Ike came prepared. With him were Patton's notes on the 126 case problems Patton had used to graduate the previous year with honors.

Rumors circulated in the army about the rigors of the school, including apocryphal tales of breakdowns and suicides. Ike was advised to enter a study committee or form his own two-man partnership. He and Gerow teamed up.

General Conner had told his protégé that he would finish right near the top because Ike, under Conner in Panama, had mastered the art of writing a succinct five-paragraph field order or operations plan. Eisenhower made Conner a prophet. Ike finished first (his friend Gee was eleventh).

Ike's pen landed him his next assignment, again at the general's recommendation: to write a guidebook for the American Battlefields and Monuments Commission, which had been created to build and maintain cemeteries for the Americans buried overseas. The new cemeteries were certain to attract families of the buried veterans, as well as tourists.

In six months in Washington Ike wrote a 282-page book. The general whose writing had most captured Eisenhower's eye was Grant, and Eisenhower emulated the muscular style of Grant's memoirs. The result was a detailed but easily readable account. The unbureaucratic tone impressed General Pershing, who had asked Eisenhower to give him some advice for the memoirs he was writing. Eisenhower told him to abandon the form of his diary for a more readable chronological treatment and then wrote a chapter as an example. Col. George Marshall disagreed with Ike's recommendation, but both were proved right: the "diary" approach won Pershing a Pulitzer Prize, but the book bombed in the bookstores.

Pershing, known for his economy of praise, extolled Ike's guidebook and recommended that he write a new revised and expanded version, based on his firsthand study and observations of the battlefields. Eisenhower resisted. A position on the General Staff in Washington was also being offered. A tour in Paris would not lead to any star on his shoulder.

But to Mamie, Paris was filled with stars, famous authors, and exiled royals. In 1928 Paris dazzled more than any city of the world. Mamie did not speak a word of French, but she was going to see "the City of Lights."

Ike was equally adamant. First he had been pegged in the Army as "Coach Eisenhower," and now he would be tagged as "Ike the writer." Neither category steered him toward the top.

Ike and Mamie had another pitched battle like the poker night in Abilene, and the soldier lost. But Ike benefited by Mamie's ultimatum. France became for Ike the liberal arts education that he never received at West Point.

France vaunts itself as the center of Western civilization, and it can rightfully boast of having been the arena of Europe's epic battles ever since. Caesar conquered the Gauls there. It was in France that Charles Martel, "the Hammer," beat back the Moors in the eighth century.

As he had in Gettysburg, Ike took out his history book and maps to examine the terrain of the famous battle and the decisions of opposing generals. At Agincourt he added Shakespeare's *Henry V* to his homework, as he and Mamie toured the battlefield where the new English longbows defeated the French knights.

He and Mamie also drove over the road that took Napoleon to Italy, as well as the highway that goes north to Belgium and a town called Waterloo. In the course of his weekend journeys, he got to know the roads and rivers of France better than he knew Kansas. In fifteen years that knowledge would prove invaluable. Later, looking back, he told his grandson David, "Paris was the most fun of my life."

II DOWNING STREET

Politicians know they are but the creatures of the day.

WINSTON CHURCHILL

IN THE 1920s Churchill also spent much of his time writing. On leaving Parliament, he had taken up the pen. Inactivity was an anathema to Churchill, and he now threw his energies into writing about the Great War.

Although Lord Balfour, typically sardonic, called *The World Crisis* "an autobiography disguised as a history of the universe," a more apt description might be "oratory in the garb of history." The book, written in Churchillian rhetoric, reverberates with the thunder of terrible events. His previous writing experiences shaped the studied nature of his early speeches, but it is the majestic sweep of Churchill the rhetorician that is heard in *The World Crisis*. He didn't actually write it—he dictated it. Puffing a Havana cigar, he paced up and down the study declaiming in bursts, while a nervous secretary struggled to record all his rich phrases in Pitman shorthand.

For Churchill, such literary exercise was not a chore but a lark he could not bear to end by sending it off to the printer, and when it returned in galley form he viewed it as another draft instead of a proof to be checked for accuracy. Galleys were returned, their margins bulging with whole new paragraphs to be inserted.

But the final draft was, for the most part, well worth the cost. Listen to his conclusion of a colossal military epic when he prophesies, with a rhetorical "nay," the specter of nuclear apocalypse:

> It is probable—nay, certain—that among the means which will next time be at their disposal will be agencies and processes of destruction wholesale, limited and perhaps, once launched, uncontrollable.
>
> Death stands at attention, obedient, expectant, ready to serve, ready to shear away the peoples en masse, ready, if called on, to pulverize, without hope of repair, what is left of civilization.

His workshop for the bestselling *The World Crisis* and its sequel, *The Aftermath*, was a new house. With the loss of his seat in Dundee in 1922, Churchill at forty-eight was no longer a young man of promise but a relic of the past. The hair, still sandy, had thinned and made no pretense of covering the scalp except on the sides, and his slouch, which had once given his youth a purposeful cast, now seemed less a mannerism than a mirror of age. The days of adventure and greatness were behind him. At that time of life when most men find the security of career replacing the dreams of youth, Churchill had neither. The moorings were missing, not only those of politics and party but also the personal ones of property and household.

For most of his life Churchill had been rootless. He had fought in many countries, occupied many ministerial posts, and lived in many houses and apartments. As head of his family he yearned to settle down and seek the solace of the countryside in a home that was his own, where his children could run and romp.

On a November Sunday in 1922 he took his family on a drive from London to see an estate in Kent. Not until their return did he reveal, grinning, that the house, Chartwell, was already theirs; he had bought it with a recent legacy from his great-grandmother, the Marchioness of Londonderry. The Victorian manor was not an architectural splendor, but the view was. A hilly crown wooded by expansive spreading chestnuts and resolute oaks overlooking the green of an English heath, the site suggested much of Churchill himself.

It was also where Churchill wrote his two top sellers, *The World Crisis* and *The Aftermath*. Like a farmer who rotates his crops for more productivity, he alternated his pen and brush. After a stint of painting, Churchill found he could return to his study revived. The secret to his titanic output was in no small way this rhythmic rotation from library to landscape. As he explained in *Painting as a Pastime*,

> Change is the master key. A man can wear out a particular part of his mind by continually using it and tiring just in the same way as he can wear out the elbows of a coat by rubbing the frayed elbow; but the tired part of the mind can be rested and strengthened, not by merely rest, but by using other parts.

The habit of a midday nap served to extend his working day, and the hobby of painting generated more hours of creativity in that day.

During those bleak days of political limbo, Churchill also threw himself into the task of restoring the grounds and the manor house that rested on them. Just as an orator will strike the clumsy word, revise the awkward phrase, and redress the unbalanced sentence, so Churchill hacked the Victorian gables off the roof, sliced off the ponderous oriels of the windows, and cut away the brush of ivy on the sides to reveal the simpler tones of a Tudor house.

Churchill plowed the royalties of his two books back into his Chartwell renovation. In untypical modesty, calling *The World Crisis* a potboiler, he sent copies to friends. Lawrence of Arabia wrote back, "Some pot!" (In recounting the incident to friends, Churchill, after the initial laugh, would add, "some boiler," which no doubt was the origin of his "some chicken, some neck" aside to the Canadian Parliament in 1941.) The success of this pot-boiler stirred up renewed interest about its author.

Yet more than being read, Churchill wanted to be listened to. For that, he needed a forum. Since the Liberal Party debacle of 1922, Churchill had been without a parliamentary seat and virtually without a party. Although Churchill was still a Liberal in name, the old domestic issues of reform were faded yellowed clippings in a mind now transfixed by the glaringly recurrent headlines of war and peace. Yet even more than the weakening of his ties with the Liberal Party, the Liberal Party itself was weakening. Not only had the Labourites replaced the Liberals, but also what remained of the dwindling Liberal ranks had bitterly split into Asquith and Lloyd George factions. Churchill was grateful to the feisty Welsh leader who had brought him back to the Cabinet after Gallipoli; although a follower of Lloyd George, however, he was not eager to follow him in his accommodation with the left. It was one thing to fight the lords, but it was another to yield to the rising union demands. Special privilege for any class, be it by heredity or majority, was wrong to Churchill, yet that was what the egalitarian tenets of British socialism seemed to demand. If, in the face of Liberal Party disintegration, the struggle for the future lay between Labour and Conservatism, Churchill had no difficulty in making a choice.

He told one group that "The American Declaration of Independence states that all men are created equal, but the socialists want to say that all men should be kept equal. I'm for equality at the starting gate, but not at the finish line."

But would the Conservative Party take him back? As Churchill himself said, "It is one thing to 'rat' but another to 're-rat.'" After all, the Churchill stock was not exactly bullish. Since his defeat in Dundee in 1922, he had lost again as a Liberal at West Leicester in 1923. Nevertheless, Churchill asked the Conservative Party to adopt him as the candidate when a vacancy arose in the historic seat of Westminster. Because the constituency was right in the heart of London, which included Westminster Abbey and the Houses of Parliament, it was rather like asking for the party nomination in that part of the District of Columbia where the Capitol, cabinet departments, and White House lie. Not unexpectedly, he was turned down. Undaunted, Churchill created his own one-man party, the Constitutionalist, and ran anyway. Aided by his campaign manager, a young redhead named Brendan Bracken, Churchill took on the political organization of the Conservatives, as well as those of the Liberal and Labour Parties, in what may have been the most colorful campaign in parliamentary history.

In a district that included the toughs of Soho as well as the theater set of the Strand, the poor as well as the peers, Churchill mobilized for the ten-day campaign the unlikeliest collection of political volunteers a British election had ever seen. Duchesses in diamonds went door-to-door, show girls stayed up all night after performances stuffing envelopes, jockeys and prizefighters took to the stump for Churchill, "the man against the machine." Churchill himself, in a posh version of the American sound truck, rode around the district in a four-in-hand carriage with a standing uniformed trumpeter proclaiming his arrival. The American wife of a Conservative MP had hung in her townhouse windows huge posters of Churchill's baby daughter Mary, saying, "Vote for my Daddy."

If Londoners and their press, almost all of which endorsed the Churchill candidacy, warmed to the American-style campaign, Churchill positively glowed. In earlier campaigns he had been inhibited by the strictures of party conformity, but this time he could be completely himself. He had a cause. As a centrist with his own Constitutionalist Party, he would show hidebound Tories and complaisant Liberals how to fight socialism. To his London voters he proclaimed,

> Westminster has it in its power to send to our friends and allies an important message that Britain and the British people, to whom the whole world looks for example and guidance, is not going to slide and slither weakly and hopelessly into socialist confusion.

But Churchill reserved his greatest contempt for the government's recent recognition of the Soviet government in Moscow:

> In a few weeks a Bolshevik ambassador will reach these shores and be rapturously welcomed by the socialist minister. He will be applauded by every revolutionary, and will be conducted to the presence of the sovereign. He represents a government, which has reduced a mighty, and noble nation to a slavery never witnessed since the Middle Ages.

The zest of the candidate spurred on his volunteer army of celebrities and chorus girls. Almost all the press chimed in, calling for the return to the Commons of that "debating force and volcanic energy." Finally, on the eve of the election, one-time Conservative leader Arthur Balfour broke ranks and gave his support to his one-time tormentor from the back benches. Balfour, now an earl, was an erudite statesman who felt a disdain for the cant and histrionics of electioneering but recognized Churchill's uncommon talents and indicated his "desire to see you once more in the House of Commons, once more able to use your brilliant gifts in the public discussion."

But it was not to be Westminster itself that returned Churchill to Westminster. Despite all the glamour and glitter of a spectacular campaign, he lost by 43 votes out of the 22,000 cast. Yet wrapped in the defeat was a victory. Churchill had fought his way back to national recognition and esteem. The Conservative leader, Stanley Baldwin, constrained to acknowledge the potential of his leadership, assigned him a safe Conservative seat in Epping, which Churchill easily won.

When Conservatives later that year swept into office with a massive victory, Baldwin, as the new prime minister, sent for Churchill to come to 10 Downing Street. "Well, Winston," asked the bluff Yorkshire man between puffs on his pipe, "will you take the chancellorship?" In his eagerness to be welcomed back in Conservative Party councils, Churchill, although thinking Baldwin meant the ceremonial sinecure as chancellor of the Duchy of Lancaster, accepted. Not until later did he realize he was being offered the powerful Exchequer. The chancellor of the Exchequer has the prestige of a head of the U.S. chief justice, with the combined power of treasury secretary, budget director, and chairman of the Federal Reserve. The prodigal son had been awarded the most coveted seat. Churchill now donned for investiture the same black robes of the chancellorship that Lord Randolph had once worn. His mother had never returned them but had carefully saved them for her son.

At fifty, Churchill had reached the pinnacle that his father had gained at a younger age some thirty-eight years before. As in Lord Randolph's case, Churchill's tenure was not distinguished by success. At the end of the ministry, Churchill said, "They said I was the worst Chancellor in history," and then after a pause he added, "You know, they're right." The Exchequer did not suit his talents. As a young man he had described his befuddled approach to the arcane of mathematics:

We were arrived in an "Alice-in-Wonderland" world, at the portals of which stood "A Quadratic Equation" followed by the dim chambers inhabited by the Differential Calculus and then a strange corridor of Sines, Cosines and Tangents in a highly square-rooted condition.

For the first time in his ministerial career, Churchill was wholly dependent on his advisers, the career economists of the Exchequer department. Virtually every financial expert, into whose ranks a dubious fiscal heretic named John Maynard Keynes was not admitted, recommended that Britain return to the gold standard. The deflationary move was the singular if questionable achievement in Churchill's four-year supervision of a depressed British economy.

If economics is "the dismal science," as historian Thomas Carlyle wrote, the Churchill prankishness belied it. On the occasion of his first budget as chancellor, he paused and filled a glass beside the dispatch box next to him, not with water but with whiskey, saying, "It is imperative that I should first fortify the revenue, and this I shall now, with the permission of the Commons, proceed to do."

Considering the times in which he presided, Chancellor Churchill might be forgiven for resorting to spirits. The country was in depression, or as he called it, "an economic blizzard," and in 1926 a general strike paralyzed the nation. Churchill's hard line against the massive labor walkout was characterized by his statement, "I declare utterly to be impartial as between the Fire Brigade and the fire." When newspaper presses shut down, Churchill even put out a government organ. The paper, entitled *British Gazette*, gained a huge circulation, even though some felt that it lowered Churchill's literary reputation.

Generally, though, the stint at the Exchequer was not a happy one for Churchill. The cause of financial orthodoxy did not invite the flair of his genius. The everyday burden of mastering budgetary details began to weary him, and he was almost relieved when the Conservative government was swept out of office in 1929. The mood of the 1920s, spent by the sacrifice of war, craved mediocrity as a sign of stability. In such "normalcy" Churchill was out of joint with the times. To friends, he remarked, "I'd quit politics altogether if it weren't for the chance that someday I might be prime minister."

CHAPTER 12

MALACAÑAN PALACE,
THE PHILIPPINES

Douglas MacArthur wrote and spoke in purple splendor.

DWIGHT DAVID EISENHOWER

RETURNING TO WASHINGTON in 1930 after Paris in 1929 was like a hangover after a night of drinking champagne. Like Winston Churchill's tenure as chancellor of the Exchequer, President Herbert Hoover's prescription for unemployment was a failure. High tariffs and lowered expenditures did not revive trade or economic growth, and the cuts in the War Department's budget did not brighten the future of career majors such as Eisenhower.

The increasingly isolationist nation was beginning to believe that U.S. intervention in the Great War was the work of English propagandists and U.S. munitions makers. In that climate, Eisenhower's assignment in the War Department was an affront to public sentiment. To be in the military was, by definition, to be a militarist. Ike was preparing contingency plans for the next war—specifically, for the mobilization of private industry. Business leaders, however, were cool to questioning by the War Department on procurement problems in time of war. Just the idea of another war was unacceptable, and any thought of intervention by government into private enterprise, even in wartime, seemed to violate the Constitution.

Eisenhower, though a conservative in political thinking, was a pragmatist who disdained doctrinal rigidity. He believed that the interests of the private sector should yield to the greater public good in time of emergency. Far from being hostile to business, he was entranced by it and in his later years sought out for companionship leaders from the corporate and industrial world, much preferring them to lawyers and politicians. The beginnings of an industrial college had been established in the War Department, and Eisenhower took up with relish the case studies for converting peacetime manufacturing plants to wartime demands and schedules. One of the main questions was the control of production during time of war. For that Eisenhower called on Bernard Baruch, who had worked as a dollar-a-year man as the World War I head of the War Industries Board.

Baruch, who had turned sixty in 1930, was already a legendary Washington figure. A tall, craggy-faced man with leonine hair, he combined financial acumen with a shrewd sense of public relations. He cultivated the image of the presidential adviser who sat on a Lafayette Park bench opposite the White House, waiting to be asked for his guidance. He counseled presidents from Wilson to Hoover and later presidents up to Eisenhower himself. He also enjoyed the role of mentoring those possible leaders in the future. One of his protégés was the playwright and future ambassador Clair Boothe (Luce).

Eisenhower, like Churchill, sought out the views of older men. As Bourke Cockran shaped Churchill, so Fox Conner molded Eisenhower. One adviser they shared was Bernard Baruch.

In Panama, contemporary officers chided Eisenhower behind his back with an ugly word for his accommodating attentiveness to Fox Conner. But Eisenhower was never an officious bureaucrat. His disdain for the go-by-the-book approach proved that. Rather, like Churchill, he was drawn to those he could learn and profit from.

Baruch's belief that World War II was inevitable echoed the words of Fox Conner and confirmed Eisenhower's opinion. Ike adopted Baruch's view that prices, wages, and costs of materials and services should be frozen immediately on the outbreak of the war—preferably in advance, to prevent soaring inflation.

Eisenhower integrated Baruch's ideas into an article called *Army Ordnance*. It called for a special organization that would set price controls and eliminate the service rivalry that impeded maximum production. Army and navy "brass" reacted as if it were revolutionary and leaked their opposition to their friends on the House and Senate Armed Services Committees in Congress. Baruch's testimony to the congressional panel helped mute the political attacks. For Eisenhower, this lobbying of businessmen backed by their military friends sowed the seeds of his future warning, in his Farewell Address, about "unwarranted influence . . . by the military-industrial complex."

A more profound influence on Eisenhower's life and career was Gen. Douglas MacArthur. Although ten years Eisenhower's senior, MacArthur had been the stuff of legend ever since his West Point days. Everyone knew how MacArthur, with his fabled photographic memory, had edged out Robert E. Lee in the all-time West Point academic record. A brigadier general in the World War, he had cut quite a dashing figure, charging the trenches with his white bandanna around his neck. Ike also admired MacArthur as the only general who dissented in the court martial of airman Billy Mitchell in 1925.

Ike's power of the pen brought him to MacArthur's attention. The general, a man of no mean literary skills himself, chose Eisenhower to write his annual report as chief of staff in 1931. Afterward, MacArthur wrote a letter that Mamie framed: "I wrote you this commendation that you may fully realize that your outstanding talents . . . are fully appreciated."

In 1931 MacArthur, as chief of staff, had need, in Eisenhower's words, for "an amanuensis"—someone to draft statements, reports, and letters for his signature. Ike received the full blast of his charisma. MacArthur was gifted with a brilliant mind that he gave stage to with perfervid oratory, theatrical gesture, and often flamboyant costume. Only a slatted door separated MacArthur's office from Eisenhower's. Later Eisenhower wrote that it was the best show in town.

MacArthur, who had a patrician nose and an actor's profile of a face, often wore a green silk Japanese robe as he unleashed to visitors a barrage of eloquence, flourishing an ivory cigarette holder for dramatic punctuation—all in front of a gilt-edged wall mirror behind his desk.

"Senator," he would declaim in his resonant baritone, "this mere functionary manifested the rank temerity of instructing MacArthur on. . . ." (MacArthur had the odd habit of always referring to himself in the third person.)

Rarely could the word 'conversation' describe MacArthur's meetings with visitors. They were monologues. This soliloquy style, but with cigar as prop, also defined the Churchill mode of conversation. Actually, MacArthur was a distant cousin of Churchill. Their American great-, great-, great-grandfather was also an ancestor of Franklin Delano Roosevelt. Perhaps their shared gene was a flair for the dramatic, because all three were innate actors.

In the November 1932 election, Franklin Roosevelt overwhelmed President Hoover. The blighting effects of the Depression had engendered a sense of despair and anger. For some, the frustration had turned to fury. The Bonus Army March in July of that year was an expression of that outrage.

Congressman Wright Patman of Texas introduced a bill that would have advanced the World War I bonus stipend, due in 1945, to instead be paid in 1932. When the legislation was defeated in the Senate, eighteen thousand veterans came to Washington and camped down in the Anacostia section of the city.

President Hoover ordered the War Department to have the army disperse the protesters. General MacArthur decided that he should personally take active command in the field. Major Eisenhower told him, "The Chief of Staff should not be involved in anything like a local or street corner fracas."

MacArthur replied coldly, "Get into your uniform, Major." (In that time army officials at the War Department had instructions to wear only civilian clothes because the display of uniforms around the capital in peacetime was deemed undesirable.)

When Ike met MacArthur at the Munitions Building, the general was in his number-one dress uniform with every badge, medal, ribbon, pin, and gold braid he had, including the Congressional Medal of Honor that had been awarded his father, Gen. Arthur MacArthur.

With MacArthur on horseback in the lead, the troops crossed the bridge into Anacostia. The Bonus Marchers disbanded except for about a hundred who refused to leave their ramshackle huts. Using canisters of tear gas, the troops dispersed the squatters and then set fire to the shacks.

The incident damaged the general's reputation and sealed the defeat of President Hoover five months later. The next March, when Franklin Roosevelt was sworn in, the new president surprised the general by not immediately replacing him as Army Chief of Staff. MacArthur, however, still did not mute his outspoken attacks on the president. One of MacArthur's first postings had been as military assistant to President Theodore Roosevelt, whom he revered. Franklin Roosevelt, was about as closely related to T. R. as he was to MacArthur. (FDR did, however, marry the president's niece, Eleanor Roosevelt.)

MacArthur quoted *New Republic* commentator Walter Lippman's assessment of FDR—"a shallow dilettante, that only managed gentleman's C's at Harvard, and had ridden to success on the Roosevelt name." To MacArthur, the new president had brought down a lot of "pink socialists from Harvard" to fill New Deal slots, and the proof of it was Roosevelt's recognition of the Communist regime in the Soviet Union.

Eisenhower was no admirer of FDR, but he was shocked by MacArthur's political indiscretion. Eisenhower was a Republican but by conviction did not vote. That was Ike's way of enforcing the principle that the military should keep its distance from politics.

For the low-ranking major, military life in the 1930s was not a happy time. Eisenhower bridled under MacArthur and chafed under the limits of his salary. Any social life in Washington was through his younger brother Milton. Milton, who had married a department store heiress, had risen to a top position in the Department of Agriculture.

Eisenhower was a little-known major in Washington, but he was highly esteemed by the press corps covering the War Department. A newspaper chain offered him a job in Washington as its Washington military correspondent at a salary of $20,000 a year, a fortune for the young man then making $3,000 a year. However, when Ike considered the frantic pace of German and Japanese rearmament, as well as Fox Connor's prediction of another war bigger than the last one, he decided to stay in the service. Ike did not want to report on that war— he wanted to fight it.

But he needed the experience of a battalion command as a line officer. In 1935 MacArthur's tour as chief of staff ended, and Eisenhower was ready for his field assignment, but MacArthur, as Ike later wrote, "lowered the boom." There was to be no battalion command in the state of Washington; MacArthur demanded that Eisenhower come to Manila with him. The Philippines wanted MacArthur to organize its army. The former territory now had commonwealth status, with complete independence scheduled for 1946.

Mamie did not want to join Ike in the Philippines. Three years in Panama was enough time spent in the tropics "Anyway," argued Mamie, "our son John should be allowed to finish his elementary school in Washington."

So Ike sailed alone to the destination he had requested two decades before. MacArthur's task was to build from scratch a Filipino army, and he gave Eisenhower, a newly promoted lieutenant colonel, the assignment of writing the organization plan. MacArthur himself was now a major general. The four-star general had lost two stars when he stepped down as Army Chief of Staff. But soon MacArthur adorned himself with the five stars of a field marshal; he had asked President Quezon to create the rank.

Eisenhower remonstrated with MacArthur directly: "General, you have been a four-star general in the U.S. Army. This is a proud thing. Only a few have had it. Why in the hell do you want a banana republic giving you a field marshalship?"

MacArthur reacted in cold fury. He told Eisenhower, "It would be an insult to the President if [I] turned the Field Marshal rank down." (Later, Eisenhower learned that it was not Quezon's idea but MacArthur's alone.)

Eisenhower found later that although MacArthur shared with Churchill a love of dress-up and fancy uniforms, the Englishman could laugh at himself while doing it. MacArthur demanded sycophants, whereas Churchill despised them.

For the ceremony at Malacañan Palace, the new field marshal was sworn in, resplendent in a sharkskin uniform of black trousers and a white dress coat with braids, five stars, and intricate designs on the lapel. He accepted his gold marshal's baton from Mrs. Quezon.

In the White House years later, President Eisenhower told an aide, "You know, Mac had an 'eye' problem." The assistant immediately thought of glaucoma or a detached retina. Eisenhower continued, "He had a fatal addiction to the perpendicular pronoun."

If working under MacArthur offered Eisenhower lessons in leadership, most of them were negative ones. MacArthur's vision and knowledge of history were the gift of a mind that approached genius, yet his flaws offered case examples of what a general should not do.

The general's meddling in U.S. politics, his demand for adulation, and his parading of ego were noted in Ike's diary, which helped release his mounting frustration as MacArthur's deputy. In the 1952 campaign, when Governor Dewey criticized presidential candidate Eisenhower's flat and dry delivery and recommended more gestures and rhetorical pauses, Ike bristled: "Don't give me that, Governor, I had four years in the Manila Theater of Dramatic Arts." To Eisenhower in the Philippines, Field Marshal MacArthur, bedecked in his glittering regalia, was an affront. Eisenhower chose to be buried in a $95 casket—the same as was supplied to every GI who died under his command in Europe.

It was during this time of exile and separation from his family in Washington that he took up flying. If Mamie had been in Manila, she might have put her foot down, but for Eisenhower it was another safety valve to vent his disaffection. Even if he made his wings as part of the Philippines Air Force and not the U.S. Army, nevertheless he became the first president to be a pilot. (The two Bush presidents were the next commander in chief pilots.)

In September 1936, Mamie and their fourteen-year-old son, John, arrived in Manila. To hug his wife, Ike took off his Panama hat. Mamie screamed, as she saw that Ike's head was as shiny and smooth as a cue ball.

"Ike," asked Mamie, "what have you done with your hair?"

Ike grinned. "It's so hot over here that I shave my head when I have to shave my face."

Now life brightened, at least his personal life. "Club Eisenhower" Chez Mamie resumed. The availability of a huge Filipino staff afforded her a vast improvement over her days in Panama. Mamie also liked MacArthur's new young wife, Jean, who was about six years her junior. Their friendship smoothed the strained relationship between their husbands.

As the presidential election of 1936 neared, MacArthur's diatribes against Roosevelt increased. MacArthur was convinced that Governor Landon of Kansas would win and cited the polls in the *Literary Digest* as proof. Eisenhower told MacArthur that Landon would not even carry Kansas, his and Ike's home state. MacArthur berated Ike for his refusal to face obvious facts.

When Roosevelt carried Kansas and forty-five other states, Ike's correct prophecy did not endear himself in the general's affections. The following year, relations froze when the general told Ike to begin writing plans for a huge parade. In MacArthur's conception, the 40,000-strong Filipino army would march through Manila behind fluttering flags and blaring brass.

Eisenhower's questions to MacArthur about the costs to the impoverished Filipino government were dismissed. Eisenhower asked how the Filipino army could be fed and housed for a week in the capital city. MacArthur brushed him aside. But when President Quezon rejected the plan, MacArthur agreed, insinuating that it had been Eisenhower's idea.

Ike was outraged. "General, all you are saying is that I'm a liar and I am not a liar. So I'd like to go back to the United States right away."

MacArthur put his arm around Eisenhower's shoulder and smiled. "It's just fun to see that Dutch temper of yours."

Unlike some of the general's staff, Ike did not idolize MacArthur. He resented being used and lied to. He wanted to go home. Mamie, however, liked Manila. The salary given by the Philippines was greater than her husband would receive back home—not to mention the servant staff.

But Manila was becoming intolerable. Eisenhower was caught between *El Presidente* and Field Marshal MacArthur, who were no longer on speaking terms. Quezon begged him to stay and set his own price. MacArthur, despite their bitter disputes, knew that Ike was his indispensable officer.

Eisenhower stood adamant on his refusal to extend his tour. So orders were cut for him to report to Fort Lewis, Washington.

CHAPTER 13

_____

CHARTWELL

Unwisdom prevailed.

WINSTON CHURCHILL

THE 1930S WERE for Churchill a period of exile but not one entered regretfully. Churchill, in packing away the robes of chancellor, could now again don the painter's smock and brick-layer's apron, and Chartwell country squire was a role he had sweetly anticipated in the last dreary days of 11 Downing Street. His relations with the stolid occupant next door, Prime Minister Stanley Baldwin, though superficially correct, were strained in a clash of temperaments. Churchill once said of the play-it-safe Baldwin, "He keeps his ears so close to the ground that they're full of grasshoppers."

Churchill knew that the rank and file of the party had no use for him. His chances for prime minister were remote even if the Conservative Party should return to power. Churchill was too clever to be trusted, and his acerbic wit won him few friends. On one occasion after he left the Cabinet, he told the House that as a boy he always looked forward to the London arrival of the American Barnum and Bailey Circus.

"But," added Churchill, "there was one show that my nanny would not let me see. She said it was 'too revolting a spectacle for the human eye.' The sideshow was called 'the Boneless Wonder.' Now, after thirty-six years, where do I finally find this freak show? In the circus, no—but in the House of Commons, sitting on the front bench—'the Boneless Wonders.'"

His unpopularity at that time was attested to by the Irish playwright George Bernard Shaw. The dramatist sent him two tickets in 1932 for the opening of his play *Too Good to Be True.* Shaw added a note: "Bring a friend—if you have one."

Churchill replied, "Unfortunately, G.B.S., I have another engagement on opening night. But I would like tickets for the second night—if there is one."

As chancellor of the Exchequer, Churchill had seen the savings in his own family exchequer dwindle. Politics was his occupation, but writing was his livelihood. The responsibilities of family, not to mention the maintenance of Chartwell, necessitated income. In 1930 he wrote more than forty articles for newspapers and magazines, nearly half of them for the *Daily Telegraph.* He wrote the wide-selling *My Early Life*, which in America was called *A Roving Commission.* The next year he actually increased his output. An abridged version of *The World Crisis* went on the stands, as did *Eastern Front* (in America, *The Unknown War*). Not surprisingly, this work kept his attendance in the House of Commons as the member from Epping to the obligatory minimum.

He also made some speaking tours in America, earning a pretty penny. On one of those trips he consulted with his friend Bernard Baruch, who had taken over Churchill's investment portfolio. After he left Baruch's office on Park Avenue, he crossed the street, but as an Englishman he by habit looked the wrong way for oncoming traffic. He was run over and rushed by ambulance to the hospital. He said of his bloody body, "I felt like a crushed blueberry." He had to postpone his return to England. He begrudged the trips to London away from his beloved Chartwell, where he could write and paint in the company of Clementine and his children. The older ones, Diana and Randolph, were now already adults.

The 1930s were the heyday of magazine writing, and Churchill, according to one account, was averaging about $100,000 a year, of which most came in the form of advances from newspaper and magazine editors. The rest of his income was from the semiannual royalty checks from his book publishers and the fees from his lectures, particularly those in America.

Churchill needed every penny of those checks to support his opulent tastes. As he himself wrote, "I am easily satisfied with the best." He had by habit and desire acquired the appetites of a duke—the best horses for his stable, the finest wine for his cellar, and the richest food for his table. Even when he went on a painting jaunt, he took along for his picnic spread wicker hampers laden with cold grouse or venison, imported fruits, cheese, caviar, and a magnum of champagne.

At home at Chartwell, his regimen in those years out of ministerial office began with reading the morning newspaper and mail in bed while consuming a breakfast considered generous by English standards. For his pressing parliamentary and commercial correspondence, he dictated quick replies and memoranda, trying to finish the business end of his work during his morning bath. There, twirling his toes in the toasty-hot water, he began his literary dictation. Outside the open bathroom door the secretary jotted down his bursts of declamation. His sentences continued their staccato roll, uninterrupted by lathering, toweling, and whatever other morning ablutions were required. First he muttered and growled snatches of phrases until he had assembled the makings of a paragraph. Then he bawled out the whole chunk, grunting his satisfaction at the end.

The costume for this singular exercise proceeded from a loosely wrapped Turkish towel to pink silk shorts with red cummerbund, and then, anticlimactically, a white undershirt. Only occasionally was a robe put on to satisfy the delicate sensibilities of guests. Back in bed, Churchill, no doubt stimulated by the hot bath and strongly scented soap, continued his roar of dictation until the midmorning break of "elevenses." While the exhausted secretary braced herself with coffee, Churchill sipped a Scotch and soda. Thus fortified, he filled up more of the secretary's shorthand tablets for transcribing until well past noon.

At lunchtime he slipped into a robe and appeared in the dining room, if visitors were expected at Chartwell. But even if he stayed in his bedroom to eat from a tray, the menu was uncompromisingly grand—soup, fowl, or beef, washed down by a bottle of Claret, to be succeeded by a glass of cognac and post-prandial cigar. Then, after a stroll through his grounds, perhaps to feed the goldfish and greet the swans, he returned to his study to find a tense stenographer, poised with pencil for the afternoon session.

With only a tea break at four, which for him meant brandy or a whiskey and soda, Churchill, cigar in hand, by puffing and pacing, turned thoughts to words. Only occasionally did he stop to check the Oxford dictionary or look at a source book propped up on a desk opposite his writing table. The rest of the time he was, to his secretary, a walking volcano whose spasmodic eruptions had to be hastily scribbled down before the torrent of phrases flooded the limits of her memory.

An hour and a half nap at five was no doubt as welcome to the stenographer as the writer. Another spicy, hot tub and Churchill was ready for dinner, the only meal he regularly dressed for. He met dinner guests with the velvet-trimmed smoking jacket, but alone his raiment might be battle fatigues, a tunic, a lounge coat, or an occasional suit.

Then, after a repast even more Lucullan than the lunch, he lit up a Havana cigar for the nightly backgammon or bezique match with Clementine. When she retired at eleven, Churchill began his next dictation shift with a new secretary. Not until two or three in the morning, when the relief secretary had been pushed to the limits of exhaustion, did Churchill himself turn in for his six or so hours' sleep.

During these Chartwell years, rumors in London political circles abounded that an over-the-hill Churchill was sliding into habitual drunkenness. Churchill did nothing to scotch these stories. Unlike the alcoholic who carefully conceals his number of drinks, Churchill broadcast them, constantly pressing his guests to accept another round. With furtive glee, he, who never drank cocktails or mixed drinks, handed out stiff concoctions to visitors while refreshing his own brandy or whiskey from the seltzer siphon. Yet despite the weak whiskeys, Churchill's rambling discourses seemed to reinforce the bibulous impression. Away from the public forum, his rhetorical guard was let down in conversation. His monologues on history or political issues became slathered with lisps and often shaken by a vehement stammer.

But the best refutation of those tales of the gargantuan drinking bouts at Chartwell is the prodigious writing output of Churchill at that time. The principal part of that production was Churchill's massive six-volume biography, *Marlborough*. Although research assistants presented memoranda and combed source books, marking relevant passages for examination, Churchill himself dictated the first and succeeding drafts and then revised the publisher's galleys. Unlike professional historians, who interminably delay writing in their search for new leads of documentary evidence, Churchill liked to get something down on paper early, knowing he could revise factual accuracy in later drafts. That is not to suggest that Churchill was slipshod with facts, for he was a stickler on verification and reverification of the final copy; but it does account for a productivity that far outstripped that of academic scholars.

Critics complained not of his facts but of his rhetorical flourishes. In *Marlborough*, Churchill the writer never frees

himself from Churchill the orator. The rhythm is almost re-
morseless, and sentences spring to attention like soldiers on
parade. As if in a battle, Churchill marshaled his adjectival artillery for a purpose: to reclaim the lost ground in his ancestor's reputation. It was a labor of love and family piety.

If the hero of the book was John Churchill, the villain was
Louis XVI:

> Better the barbarian conquerors in antiquity, primordial fig-
> ures of the abyss, than this high-heeled, beperiwigged dandy,
> strutting amid the bows and scrapes of mistresses and confes-
> sors to the torment of his age. Petty and mediocre in all ex-
> cept his lusts and power, the Sun King disturbed and harried
> mankind during more than fifty years of arrogant pomp.

Possibly Churchill's description of the pompous strutting
of the seventeenth-century French autocrat was occasioned by
a squalid twentieth-century perversion now on the political
horizon—the German Führer. A frustrated artist, Hitler had
given up house painting more than a decade before Churchill
learned to paint in the south of France. Churchill's defeat in
1922 had happened a year before the Munich putsch landed
Hitler in prison. While Churchill was writing *The World Crisis*,
Hitler was putting together *Mein Kampf.* At the time Churchill
reentered public life in 1924, Hitler was leaving jail to resume
his political activities. Before Hitler ever actually assumed
power, Churchill was warning Britain of German resurgence
in a 1932 speech, which most of his House of Commons audience found too pessimist or alarmist:

> Now the demand is that Germany should be allowed to
> rearm. Do not delude yourselves. Do not believe that all that
> Germany is asking for is equal status. . . . That is not what
> Germany is seeking. All these bands of sturdy Teutonic

youths, marching through the streets and roads of Germany, with the light of desire in their eyes to suffer for the Fatherland, are not looking for status. They are looking for weapons, and, when they have the weapons, believe me, they will then ask for the return of lost territories and lost colonies.

We watch with surprise and distress the tumultuous insurgence of ferocity and war spirit, the pitiless ill-treatment of minorities, the denial of the normal protection of civilized society to large numbers of individuals solely on the grounds of race.

Churchill's only chance of ever meeting *der Führer* came in 1932 while retracing Marlborough's maneuvers on a battlefield near Munich. In the course of his stay he met Ernst Hanfstaengl, a Harvard graduate, art publisher, and close friend of Hitler's. Yet when Churchill closely questioned Hanfstaengl on Hitler's attitudes toward Jews, the proposed encounter with the Nazi Party leader was canceled.

In the 1930s, Churchill's audiences, whether in the House of Commons or in a constituency meeting, knew before he even arose to speak that he would be expounding on some variation of the British preparedness theme: the resurgence of German militarism, the ineffectuality of the League of Nations to contain it, the inadequacy of the Royal Air Force, the need for Anglo-French cooperation, or the dangers of British pacifism.

There was nothing cursory or casual about these Churchill speeches. All the available statistics on comparative defenses and historic parallels with the past were brought to bear on one overriding conclusion. In this strenuous process of putting his impressions on paper for a speech, speculation became certainty and inferences turned to facts. Like a scholar who labors with his doctoral thesis or a mother with the birth of a child, Churchill had the unshakable faith in the finished product of his work that only such mental and emotional investment can bring.

To his listeners, Churchill's excess of energy seemed more like an obsession. Rearmament and the threat of another world conflict was a message that a war-spent and economically depressed nation did not want to hear, particularly from one whose judgment was already suspect. Public confidence in the minister who had orchestrated the Antwerp Circus and planned the Dardanelles disaster was not unbounded. Better to trust the words of Stanley Baldwin, Ramsay MacDonald, or, later, Neville Chamberlain, whose dependability was never tainted by imagination and whose respectability was never sullied by genius.

But the blame did not rest solely with the audience. The fervid imagination of a Churchill had its fallible side. His fulminations against Gandhi and Indian self-rule were too strident, and his misplaced loyalty to Edward VIII during the nine-day abdication crisis of 1936 was too impulsively romantic. Churchill, faithful to his long-time friend the Prince of Wales, had urged him to play for time and build popular support against a prime minister who insisted that marriage with the divorced American Mrs. Wallis Simpson meant no monarchy. Fortunately for the nation, Edward chose to give up the throne. Churchill went to Edward's retreat at Fort Belvedere and helped him compose the abdication speech. Among the phrases he contributed were "bred in the constitutional tradition by my father" and "one matchless blessing, enjoyed by so many of you and not bestowed on me—a happy home with wife and children."

What was left of the Churchill prestige dwindled in the aftermath of the abdication. Still, there remained a band of adherents who made their trek to Chartwell. To them, Churchill was not just a sexagenarian politician past his prime. Foremost among Churchill's friends were the three Bs: Baruch, Beaverbrook, and Bracken.

Bernard Baruch was the U.S.–Jewish financier whom Churchill had met during World War I when he was munitions minister and in the process of coordinating the war effort with the United States. Baruch was helpful to Churchill in bringing some financial stability into his chaotic finances.

Lord Beaverbrook had been born Max Aitken. A Canadian entrepreneur who suffered from asthma as well as a stutter, he had built the Tory *Daily Express* to the number-one newspaper in British circulation. Although the opinionated Beaverbrook often clashed with an equally outspoken Churchill, Winston called the Scottish-Canadian his "foul-weather friend" for his steadfast loyalty in time of crisis and despair.

Brendan Bracken, the youngest of the group, came out of nowhere to help Churchill in his election campaigns in the early 1920s. In the next decade Bracken became Churchill's eyes and ears for political intelligence, as well as a one-man fan club, promoting the virtue of his leader to anyone who would listen. The fanatic loyalty of the carrot-topped, black-spectacled Bracken gave rise to the ridiculous rumor that he was Churchill's bastard son. Bracken was not unhappy with the tale.

Whether it was the financial wisdom of a Baruch, the newspaper mind of a Beaverbrook, or the political savvy of Bracken, Churchill sought as his friends those who had more to contribute than just congenial amenities and social breeding. He had no time for the effete members of his own background who had not proved their worth or ability. A frequent visitor to Chartwell described the nature of the guest list there. "The full truth is, I believe, that Winston's 'friends' must be persons who were of use to him. The idea of having a friend who was of no practical use to him but being a friend because he liked him had no place." The speaker was Sir Desmond Morton, who, along with Professor Lindemann, headed a second tier of advisory friends from whom Winston absorbed scientific and military data. Morton, a nearby neighbor at Chartwell, was a former aide to Field Marshal Haig in World War I. An intelligence expert, he began collecting for Churchill estimates on German industry and defense.

Lindemann, a brilliant Oxford physicist, was Churchill's interpreter of nuclear mysteries and emerging technical developments. Once a visitor bet Lindemann that he could not explain the quantum theory in five minutes. The Churchill children timed the professor with a stopwatch and applauded vociferously when he succeeded. Like the Churchill cigar, the slide rule was an appendant prop of the "Prof."

While enjoying his postprandial cigar and brandy in a hotel, Churchill once asked Professor Lindemann, "If all the wine and spirits that I have drunk in a lifetime was poured into this room, do you think it would reach the ceiling?" Lindemann, who had been a mathematics professor before being commandeered by Churchill to serve as his scientific consultant, drew out his ever-present slide rule and made his calculations.

"Prime Minister, if all the alcohol you have consumed in your life were to occupy this room, I estimate that it would only attain the level of your eye."

A disappointed Churchill muttered, "As I gaze at the ceiling and contemplate my sixty-five years, my only thought is— how much left to do and how little time to do it."

Experts such as Lindemann and Morton were, in a way, human fodder for Churchill's speeches. He relied on them not only for their input of technical assessment of facts and trends but as an audience before whom he could present his conversational monologues, which were often rehearsals of later speeches.

What Churchill did in these years out of ministry was to organize his own staff operation. One frequent visitor to Chartwell in the 1930s was the young Conservative member of Parliament Harold Macmillan. To him, Chartwell seemed like a government in exile. Everywhere were maps, charts, and graphs denoting production of German munitions. Temporary filing cabinets bulged with folders on various aircraft and memoranda on selected members of the German high command. A European politician would arrive for an appointment and meet a scientist or military adviser on his way out. Behind every Churchill philippic on Hitler and the German threat were a juggled schedule of appointments and an assortment of "white papers" on German military mobilization.

Many of Churchill's warnings at the time began to focus on Germany's growing superiority in the air. As early as 1935 he told the Commons, "Germany has the power at any time henceforward to send a fleet of airplanes capable of discharging in a single voyage at least 500 tons of bombs upon London."

But the government dismissed the threats and delayed re-equipping and reinforcing the depleted RAF. Churchill in 1937 excoriated Prime Minister Baldwin for his timid vacillation:

The government cannot make up their minds, or they cannot get the Prime Minister to make up his mind. So they go in strange paradox, decided only to be undecided, resolved to be irresolute, adamant for drift, solid for fluidity, all-powerful to be impotent.

A little later, when Baldwin took ill, a Conservative Party member lamented to back-bencher Churchill, "What would happen if our beloved Stanley would die?"

Churchill replied, "Embalm, cremate and bury him—take no chances."

The British political reaction to Churchill's call to arms ranged from skittish to spineless. Parliament's Leader of the Labourites said that Britain should disarm as an example to Hitler, and the Leader of the Liberals termed the Churchill proposal to double the RAF "the language of Malay tribesmen running amok." These were, in Churchill's biblical phrase, "the locust years," when the British ate up years of possible war preparation.

In 1938, after the fall of Austria, Churchill rose from his habitual front-corner seat in the House and, head thrust forward, thumbs in his vest pocket, lectured the House Conservative government on the five years they had wasted failing to rearm:

> For five years I have talked to this House on these matters—not with very great success. I have watched this famous island descending incontinently, recklessly, the stairway which leads to a dark gulf. It is a fine broad stairway at the beginning, but aft a bit of the carpet wears, a little farther on there are only flagstones, and a little further on still, these break beneath your feet.

An embarrassed silence greeted Churchill as he ended. Then members, anxious to turn to more pleasant thoughts, rattled their papers, stood, and shuffled out to the lobby—many heading for tea. One member told his Visitor's Gallery guest, Virginia Cowles, "It was the usual Churchill filibuster—he likes to rattle the saber and he does it jolly well, but you have to take it with a grain of salt."

After Austria, the next country to feel the boot of Hitler's tyranny was Czechoslovakia. To avert the war, Prime Minister Chamberlain traveled to negotiate with Hitler at Munich. He returned with a settlement proclaiming that he had achieved "peace with honor."

Massive crowds turned out in London to hail Chamberlain for averting war. There was no more fervent admirer than King George VI. When Chamberlain reported to Parliament on the results of his meeting with Hitler, the House of Commons exploded with cheers.

Lady Astor cried, "He is a Prince of Peace."

Churchill uttered to the side, "I thought the Prince of Peace was born in Bethlehem, not Birmingham, England."

The next day Churchill rose to denounce the sellout.

All is over. Silent, mournful, abandoned, broken, Czechoslovakia recedes into darkness. I think you will find that in a period of time, which may be measured by years, but may be measured only by months, Czechoslovakia will be engulfed in the Nazi regime.

This is only the beginning of the reckoning. This is only the first sip, the first foretaste of the bitter cup, which will be proffered to us year by year, unless, by a supreme recovery of moral health and martial vigor, we rise again and take our stand for freedom as in the olden times.

Churchill later added his summation of Chamberlain's mission to Munich: "You were given the choice of war and dishonor. You chose dishonor and you will have the war."

But the appeasers were in full sway. One leader of the pro-German faction was Lady Astor; her coterie was called the Cliveden Group, after her manor estate near Bath. Churchill growled, "An Astorite is an appeaser and an appeaser is one who feeds the crocodile hoping it will eat him last."

Shortly thereafter, he found himself at Cliveden for a black-tie banquet.

After dinner, Lady Astor presided over the pouring of coffee. When Churchill came by, she glared and said, "Winston, if I were your wife, I'd put poison in your coffee."

"Nancy," Churchill replied to the acid-tongued Astor, "if I were your husband, I'd drink it."

The British establishment hoped that Hitler was a responsible German nationalist and characterized Churchill as an irresponsible back bencher for attacking the government position. The prevailing opinion was peace at any price. At

Oxford Union they debated a proposed military draft. Over 90 percent of the students voted it down.

Three successive prime ministers had closed their eyes to the arming of Germany. After the laissez-faire of Stanley Baldwin, the pacifism of Ramsay MacDonald, and the appeasement of Neville Chamberlain, a day of reckoning came. A price would have to be paid for those somnolent years and squandered opportunities. The price was war.

War came on September 1, 1939, when German Panzer divisions rumbled past the Polish frontier in the very early hours of that Sunday morning. A shaken Chamberlain government, desperate for unity, at least in its own ranks, asked its principal assailant to join the Cabinet as First Lord of the Admiralty. To the ships at sea, the wire was sent out: "Winston is back."

For Churchill the years in the wilderness had been oddly luxuriant and fruitful. Far from the corridors of power that had darkened with dishonor, he had at last ripened with wisdom and respect. His provident detachment from ministries, whose mediocrity would only have encumbered him, had allowed the writer to become a historian, orator, statesman, critic, and prophet. He had chosen to await fate, and it now awarded him his hour.

CHAPTER 14

FORT SAM LEWIS, WASHINGTON

*The maneuvers fortified my conviction that I belonged with troops;
with them I was always happy.*

DWIGHT DAVID EISENHOWER

WHEN EISENHOWER'S SHIP, the *Cleveland,* arrived in San
Francisco from Manila on January 5, 1940, it was met by a staff
car driven by a major. The major took him a bit south to Monterey Bay. In the car Eisenhower learned that his orders had
been altered. His hope and dream of commanding a regiment
was on hold. (In the infantry no one advanced to general without commanding a regiment first.)

On the beach at Monterey, Lt. Gen. John DeWitt came
bustling to greet him. DeWitt was the one who had changed
his orders. With DeWitt, a bald and bulky man wearing round
black spectacles, was another general who towered over De-
Witt—George Calett Marshall.

Marshall, who had a lugubrious basset hound face, asked,
"Eisenhower, have you learned how to tie your shoes again since
returning from the Philippines?" Marshall's query was a dig at
the retinue of servants supplied for duty in the Philippines.

Ike smiled. "Yes, sir. I think I can manage that chore."

Marshall told Eisenhower that U.S. entry into the war was only a matter of time, whether in Europe or Asia. The Nazi army had already blitzkrieged its way across Poland, while the Japanese had bombed and stormed the Chinese cities of Nanking and Shanghai.

The next war, said Marshall, would entail amphibious assaults—something the last war had not witnessed. Marshall had therefore ordered the staging of an amphibious assault by the Fourth Army against National Guard units entrenched at Monterey Bay.

The problem was that the Fourth Army was stretched out from Minnesota to California. Army specifications had already set up one obligatory entry base by rail in California to receive the troops, but there were too few trains. A shuttling back and forth of troop trains would consume too much time. Eisenhower's solution: set up another entry base. The colonel in charge refused: "I'm accustomed to following orders—there will be no change from specifications."

Eisenhower went to DeWitt, showed him his plan for two concentrations of troops, and got it approved. The troops reached California in time for the maneuvers. Eisenhower knew when to slice through the Gordian knot of rules.

Although a month late, Eisenhower finally was given his regimented command: Fort Lewis in Washington State. As Eisenhower later wrote, "The stumps, slashings, fallen logs, tangled brush, pitfalls, hummocks and hills made the land a stage setting for a play in Hades."

Yet Ike was now the happiest he had ever been in his life. He had his command of a battalion. Although he froze at night and sweated through the dust every day in the maneuvers of the Fifteenth Infantry Regiment, he glowed with the satisfaction of being with his troops.

After the comforts of Manila, however, camp life was not for Mamie. She and seventeen-year-old John retreated to Tacoma, Washington, the home of Edgar "Big Ike" Eisenhower. On weekends Ike visited his brother's home. Sibling rivalry always simmered under the surface with the Eisenhower brothers, but with Dwight and Edgar it sometimes erupted.

Edgar Eisenhower had built one of the biggest law practices in the state of Washington. His three-piece suit with watch chain bespoke his wealth, which then approached a million dollars.

Dwight, on a lieutenant colonel's salary, seethed as his older brother Edgar spoke expansively to John Eisenhower on the law profession as a career the youth should choose. "Why," said Uncle Edgar to his nephew, "I'll pay for your college if you choose to be a lawyer and then you could practice with me. You'd make a pot full of money."

On free Sunday afternoons Ike tried to vent his pent-up feelings by playing golf with his brother. But even then Edgar's score, in the seventies, beat Ike's by ten. Ike's son John, however, racked up the highest score in the competitive exam for West Point conducted by the office of Sen. Arthur Capper of Kansas. John had chosen the career that would win the approval and, he hoped, the affection of his unsparing father.

In the fall of 1940 Ike turned fifty. Although he was almost completely bald, with only a little light brown hair on the back and sides of his head, the pink baldness somehow added to the flash of his complexion and balanced the broad grin on his face. Friends thought he looked ten years younger than his age.

Ike exuded energy. He was at his post eighteen hours a day, seven days a week. He organized schedules, supervised full exercises, and lectured his junior officers. At night he studied the map of Europe in his office and pored over the accounts of the war in Europe, where Hitler's armies were invading the Low Countries of Belgium and Netherlands and the Scandinavian nations of Denmark and Norway. The next day he would try to apply the lessons of these battles to the training in his units.

In March 1941 he received his promotion to full colonel. At Fort Lewis, Mamie and son John held a surprise party for him. A fellow officer came up to him and said, "Ike, the next thing you'll have is a star on each of your shoulders."

"Dammit!" Ike griped later to his son John. "Why can't they let a guy be happy with what he has? They take all of the joy out of it."

By June 1941 the army was gearing up for the biggest maneuver in its history. Entire armies numbering 1.5 million men prepared to engage in mock combat. The Second Army, headed by Lt. Gen. Ben Lear, would battle it out with the Third Army, led by Lt. Gen. Walter Krueger in Louisiana.

Krueger's selection for his second-in-command was Colonel Eisenhower. Eisenhower was back in Fort Sam Houston again, where the Third Army made its headquarters.

There Ike devised a strategy for the Third Army to win. His army had double the force of the Second Army. But the Second Army had the greater advantage—it had tanks and an air force to control the air. In addition, the Second Army's forces were mostly regular army, whereas Krueger's army was largely National Guardsmen who were desperately short of training.

On the first day of the maneuvers Ike's Third Army, instead of fighting a defensive battle, charged. The unexpected attack took control of the key bridges. Lear's army found it difficult to deploy his forces into action.

First the Krueger army stopped Lear's Second Army, then annihilated it. A maneuver that was to take a week ended in three days. Eisenhower had made his point: attacking troops, properly deployed, could stop a tank attack.

The success landed the name of Col. Dwight D. Eisenhower in the national news. Reporters swarmed into Fort Sam Houston to interview him. Unlike most military men, the affable Ike was accessible. The result was that his picture was splashed across newspaper accounts—even though the name accompanying it was often misspelled. One of the more interesting captions under his photo was Lt. Col. D. D. Ersenbeing. Eisenhower's face was the new army—bold and unbureaucratic in style.

Brig. Gen. Mark Clark led the final critique. The Third Army proved the tank could be stopped. When he concluded, Clark read out a list of promotions of new brigadiers and colonels.

When he finished, murmurs of congratulations filled the room. Then Clark banged the gavel down hard. The men froze.

"I forgot one name," said Clark. "Dwight D. Eisenhower."

Later Ike approached Clark: "I'll get you for that—you sonofabitch." They both laughed.

A star meant that a new assignment would be coming. Meanwhile, Ike and Mamie moved into a new house at Fort Sam Houston. "We have a house as big as a barn," he wrote a friend.

On Sunday morning Ike went early, as usual, to his office to catch up with paperwork. With a cup of coffee, he perused the newspaper. The U.S. Navy was tracking Nazi U-boats. The Japanese and Americans were holding peace talks in Washington.

At noon he was tired. "I'm beat," he told a major. "I'm going home to have a bite and take a nap—call me if anything happens."

He had just dozed off when the major woke him up.

"General," the major proclaimed, "the Japs have just bombed Pearl Harbor."

Ike got up. His response was matter of fact: "Well, boys, it's come."

CHAPTER 15

---

10 DOWNING STREET

Let us brace ourselves to our duties and so bear ourselves that if Britain and its commonwealths last for a thousand years, men will still say, "This was their finest hour."

WINSTON CHURCHILL

ON FRIDAY, SEPTEMBER 1, 1939, Churchill turned on his radio in his library at Chartwell. The BBC commentator was saying, "Early this morning German Panzer divisions crossed the Polish Frontier...."

The Chamberlain government immediately sent an ultimatum to Hitler. When no answer was received, Chamberlain announced mournfully on the radio, "A state of war exists between our nation and Germany." That same Sunday, Prime Minister Chamberlain asked his archcritic Churchill to join the War Cabinet as First Lord of the Admiralty.

As Winston Churchill assumed his old desk in the Admiralty in September 1939, it was a case of history repeating itself, not so much with a vengeance as with a pardon. For here was Churchill, once more sitting in the same chair from which he had been so ignominiously dismissed after Gallipoli in 1915. Behind him was even the same map of the North Sea on which he had then plotted the deployments of the German fleet in World War I.

· 149 ·

In the fall of 1939 the situation hardly qualified as a full-scale war. It was, as Churchill called it, "The Trance" or the "Twilight War." On land French troops remained poised behind the Maginot Line as if in a catatonic standstill, while in the almost perpetual dusk of the North and Baltic Seas the ships of Churchill's fleet passed in silent convoy through the U-boat-infested waters.

As in World War I, the restlessness of the First Lord of the Admiralty impelled him to contemplate an action whose outcome was a severe naval disaster. Churchill foresaw Germany's increasing dependence on steel supplies shipped from neutral Sweden. Thus, in a move to block the trade, he argued in 1940 for a landing at Narvik, a major Norwegian port. The operation, although it damaged German shipping through British mines and submarines, failed to halt the Nazi invasion of Norway and Denmark. A quickly assembled British expeditionary force was dispatched ashore on the Norwegian coast. It was again a case of too little, too late. Without air cover the English troops, fighting under insupportable hardships, could not win and withdrew in defeat.

The political reaction bore a familiar ring. Yet ironically, this time the dissatisfaction, triggered by what some called "the second Gallipoli," brought about the dismissal of the prime minister and not the First Lord of the Admiralty. There was an odd justice to the rewriting of the Dardanelles disaster at Narvik in May 1940. If Churchill was unfairly pilloried from the Cabinet in 1916, he virtually escaped the wrath of Parliament and the press in 1940. The reason had to do with the growing public perception of Chamberlain and Churchill in the spring of 1940.

The defeat in Norway triggered a debate on Chamberlain's suitability as prime minister. On May 7, the veteran Conservative back bencher Lew Amery hurled at the Chamberlain Parliament, "You have sat too long here for any good you have been doing. Depart, I say, and let us have done with you. In the name of God, go!"

When Chamberlain's pitiable response was that his friends should not desert him, the aging Lloyd George the next day replied, in his last great oration, "I say solemnly that the Prime Minister should give an example of sacrifice, because I tell him that there is nothing that would contribute more to victory in this war than that he should sacrifice the seals of the office."

On May 10, while the Hitler Panzer divisions rolled their wide swath of destruction into Holland and Belgium, Chamberlain called Lord Halifax, the foreign secretary, and Churchill to discuss the prime minister question. Chamberlain preferred Halifax, but Clement Attlee, speaking for the Labour Party, would not consent to a premiership from the House of Lords. So King George VI called Churchill to Buckingham Palace to form a coalition government.

Never had a prime minister assumed office in such a grave hour. The blitzkrieg was sweeping like a tornado across Europe. Each hourly newscast of the BBC reported the latest tidings of disaster from Holland, Belgium, and now France. Churchill's "Inaugural" to the House of Commons was brief but brilliant in its electric effect on the nation:

> I have nothing to offer but blood, toil, tears and sweat.
>
> You ask, What is our policy? I will say: "It is to wage war, by sea, land, and air, with all our might and with all the strength that God can give to us; to wage war against a monstrous tyranny, never surprised in the dark, lamentable catalogue of human crime. That is our policy."
>
> You ask, What is our aim? I can answer in one word: Victory—victory at all costs, victory. In spite of all terror, victory however long and hard the road may be; for without victory there is no survival.

The pent-up frustration of hundreds of days of impotence and indecision broke. Grown men wept, not with despair but with relief. They took his promises of blood, sweat, and tears as if they were grants of nobility. If words of hope were all he had to offer, he gave them in the richest measure of English expression heard in centuries. To Churchill, words were weapons and speeches deeds. The military arsenals of Britain were bare, but the armory of its language and literature was laden with treasure.

On May 19, as French forces were reeling from the Germans breaking through the defenses at Sedan, Churchill, in his first radio address as prime minister, called on the peoples of Nazi-occupied Europe to rally to the allied cause.

> Behind the Armies and Fleets of Britain and France gather a group of shattered States and bludgeoned races—the Czechs, the Poles, the Norwegians, the Danes, the Dutch, the Belgians—on all of whom the long night of barbarism will descend unbroken even by a star of hope unless we conquer we must, as conquer we shall.

Churchill knew his words might spell the difference between defeat and resistance. Any hesitation or faltering might have meant collapse. Except for the Channel, Britain was defeated, and all Europe lay at Hitler's feet. On June 2, most of the British troops were trapped on the beach at Dunkirk. The English people, their will no longer unfocused, their courage tapped, responded. A tide of English vessels and smaller craft moved across the Channel toward French beaches and British troops. Dories, dinghies, skiffs swelled the ranks of the 860-boat flotilla in its rescue operation. Churchill labored that Sunday evening in the book-lined Cabinet room at 10 Downing Street.

On Tuesday he had to give his report on Dunkirk to the House of Commons. At the far side of the room his secretary waited at her typewriter.

Reflectively, Churchill opened:

We must be very careful not to assign to this deliverance the attributes of a victory. . . .

Then, pacing from the fireplace at the one end to the draped windows overlooking a garden at the other, Churchill dictated, first muttering under his breath snatches of words to himself, then in a burst of declamation bellowing out the complete sentence in its full majestic panoply.

By midnight the Churchill growl had faded to a croak.

We shall not flag or fail. We shall go on to the end. . . . We shall fight on the beaches, we shall fight on the landing grounds, we shall fight in the fields and in the streets, we shall fight in the hills. . . .

The words stopped. Weeping, Churchill grasped the back of a chair for a couple of silent minutes. Then, like the blare of a trumpet, he roared in deafening defiance, "We shall never surrender!"

The next day when he delivered the address he had dictated to the House of Commons, the entire membership rose to a thunderous eight-minute ovation responding to the "We shall never surrender" peroration. Amid the cheers, he muttered on side to the front bench, "And if they do land, we'll beat the bastards with the butt ends of broken beer bottles, which is bloody all we've got."

From the House of Commons Churchill went to the BBC studio at Shepherd's Bush to deliver the radio address. His speech would be carried to the Commonwealth nations of Canada, Australia, New Zealand, and the rest of the British Empire. But it was really targeted to one man, Franklin Delano Roosevelt, president of the still-neutral United States.

In his residence quarters on the second floor, the president listened with his friend and principal aide, Harry Hopkins. When the speech was over, Roosevelt turned off the radio and said, "Well, Harry, if we give aid to England, it's not like the French—money down the drain. As long as that old bastard's in charge, Britain will never surrender."

With the fall of France, Britain was alone. From the Reichstag in Berlin issued this directive from Hitler on July 2, 1940: "The Führer and the Supreme Commander has decided . . . that a landing in England is possible provided air superiority can be attained."

That invasion, called Operation Sea Lion, was postponed until mid-September, when Hermann Goering predicted that an outnumbered and overwhelmed Royal Air Force would be wiped out. From the newly captured airfields in France, the bomber squadrons of the Luftwaffe raged across southern England. As high summer deepened to fall, the contrails of the world's first major air war latticed the British skies.

At the climax of what he called the Battle of Britain, Churchill, on a September Sunday afternoon, drove with his wife from the prime minister's country residence at Chequers to Uxbridge, the underground nerve center of the Royal Air Force. On the wall was a map with red disks indicating the disposition of the German Luftwaffe bombers and blue disks indicating the British Hurricane and Spitfire fighter planes.

At about twilight the prime minister turned to the air marshal, Sir Charles Portal, and said, "Where are the blue buttons? There are no more blue buttons on the ledge tray."

The air marshal answered, "There are no more—no more reserves. All we have is in the sky."

Silence descended on the room. Of that crucial moment, Churchill wrote, "The odds were great; our margins small; the stakes infinite."

Some minutes later a wing commander entered the room and began removing the red disks from the wall.

An emotional Churchill turned his thumbs up in victory. Then with a broken voice uttered, "We've won. The Nazis are turning tail."

He took from his pocket an envelope and scribbled these words in tribute to the young men who flew up to forty hours in the sky to beat the Germans back in the Battle of Britain: "Never in the field of human conflict has so much been owed by so many to so few."

If the glory belonged to "the few" in the Battle of Britain, the credit for the endurance of the blitz of London that followed was to "the many." Beginning in September, a Nazi air armada of a thousand strong began to bomb London's industrial East End and docks. When Churchill visited the damaged docks, the workers cried, "Good old Winnie. We knew you'd come and see us. We can take it. Give it back." Churchill broke down and wept.

Because of the bombing threat, the British government persuaded a reluctant Churchill to move his command post from 10 Downing Street to the Annexe. The "Hole in the Ground" was a five-minute walk from 10 Downing Street. Originally, the honeycomb of underground rooms was a repository for old documents. Churchill's operation room was the forty-foot square War Room, whose thick wooden pillars and crossbeams painted white made it seem like a ship's mess hall for officers.

At the head of the table sat Churchill in a homely wooden chair with rounded arms and a plump cushion. In front of him were four glass inkwells, two red and two black. Between the two pairs of inkstands was an ornamental dagger used as a letter opener. The dagger, Churchill told visitors, he was saving for his personal confrontation with Herr Schicklgruber. Just past the end of the ink blotter was a propped-up cardboard sign with the words of Queen Victoria: "Please understand there is no pessimism in this house, and we are not interested in the possibilities of defeat; they do not exist."

Before Churchill ever became prime minister, he perceived that only the president of the United States could wrest his nation from its strict course of neutrality. The wooing of Roosevelt began in 1939, when Churchill, as First Lord of the Admiralty, wrote his initial letter to the U.S. chief executive. The author veiled the secret correspondence with the cryptic signature "Naval Person." The allusion touched on a common interest between Churchill and Roosevelt, who had been an assistant secretary of the navy in World War I.

A Britain that would never surrender would become the first line of U.S. defense. Although the Neutrality Act prevented the granting of military aid, the wily Roosevelt, citing an almost forgotten statute on the books, circumvented the act by leasing the needed ships for British use.

The deployment of destroyers proved mostly symbolic, but it was a symbolism not without substance. Indeed, the same could be said of the subsequent dispatch in January 1941 of Roosevelt's closest confidant, Harry Hopkins, as personal envoy to the British prime minister. Hopkins's message from the U.S. president consisted of words from the Book of Ruth: "Thy people shall be my people and thy God, my God, even to the end." On hearing it, a deeply moved Churchill turned his head away in tears.

On the steps of Hopkins came Wendell Willkie, the recently defeated Republican presidential candidate, whose visit under Roosevelt's auspices signaled the mounting bipartisan sympathy for the British cause. Churchill, in a broadcast from his subterranean cubicle, implored that the sympathy be undergirded by support:

The other day, President Roosevelt gave his opponent in the late presidential election a letter of introduction to me, and in it he wrote out a verse, in his own handwriting, from Longfellow, which he said, "applied to your people as it does to us." Here is the verse:

Sail on, O ship of State!
Sail on, O Union, strong and great!
Humanity with all its fears,
With all the hopes of future years,
Is hanging breathless on thy fate!

What is the answer that I shall give, in your name, to this great man, the thrice-chosen head of a nation of a hundred and thirty million? Here is the answer which I will give to President Roosevelt: Put your confidence in us. Give us your faith and your blessing, and under Providence, all will be well.

We shall not fail or falter; we shall not weaken or tire. Neither the sudden shock of battle, nor the long-drawn trails of vigilance and exertion will wear us down. Give us the tools, and we will finish the job.

To a Congress that had just heard the outlines of a Roosevelt-proposed Lend-Lease Act, a bottom line had never been expressed more succinctly. Ten weeks later, when Congress had passed and the president had signed the legislation, Churchill called it "the most unsordid act in the whole of recorded history."

In the early months of 1941, when British troops were being driven out of the Balkans and the Greek peninsula, the guarantee of military aid from the United States was the only good news to a bomb-ravaged Britain. At home, as the long nights of winter shortened into summer, the shine of sirens and burst of shells, which for so many months had punctuated the hours of the London dark, became sporadic. By June nothing heavier than a gentle English shower rained on the British rooftops. Soon the reason for the cessation was clear: Hitler's interest had been diverted.

On June 21, while Churchill was weekending at Chequers, the military staff telephoned him that German armored divisions were hurtling past the Polish frontier into the Soviet Union. Churchill was not surprised. Not only had he predicted the attack for the last couple of months, but he had also instructed his envoys to communicate that intelligence to a disbelieving Stalin. From the very outset he had been convinced that the deal between the two dictators to carve up Poland was a bond that would soon unravel from its own sleaziness.

As Hitler's armies invaded Russia, Churchill strolled the lawns at Chequers to ponder the new configuration in the geopolitical equation. His parliamentary secretary, John Colville, wondered aloud how the prime minister, with his record of implacable hatred of communism, could team up with the Soviet dictator.

Churchill, between puffs of his cigar, replied, "If Hitler invaded Hell, I would make at least a favourable reference to the Devil in the House of Commons."

To answer those on the left who questioned the anti-Bolshevik Churchill's reaction to the German invasion of the Soviet Union, he told the House of Commons, "We have but one aim, and one single irrevocable purpose. We are resolved to destroy Hitler and every vestige of the Nazi regime. Any man or state who fights on against Nazidom will have our aid. Any man or state who marches with Hitler is our foe."

Churchill believed that if the British and the Soviet people could hold out for the next four or five months, eventual victory was not improbable. For one thing, thought Churchill, "The Russian Bear of a winter would hug Hitler's armies to death as it did Napoleon." So by July British convoys were regularly sailing eastward to Soviet ports, carrying supplies Britain could barely spare from its own needs.

Then, in August, a different type of convoy ventured westward bearing a cargo even more vital—Churchill himself. The battleship *Prince of Wales* swept beside the president's ship, the *Augusta;* the chords of "God Save the King" sounded from the U.S. Marine Band. Standing, with the support of his son, was Franklin Roosevelt, his hand raised in salute. Churchill, whose romantic sense of the sea had been kindled by his nightly reading, while on voyage, of the adventures of C. S. Forester's Captain Horatio Hornblower, emerged on deck in a peaked sailing cap and naval jacket. With a beaming smile, he said, "At long last, Mr. President, glad to see you aboard" to Roosevelt, clad in a white Palm Beach suit.

At the sea meeting, Churchill drafted, with a few later revisions by Roosevelt, "The Atlantic Charter—which embodied initial principles of freedom." But more than in the charter, Churchill found in the Sunday church service, held on the quarterdeck beneath the battle guns, a tangible expression of their common purpose. As the sun broke through the mist that Sunday morning, the chorus of the old hymn "Onward, Christian Soldiers" rose to the sky in the mingled voices of two navies—"fighting men," as Churchill later retold to the House of Commons, "of the same language, of the same faith, of the same fundamental laws, of the same ideals and now to a larger extent of the same interests, and certainly, in different degrees, facing the same danger."

On his homeward voyage, Churchill spied in the distance a vast flotilla of merchant ships—cargo boats, tankers, whalers, and converted passenger boats—on their way to England from America, carrying the preciously needed munitions and equipment. Churchill saw his chance to say "thank you" to the ships of the U.S. Merchant Marine. In the fading light of sunset, the *Prince of Wales* plunged, cutting a lane through the six-column convoy at twenty-two knots. Not once but twice, the British battleship plowed through the motley steel ranks. Standing on its bridge was the British prime minister, with his one hand in a V-sign and the other raised in salute to the onlooking crews, whose perilous tasks were ennobled by the sight of that silhouetted figure on the distant deck.

At the historic Atlantic meeting, where the charter was almost an afterthought, the principals and their advisers mainly discussed the emergence of Russia and Japan as crucial factors in the balance of power. Churchill, ignoring the warnings of a Japanese build-up in Singapore in the Far East, told the Americans that his paramount military objective was to drive Rommel and his Afrika Korps out of Egypt.

Three months later the Americans, as well as the British, were surprised by the Japanese. December 7, 1941, found Churchill and his two U.S. guests, Averell Harriman and Ambassador John Winant, at Chequers. At 9:00 P.M. they tuned in to the BBC news. Immediately, Churchill telephoned Roosevelt.

"It's quite true," the U.S. president said. "They have attacked us at Pearl Harbor."

Churchill replied, "Well, we're all in the same boat now." Despite that shock, Churchill went to bed in an almost joyous exhilaration. Churchill wrote later, "I went to bed and slept the sleep of the saved and thankful."

CHAPTER 16

LA MAISON BLANCHE, ALGIERS

All our people from the highest to the very lowest have learned that this [campaign in Africa] is not a child's game and are ready to get down to business.

DWIGHT DAVID EISENHOWER

THE FIRST TIME Eisenhower saw Churchill was just after Christmas in 1941 at the old War Department Building.[1] Eisenhower was in a peripheral group of generals and admirals that heard an ebullient Churchill outline war aims in the big conference room on the second floor.

A day before, Churchill had electrified Congress in his address to its Joint Session. In his opening he had triggered roars of laughter when he remarked, "If my father had been American and my mother English, instead of the other way around, I might have got here on my own." Churchill had received a thundering ovation when, after reciting a litany of atrocities by the Japanese on both the British and the Americans, he asked, "What kind of people do they think we are?"

The next day Eisenhower attended the briefing in the second-floor conference room in the War Department Building.

1. The massive French Renaissance structure is now the Executive Office Building and is considered part of the White House, which it adjoins.

Churchill's radiant pink face contrasted with the dark, pin-striped three-piece suit. A blue polka-dot bowtie reflected the twinkle in his eyes. Eisenhower was surprised at Churchill's short stature—almost three and half inches less than his own six feet. Yet somehow Churchill projected as a giant. He was more dominating in presence than Franklin Roosevelt or Douglas MacArthur. Churchill's briefing was more like a lecture. The British prime minister who ended his military career as a major addressed his U.S. audience of generals and admirals as if he were the one with greater military experience. Churchill stressed that defeating Germany would be the paramount priority. It was the Atlantic Ocean—and its arm, the Mediterranean—he explained, where Anglo–U.S. fleets must first reign supreme. With control of the Mediterranean, Churchill argued, North Africa could then be the gateway to Europe and the subsequent engagement of the Allies with German troops. This campaign in North Africa, he propounded, would compel the Nazis to redirect troops away from their invasion of the Soviet Union. The Soviet army's defense of its motherland was the indispensable key, Churchill emphasized with a wave of his cigar, in dismantling the German offense.

To Eisenhower, Churchill's words sounded more powerful than the strategy. His plan seemed more defensive than defiant.

Days later the Acadia Conference (an oddly chosen name, meaning "peace," for a war planning meeting, noted Ike) opened. Although presided over initially by the prime minister and president, the meeting became the vehicle for the exchange of views between the British and U.S. high command. Some of the British generals made Ike bristle with their condescending manner and annoying habit of name-dropping geographic places in their far-flung dominions—names like the Seychelles Islands and Kuala Lumpur—British Empire outposts that they knew the Americans were not familiar with.

With his affable manner and easy grin, Eisenhower masked any irritation he felt. An attentive listener, he made friends with his British counterparts in that week of the Acadia meetings. Some of them had their doubts, however, about the American general who had no battlefield experience. Eisenhower's boss, General Marshall, was courtly but aloof with the British visitors. In contrast, Admiral Ernest King, U.S. Chief of Naval Operations, was openly hostile to them. King had been Roosevelt's voice in Washington. As former assistant secretary of the navy in World War I, Roosevelt had known King for years. King was an Anglophobe and, like just about all navy men, "a Pacific-Firster." (His daughter said of him, "Actually, my father is even-tempered. He is always in a rage about something.") The choleric King did not mince his anger at the British strategy of remaining on the defensive against the Japanese in order to concentrate on the Germans.

General Marshall had to pick someone to be a liaison with the British in London, and Eisenhower emerged as the only possible choice. Marshall once revealed his qualifications for picking generals: Marshall would assume their competence; it was their personality he studied. He rejected glory seekers, pessimists, desk-pounders, risk-avoiders, and do-it-all-yourself types. Eisenhower fit all the criteria.

On June 24, 1942, Eisenhower landed in London. The next day the commander of the U.S. forces held a press conference. For British cameramen, the photogenic Eisenhower would ever after be front-page material. The big grin and the catchy nickname of "Ike" endeared him to the British. He also won friends by his relaxed and unpretentious manner. Eisenhower would refer to his superiors as "the big shots" and would say he was "only a simple country boy." When Eisenhower was tossed a tough question, he would reply, "Well, that's just too complicated for a dumb bunny like me."

Churchill warmed to the new U.S. general too. They were soon meeting every Tuesday for lunch at 10 Downing Street or at the underground War Rooms (called the Annexe) and then just about every weekend at the prime minister's country house, Chequers.

The half-American Churchill liked his mother's countrymen, and Ike seemed to typify what he liked best about them—their directness and unrestraint. In turn, Eisenhower was enthralled by Churchill. As host the prime minister could play alternatively the role of raconteur, historian, actor, orator, and wit. He might recount to Eisenhower the battlefield strategies of William the Conqueror at Hastings or of Wellington at Waterloo, declaim soliloquies of Shakespeare, recite verses of Tennyson, or impart anecdotal tidbits about the lives of Henry VIII or Charles II.

To Eisenhower, the pink-faced Churchill in the zippered "siren suit" (the prime minister himself had designed it),[2] looked like a baby smoking a cigar. The charm was infectious. Ike said Churchill was giving him the "sun lamp treatment," and he took care to make sure its glow did not "burn" his judgment.

Ike did not agree with Churchill's North Africa strategy, and Churchill was dismissive of Ike's insistence on Sledgehammer (the code name for an invasion of France proposed for 1943). Ike did take up one Churchill suggestion, that he should have a dog at Telegraph Cottage. Eisenhower had rented the retreat, which was a forty-minute drive from his headquarters

---

2. The "siren" suit was named after the siren that signaled a German bomb attack. It took forty-five seconds to jump into this one-piece suit that zipped up from the crotch to the top of the chest. Interestingly, Eisenhower was the other war leader who became a fashion designer in World War II. Ike was responsible for "the Eisenhower jacket": it was vest length with sleeves. Ike thought the hanging drape of the old jacket looked sloppy. The jacket that waiters wore in Army mess halls inspired him to draw for tailors this new cut and shape for a military jacket.

at Grosvenor Square, as an escape from London. Churchill had as his constant companion Rufus, a reddish poodle. Said Churchill to Ike, "Rufus is my only uncritical audience!"

Ike bought himself a Scottie (like FDR's Fala) and called it Telek. Presumably, the name was a merger of Telegraph and Ike. Yet when journalists asked him the origin of the name, he said with a straight face, "It encodes a highly classified military secret."

Ike found evening solace in the mock Tudor cottage with Telek and his U.S. naval aide, Harry Butcher. The suburban house gave him a better excuse to dodge London dinner engagements. Twice a week Ike penned a handwritten note to Mamie. In one he said,

> In a place like this the Commanding General must be a bit of a diplomat, lawyer, promoter, salesman, social hound, *liar* (at least to get out of social affairs), mountebank, actor, Simon Legree, humanitarian, orator and incidentally (sometimes I think most damnably incidentally) a soldier.

He ended, "Lots of love—don't forget me."

As a promoter and salesman of the United States, Ike was supreme. Not since Benjamin Franklin arrived in London some two centuries before had the United States had a representative who so endeared himself to the English. At a time when the British had not yet met the German army on the battlefield, what Ike said and did invited almost daily coverage. An over-served U.S. general at Claridge's had bragged that the Americans would show the English how to fight. When Ike heard it, he announced, "I'm going to make the son of a bitch swim back to America," and Ike did send him back, albeit by boat.

Another press account that redounded to Ike's favorable image was the report of his demoting and dispatching "stateside" a U.S. general who had called an English counterpart "a British son of a bitch." A British general told Eisenhower that the American general had been a bit harsh in reprimanding the U.S. officer. "Actually," said the British officer, "he *is* a son of a bitch."

Ike replied, "Look, I know he's a son of a bitch, but what I dismissed the General for is that he called him a *British* son of a bitch."

There was also the leak of Eisenhower's memo, which ordered that U.S. troops in Britain should use American terms, not British: "Words should not be used such as *lorry* [truck], *petrol* [gas], *tiffin* [lunch], *torch* [flashlight], [or] *bonnet* [hood of car]."

Curiously, the English press loved it. Ike was an American "not trying to be somebody he wasn't." "Ike," one journalist wrote, "wasn't someone who'd rather be hobnobbing with the toffs. He was a jolly good bloke."

Another press story reported that the chain-smoking Ike had offended some duke at a black-tie dinner at Whites (a London private club) by lighting up a Chesterfield before the toast to the king (protocol requires the toast to come at the end of the meal). The next day it reported that Ike would be swearing off such formal banquets.

Some time later, Ike spent a weekend with his best friend among the British high military brass, Dickie Mountbatten, the admiral and cousin of the king. At Broadlands, his majestic manor, Mountbatten was in the middle of a dinner conversation when Ike suddenly pulled out a pack. As the American general flicked his lighter, Mountbatten jumped up and cried out, "To the King," and said, "Now, Ike, you can go on smoking as much as you goddamn please."

Unlike the British military brass, Ike never sounded pompous or pretentious. Even his foibles, such as his chain smoking, were fuel for endearing stories, just like Churchill's cigar. However, one military figure who did not warm to Eisenhower as Mountbatten did was General Montgomery, who viewed any press coverage of Ike as diminishing his own.

When Ike visited Montgomery, the British general announced, "There'll be no smoking when I'm around, General Eisenhower." Later, at Chequers, Ike asked Churchill if Montgomery stopped *him* from smoking! Churchill shook his head, laughing.

"Monty told me, 'Prime Minister, I don't smoke. I don't drink and I'm 100 percent fit.'

"'Well, Monty,' I said, 'I smoke, I drink, I'm 200 percent fit.'"

Churchill was an early enthusiast of Eisenhower, and he dismissed the appraisal of those generals such as Alan Brooke and Bernard Montgomery who considered Eisenhower "a desk man" because he had no command experience in the field. Lord Mountbatten also saw Eisenhower as a natural leader of men. He agreed with his long-time friend Churchill, who told him, "Dickie, Ike is more than a general—he's a born politician and innate diplomat." In Churchill's opinion, those were the qualities needed to forge an alliance. Churchill summed it up by saying, "He's a prairie prince."

Churchill came to appreciate the tact and sensitivity of Eisenhower. Once Churchill questioned a decision of General Alexander in Egypt. Churchill showed his cable to Ike, who said, "I would resign if such a cable was sent to me. You are saying you are a more competent judge 1500 miles away." Ike's suggestion was for Churchill to frame his reservations in the form of a query. Churchill took the advice.

It was Churchill's strategy to mount a landing in North Africa rather than Europe. Churchill had a code name for the campaign—"Torch."

The question was, Who should head the joint U.S.–British force? Churchill delicately hinted at Eisenhower, but Roosevelt was torn between Marshall and Eisenhower. If Marshall went to North Africa, Eisenhower would have to come back to Washington to take Marshall's place. Churchill's endorsement of Eisenhower made the difference.

The Torch initiative started at a difficult time. In late 1942 the British army had just about pushed out the Italians in Egypt when the Germans sent their armies to relieve the faltering Italians, and soon afterward they routed the British at Tobruk. It was the worst British defeat thus far.

When Eisenhower looked at a map of North Africa, it was French colonial territory stretching almost a thousand miles from Morocco on the Atlantic coast to the western border of Libya. (Egypt and the Suez Canal lay to the east of Libya.) Vichy France now administered that colonial territory. That government—which had been established with the sanction of Hitler— was not quite a puppet state, but neither was it totally free of the German domination. The aging hero of World War I, Marshal Petain, was the figurehead leader of Vichy France. His deputy was Admiral Jean Darlan, the defense minister of France.

In November 1942 Ike flew to Gibraltar to assume command of the Allied invasion of North Africa. British and U.S. troops were poised to land in a neutral territory without a declaration of war and without any provocation—and with the hope that the French colonial army would greet them not as aggressors but as liberators. Unfortunately, the French chose to resist. That meant Eisenhower had to negotiate with Darlan, who was considered a cryptofascist and an anti-Semite. To make any deal with Darlan would raise political flak from the New Deal crowd back in the United States. Before leaving to see Darlan, Eisenhower asked Churchill for advice. "Kiss him on the ass, if you have to, Ike," said Churchill. "Anything to make him surrender."

On November 13 Eisenhower flew from Algeria to meet with Darlan. Darlan promised to surrender the French army if Eisenhower would make him governor-general of French North Africa.

Hell did break loose in America. "The first move Eisenhower makes, as Commander," a newspaper screamed, "is to make a deal with a Fascist." Anthony Eden, the British foreign secretary, was also disparaging of Eisenhower, but Churchill came to his defense: "Why not take the support of Darlan in defeating the Germans; after all, we are supporting Stalin, who is certainly no zealous promoter of democracy." However, even though Darlan was assassinated in December, landings were made in Algiers, Oran, and Casablanca without incident.

In January Churchill and Roosevelt met in Casablanca. Ike flew from Algiers to join the conference. Over the Atlas Mountains, two of the four engines on his plane conked out. Ike and the crew had to put on their parachutes. The pilot, however, decided he could glide the plane without fuel the rest of the way to Casablanca. Roosevelt met Eisenhower when the plane landed and later told his White House aide, Harry Hopkins, "Ike looks strained, as if he is not up to the pressure." Hopkins explained to him that Eisenhower had just emerged from a plane that had almost crashed.

Churchill dispelled any of Roosevelt's doubts about Eisenhower. In Churchill's view, Eisenhower was doing a superb job in organizing a joint Allied command. Ike told Churchill, "I feel in headquarters that I am one-half American and one-half British."

Churchill replied, "Well, General, I feel the same way. You are speaking to the result of an English Speaking Union."

Not the least of the frictions between U.S. and British officers in North Africa were the rules in the officers' mess. The Americans liked to down their whiskey highballs before sitting down to dine but banned alcohol at the table. The British regulations forbade drinking before dinner, but during the meal officers enjoyed their bottles of wine at the table.

Churchill announced his Solomon-like solution to the impasse. "Before dinner," Churchill ruled, "we British will have to defer to the American rules and imbibe, but at the table, you Yanks must abide by our British regulations and drink." As

Churchill raised his own glass of whiskey and soda at the mess bar, he observed, "I hope this felicitous arrangement for the fraternity of Anglo-American relationships will be accepted in good 'spirits' by all."

At the Casablanca Conference, Eisenhower complained to Churchill about the intransigence of Charles de Gaulle. De Gaulle, who had appointed himself head of the French Resistance, balked at being paired with Henri Giraud as the co-leaders of the Free French. Roosevelt, who detested de Gaulle, leaned toward excluding the prickly French general altogether.

Charles de Gaulle, whose very name suggests the ancient glory of Charlemagne and Gaul, believed he was the embodiment of French history and pride. Churchill remarked to Eisenhower, "It's a cross we have to bear—no, it's a double cross, the Double Cross of Lorraine."

"De Gaulle," continued Churchill, "seems to think he's Joan of Arc, and my problem is that my bishops won't allow me to burn him!" But Churchill agreed to talk to de Gaulle. Glaring up at the towering figure of de Gaulle, Churchill delivered his bastardized concoction of "Franglais," with additions to the noble Gallic tongue even more atrocious than his accent: *"Si vous m'obstaclerez, je vous liquiderai"* ("If you obstacle me, I will liquidate you"). A bewildered de Gaulle backed down.

Eisenhower, however, was under real pressure by Churchill to engage the U.S. and British troops under his command with the German army. Even a fervent Eisenhower backer such as Churchill reflected the impatience of British public opinion. "The Americans," complained Churchill, "should be using North Africa as a spring board, not a sofa."

In February an American opportunity arose. After their defeat at El Alamein in Egypt, Field Marshal Rommel and his Afrika Korps were in retreat. Churchill had said of the British victory, "This is not the end, nay, not even the beginning of the end, but it is perhaps the end of the beginning."

A fleeing Rommel now tried to march through Kasserine Pass to a major supply base at LeKef in northern Tunisia. Eisenhower dispatched his army to stop Rommel, but the first U.S. Army effort was pushed back. Kasserine was Eisenhower's first real battle, and only U.S. artillery and German shortages saved Eisenhower from a humiliating defeat.

Churchill was more understanding than his own generals Montgomery and Brooke. Even General George Marshall in Washington conveyed to Eisenhower his dissatisfaction. Yet in Churchill's mind, Eisenhower had achieved his chief priority. He had welded together a military command of the two countries. As for the defeat, it was more a skirmish than a battle. Anyway, Churchill was content to let Ike take the heat. Churchill could defend a U.S. general far more easily against second-guessing attacks than he could a British general. He squelched further carping by British officers by stressing, "General Eisenhower is my man."[3]

At any rate, the U.S. effort in Africa had forced Hitler to divert some German troops and supplies from the Soviet front and dispatch them to North Africa. That, if not a victory, was valuable in itself. The German shift of some forces pleased the Kremlin.

Churchill, however, did not regard "Uncle" Joe Stalin with any familial affection. After a dinner with the Allied command, Churchill asked his resident minister in Algiers, Harold Macmillan, to come back to his hotel suite to join him for a drink. "Harold," he asked, "what do you think of Cromwell?"

Macmillan, not quite sure of what to say, replied cautiously, "Rather ambitious chap wasn't he, Prime Minister?"

---

3. John J. McCloy, secretary of war and later high commissioner of Germany, told the author about Eisenhower's ability to ingratiate himself with his superiors, "For a while Ike was simultaneously 'MacArthur's man,' 'Marshall's man,' and 'Roosevelt's man.'" They all thought Ike was their own special protégé: "It was Ike's smile and suppression of his ego."

"Harold," Churchill replied, "Cromwell was obsessed with Spain but he never saw the danger of France."

Macmillan later observed to Winston Churchill II, the Prime Minister's grandson,

> Here we were at a time when we were still, frankly, losing the war, but Churchill already was confident of eventual victory. He had factored in the American entry into the war and the Germans' likely failure to conquer Russia. He was already focusing on what we would later call the 'cold war' after the Allied victory over Germany.

Weeks later Foreign Secretary Anthony Eden wrote in a memorandum that the United Nations must include the Big Four Powers: the United States, Britain, China, and the Soviet Union. Churchill was dubious. He memoed back, "We cannot, however, tell what sort of Russia and what kind of demands we shall have to face. It would be a measureless disaster if Russian barbarism overlaid the culture and independence of the Ancient States of Europe."

Eisenhower, if not as prescient as Churchill, did challenge Gen. Sir Alan Brooke's view that a cross-channel invasion of France would be unnecessary "since the Russian Army would grind the Germans into the dust."

Ike then asked the British general, "But what if you find all of central and Western Europe have been overrun by the Soviets?"

"Oh," answered Brooke, "Stalin wouldn't want to hold anything beyond Russia's border." Eisenhower shook his head.

Montgomery's armies were now pushing Rommel's Afrika Korps back in the north of Libya, so Eisenhower wanted to engage Von Arnem's armies to the south. Alexander tried to dissuade Eisenhower: "You Americans did not actually prove yourselves in Kasserine, did you? Your place is in the rear, backing us up." In reply, Eisenhower argued the line he had heard Churchill once use: If the American people ever came to believe that their troops would not play any substantial role against the Germans, they would be more inclined to insist on a Japan-first strategy.

Eisenhower now had his next battlefield test. He needed two U.S. generals to beat the Germans at Bizerte. They were Omar Bradley and George Patton. In the *Howitzer*, the 1912 West Point yearbook, Ike had once written, "Someday we will be able to say, 'Yeah, I knew General Bradley.'" Bradley's expertise was infantry tactics. He knew how to employ intelligence, transportation, and supply to move his infantry. Patton, the maestro of mobile armor, was to lead his tank corps in North Africa.

By May 7 the Americans entered Bizerte in victory. The same morning Montgomery's British army captured Tunis. On May 20 the Americans, British, and Free French marched in a victory parade through the palm tree–lined boulevards of Tunis. Afterward Eisenhower joined Harold Macmillan, his British adviser, for a flight back to headquarters in Algiers.

As their Flying Fortress flew over Bizerte, they could see a huge Allied convoy proceeding unmolested toward Egypt. Macmillan touched Eisenhower's arm. "There, General, are the fruits of your victory."

Eisenhower smiled, with tears in his eyes, and said, "*Yours*, you mean *ours*, Harold."

Also on May 20, Churchill flew to Algiers to tell Eisenhower that the next step should be Italy. For a week he monologued at Eisenhower. "Sardinia," declared Churchill, "would be a mere convenience but Italy a glamorous campaign."

At a luncheon and then dinner at his hotel, Churchill painted visions to Ike about the conqueror of Rome in future history books. About a half hour before midnight, just as Eisenhower was preparing for bed in his suite at the St. George's Hotel, the phone rang. It was Churchill, asking him to come over to his hotel, the Anfa.

For two more hours Churchill argued for Sicily as "the gateway to Rome." The next morning when the British general Alexander noted a bleary-eyed Eisenhower, he smiled sympathetically, for Churchill had given Alexander the same treatment the day before.

Eisenhower said years later in a television interview by Alastair Cooke, "The man used pathos, humor, anecdotes, history, anything to get his own way."

Churchill was insistent on invading Italy because the Italian campaign could lead to "the underbelly of Europe." Central Europe should be the next step beyond a conquered Italy. Churchill hoped to free the Balkans before the Soviet armies entered them. That might keep Eastern Europe from falling under Soviet control.

Operation Husky was the code name given to the Sicily invasion. British intelligence made the armada landing a little easier by floating up the Spanish coast the body of a dead British major, carrying a letter to General Alexander that referred to the code name "Husky" as an Allied invasion of Greece. The invasion fleet, said the letter, would feint north toward Sicily before heading east. Hitler fell for it and sent reinforcements to Albania and Greece.

On July 9 the Allied armies assembled in the waters off Malta. In his headquarters, Ike saw the barometer fall. A storm would jeopardize the landing. He rubbed his lucky coins in his pocket—the six coins of the Allies: United States, Britain, Canada, Australia, New Zealand, and South Africa. Despite the threatening weather, Eisenhower then told his generals, "OK, let's go."

Landings took place on the Sicilian coast. A month later, British tanks would roll into Palermo, Sicily.

As the Allied armies were now poised to invade Italy near Naples, another awkward problem, similar to the Darlan Deal, arose. General Castellano, head of the Italian army, was hinting through diplomatic channels an interest in declaring war against Germany, Italy's former Axis partner, in exchange for an armistice. Castellano had just organized a coup d'état against Mussolini, placing Marshal Badoglio as head of the Italian government. Castellano's main fear was the revenge Hitler might take with his armies to destroy Rome and its antiquities. Ike drafted terms for an armistice, but it was vetoed by Roosevelt. "Unconditional Surrender or Nothing," wired back the White House.

Eisenhower with his top deputy, Gen. Beedle Smith, drafted the words for "an armistice" on September 3, with a codicil that virtually spelled out the terms of an "unconditional surrender," without using the exact words. On September 9 Marshall Badoglio reneged. An angry Eisenhower told Badoglio, "I intend to broadcast the existence of an armistice at the earlier agreed time. I do not accept your message."

Badoglio backed down. Afterward Ike announced to an aide, "One down—two to go."

In Algeria Ike had moved from St. George's Hotel to a modest white villa known as La Maison Blanche. His staff called it by its English translation, "the White House." Eisenhower awaited word from Teheran, where newspaper photos featured a dark-caped Roosevelt with a cigarette holder, Stalin in his white tunic smoking a pipe, and Churchill wearing a naval uniform and puffing a cigar.

Clouds of controversy had darkened the first meeting of the Soviet premier with Roosevelt and Churchill. Stalin was contemptuous of the Italian operation and angrily opposed any move eastward from Italy into the Balkans. The Soviet premier's hints that he wanted Poland under his control alarmed Churchill. Most of all, Stalin was demanding a "second front" soon—that is, an invasion of France by the following spring.

Churchill and Roosevelt promised Stalin such a cross-channel invasion for no later than the following spring. Its code name would be Operation Overlord.

Later, in Cairo, Churchill and Roosevelt discussed who would direct Overlord. Marshall, the U.S. Army Chief of Staff, was again the obvious choice. Churchill knew, however, that Roosevelt in Washington leaned heavily on Marshall. Churchill implied to FDR that he would not be unhappy with the choice of Eisenhower. Brooke and Montgomery still had their doubts about Ike as a general, but they had come to like him, as most all British did. Most of all, they trusted him. He was a team player who had fused together a joint Allied command. Roosevelt chose Ike.

From Cairo, Churchill flew to meet Ike in Algiers on December 10. The fights with Stalin over Poland had drained every ounce of energy out of Churchill. As Eisenhower ushered him into his armored Cadillac, Churchill said in a tremulous voice, "I'm afraid that I'll have to stay with you longer than I planned. I am completely at the end of my tether."

Churchill had come down with pneumonia. He wired FDR: "Am stranded amid the ruins of Carthage." Two days later the British prime minister suffered a slight stroke. He told Eisenhower, "If I die, don't worry—the war is won." He slipped to the very edge of life before he rallied. Days passed as Eisenhower supervised his recovery. He even lent Churchill some of his Western paperback novels to read. When Ike was sure that Churchill would survive, he flew to Italy to confer with Gen. Mark Clark, who was heading the U.S. Army campaign in Italy against the German army.

On Christmas Eve Eisenhower took a ride on a destroyer from Africa to visit Capri, which he had set aside for "R&R" for American GIs. He saw no enlisted men but did note a huge villa atop a hill. "Whose is that?" asked Ike.

"Yours, sir," said the U.S. Navy officer.

"And that one?" Ike pointed to an even bigger villa.

"That belongs to General Spaatz." (He was the U.S. Army Air Force head.)

"Goddamn it," said Ike. "That is not my villa, and that's not General Spaatz's. This is supposed to be a rest center for combat men—not a goddamn playground for brass."

Back at La Maison Blanche, Eisenhower had Christmas dinner with Churchill. It was the first time in two weeks Churchill had felt strong enough to get out of bed. Churchill toasted the king, the president, Ike, and then the success of Overlord.

Four days later, a telegram arrived from General Marshall. Ike was ordered home. "You'll need to be fresh, mentally," said Marshall.

Ike and his U.S. naval aide, Harry Butcher, arrived the day after New Year's Day in 1944. With them were two Scottie puppies with Scottish plaid collars—the issue of Telek. Butcher's wife was Mamie's good friend, who lived in the next apartment to hers in the Wardman Park Hotel. (It is now the Sheraton Park in Washington.)

The new Eisenhower puppy won no reprieve from Mamie when the cute canine defecated on her favorite oriental rug from the Philippines. The Eisenhowers first visited their son John at West Point and then took a weekend at White Sulphur Springs in West Virginia (General Marshall had reserved their suite and ordered them to go there).

Then the Eisenhowers flew out to see Ike's brother Milton, the new president of Kansas State University in Manhattan, Kansas, where Ike's aging mother was visiting. Ida Eisenhower hardly recognized her son at first. "Is that you, Ike?" she asked.

Ike now was ready to leave and assume the greatest military undertaking in history: the landing of half a million soldiers on an enemy coast.

CHAPTER 17

TELEGRAPH COTTAGE, ENGLAND

People of Western Europe: A landing was made this morning on the coast of France by the troops of the Allied Expeditionary Force. This landing is part of the concerted United Nations plea for the liberation in Europe.

DWIGHT DAVID EISENHOWER

THE SPRING OF 1944 was the deadline for D-day. Four months from January still gave the Allies enough time to mobilize and train the troops in the British Isles, but it was early enough in the spring to allow some summer months for battle campaign weather in France before the autumn rains. Allied meteorological experts in ocean tides told the planning staff that the date would have to be the first week in May or the first week in June—the two times for low tides in the Channel. Normandy was chosen for the beach landing because the "Atlantic Wall" of German defenses was heaviest around Calais—which was the shortest distance from the English coast and where the Germans expected the invasion to take place. Finally, it was determined that dawn was the best time of day because it would allow the navy fleet to cross the Channel in darkness and then enjoy a full day of light for establishing a beachhead.

During Tuesday luncheons at 10 Downing Street (or at the Annexe) and then Friday dinners, mostly at Chequers, the prime minister's weekend home in Buckinghamshire, Ike hashed out the various planning decisions with Churchill. Sometimes senior military leaders such as General Beedle Smith or Carl "Toohey" Spaatz on the U.S. side joined them, along with Admiral Sir Andrew Cunningham and General Sir Alan Brooke of the British.

Churchill's style at these meetings would be to sit down and say, "Now gentlemen, we have this proposition." And he would bring it out himself. Then he would invite discussion on a topic usually selecting the officer most concerned. "It was very informal," Eisenhower would say later. "There was no punctilio protocol."

The biggest logistical problem was too few landing craft. Before the war, Admiral King had lobbied in Washington for building more battleships and aircraft carriers. But when the Pacific war turned out to be an island-hopping campaign, King hoarded the few available landing boats for the Pacific. The European campaign was thus shortchanged. A New Orleans inventor had come up with an LST, a troop carrier that could move back and forth from ship to shore without the excess time of turning the craft around (which would make the sea vehicles more vulnerable to enemy aircraft). The navy originally dismissed the inventor's troop carrier but later adopted it. Yet the factory in New Orleans, working around the clock, couldn't produce enough of them. Churchill said to Ike in late January, "The destinies of two great empires seemed to be tied up in some goddamn things called LSTs." The LST shortage forced Ike to push D-day back from May to June.

Sipping brandy and smoking his Romeo and Juliet cigar at Chequers when Ike was his only guest, Churchill expressed his reservations about Overlord. Between puffs of his cigar, he became almost tearful.

"When I think of the beaches of Normandy choked with the flowers of American and British youth and when in my mind's eye I see the tides running red with their blood I have doubts." Shaking his head, Churchill repeated, "I have my doubts, Ike. I have my doubts."

Ike usually never let the smile of optimism fade from his face, but he, too, could not totally put aside the fate of those young men who would never return to their families.

The general and admirals planned the attack and organized the logistics, but Ike knew the success would rest on the soldier carrying his rifle over the beaches of Normandy. If the infantrymen drove forward in the face of German fire, D-day would succeed.

For that reason Ike spent much of his time in these preinvasion months visiting troops. He wanted to make certain that as many soldiers as possible got a look at the man who was ordering them into battle at the risk of death. From February until June he visited, on his special train called "The Bayonet," twenty-seven divisions, twenty-three air bases, five warships, and innumerable depots, hospitals, and other military grounds. On those visits he delivered a short talk to those assembled and then went around shaking the soldiers' hands.

Other generals did this, too, but not as much as Ike and not in the same way. A Patton or Montgomery would inquire about soldiers' military specialty, their training, or their unit. Ike's first question would be, "Where are you from?" Then he questioned them about their family. What kind of job did they have? What were their plans after the war? He loved talking with them about cattle ranching in Wyoming, growing corn in Iowa, dairy farming in Vermont, or logging in Idaho.

But once while visiting a troop unit, he did follow up on their specialty. He was asking several of the soldiers where they hailed from. One answered, "Pennsylvania, Sir," another "Texas," and then a blond private said, "Kansas."

Ike's face lit up like a light bulb. "Where?" he asked.

"Dodge City," the private replied.

"What do you do?"

"I'm a marksman."

"Are you good?" asked Ike.

"Best one in the company," was the reply.

"Is that what the guys in the company say?" asked Ike.

"The smart ones do," the soldier answered.

Ike laughed. "Well, go get 'em, Kansas!"

Ike once said that the best appearance he ever made before troops was in Norfolk. It was a rainy March morning. As General Eisenhower made his way to the little platform from which he would deliver a few remarks, he slipped in the mud and went down back-ass-ward. The troops tried to stifle their reaction as Ike got back on his feet and wiped the mud off his seat. When he finished, Ike let loose a big guffaw. That triggered gales of laughter from the soldiers. Ike then gave his two-armed wave and pushed his way into the troops, shaking hands. There were no remarks delivered. Ike said it was the best morale-lifting appearance he ever made.

In the same month, Prime Minister Churchill, visiting a bombed East London church, pinned a Victoria Cross on a one-armed Home Guard volunteer who had rescued children from a fire-burned rubble of a house. "You honor me," said the grizzled old man as the medal was pinned on his chest.

"No," growled Churchill. "You are the one who honors me."

Eisenhower himself once referred to the sensitive side of Churchill. Once at Checquers, Eisenhower recalled a logistical presentation. The officer used the phrase "so many thousand bodies." "Churchill broke in," said Eisenhower, "with great indignation. 'Sir, you will not refer to personnel of His Majesty's Forces as bodies. They are live men. I want to hear no more of that word.'"

At a luncheon at 10 Downing Street, a worried Churchill confided to Eisenhower, "General, it's good for commanders to be optimistic, else they would never win a battle but I must say to you if by the time the snow flies, you have established your armies in Brittany on the Normandy coast and have the port of Cherbourg firmly in your grasp, I will be the first to congratulate a wonderfully conducted military campaign."

Then Churchill took another puff of his cigar and added, "If, in addition, you should have seized the port of Le Havre and have extended your holdings to include all the area including the Cotentin Peninsula and the mouth of the Seine, I will proclaim that this is one of the finest operations in modern war.

"And finally," expanded Churchill, "if by Christmas, you have succeeded in liberating our beloved Paris—if she can by that time regain her life of freedom and take her accustomed place as a center of Western European culture and beauty, then I will proclaim that this operation is the most grandly conceived and best conducted campaign known to the history of warfare."

To this Eisenhower replied, "Mr. Prime Minister, we expect to be on the borders of Germany by Christmas, pounding away at her defenses. When that occurs, if Hitler has the slightest judgment or wisdom left he will surrender unconditionally to avoid complete destruction of Germany." Ike smiled. "Because of this conviction, I made a bet with General Montgomery some months ago. The proposition was that we would end the war in Europe by the end of 1944. The bet was for five pounds and I have no reason to want to hedge that bet."

The prime minister's face curved upward into a splendid smile. "My dear General, I pray you are right."

Because of the easy intimacy that had grown between the two men, their friendship could weather any storm of difference. A major argument arose about bombings in March and

April on coastal France. Churchill sided with British Air Marshal Arthur Harris and U.S. Army Air Force General Spaatz. They both believed that heavy bombardment might turn the sentiments of the French population against helping the invading Americans and British. Moreover, Churchill wanted the bombers to concentrate on the German V2 emplacements. The rocketing bombs had been terrorizing London.

De Gaulle sided with Eisenhower, "If that [the bombing of the French coast] was the price of liberation," said de Gaulle, "the French would pay it without regret or complaint."

During March, Air Marshal Harris had turf battles with General Spaatz over power and policy. In frustration, Eisenhower called his friend Royal Air Force Vice Air Marshal Tedder. "Arthur, I am tired of dealing with a lot of prima donnas. By God, you tell that bunch that if they can't get together and stop quarreling like children, I will tell the Prime Minister to get someone else to run this damned war!" As Supreme Allied Commander, Eisenhower had to have control of the air forces. Ike knew General Marshall would back him on this, and he did.

When Eisenhower left for North Africa, he turned Telegraph Cottage over to his closest British military friend, Vice Air Marshal Tedder. When Ike returned, he took over Telegraph Cottage once again and gave Tedder the large manor home that the Allied command had thought more appropriate for the Supreme Allied Commander.

Capt. Harry Butcher worried about his housemate's high blood pressure. At Butcher's urging, Ike made himself not go to the office once a week. That day he rode a horse in Richmond Park. At night he tried to relax by listening to music from the BBC and reading, occasionally a C. S. Forester novel but usually a pulp magazine of short stories about the old West. Twice a week he penned a letter to Mamie and signed it, "Your lover." One time he wrote, "Every time someone brings me news of the way you handle yourself, I'm prouder of you . . . you are a thoroughbred, and incidentally, I love the Hell out of you."

One morning in Grosvenor Square Eisenhower received a call from George Allen. Officially Allen served as a Washington, D.C., commissioner, but mostly he was a martini-drinking mate of President Roosevelt's and chief purveyor to the president of the latest rumors and off-color stories. The Mississippi-born "General" Allen drawled on the phone, "You don't know me, General, we've never met, but I wanted to ask you a big favor."

"Oh, I know who you are," replied Ike. "How can I help you?"

"Well, a couple of years ago," said Allen, "when I got back from London, my friends wanted to know what was the inside scoop?

"I'd lean over and whisper, 'Eisenhower—I can't say anything more.' Hell, I didn't know who or what it was. It could have been the name of a new tank.

"My problem is this," continued Allen. "The Americans here think I'm a big insider, and if I run into you in London in the next couple of weeks and people see you don't recognize me, my reputation in Washington is ruined."

"George," said Ike, "I haven't been to the Savoy for lunch for six months. You get there at one o'clock. I'll arrive at one fifteen. As soon as I walk into the Grill Room, I'm going to yell at the top of my voice, 'Hello, George,' and you'll yell back, 'Hello, Ike.'

"When I get to the table, you start writing down some of those stories you're famous for so that I can tell them. Everyone will think you're giving me orders and your reputation will be made."

It was done exactly that way: Allen became one of Ike's best friends and later bought a farm next to him at Gettysburg.

If Eisenhower gained a new friend, he was souring on an old one—George Patton. Patton had no part in planning Overlord except one—to stage a charade for the Germans. He was to star in "Operation Fortitude." Fortitude was the deception plan to convince the Germans that any landing in Normandy was only a ruse. The objective was to make the Germans keep their Panzer divisions at Calais, where Patton would supposedly land with Allied armies.

The German high command considered the right-wing, anti-Soviet Patton the top general of the Allies. Therefore, they would be inclined to believe the charade. The army had erected mock barracks, fake air hangars, and cardboard planes, like a Potemkin village, to fool the Germans from the air, and the base radio crackled with signal traffic by Patton's army headquarters.

In addition, Patton was to maintain public visibility by an active speaking schedule. On one of his many speaking invitations, on April 25, Patton went to Knutsford, a little town in northeast England. There he was to dedicate an opening of a club sponsored by British women for U.S. servicemen. Patton spoke on the importance of Anglo–U.S. relations. He remarked, "If it is the destiny of the British and Americans to rule the world—the better we know each other the better we can do." Back home, Patton's remark was played up in the *Washington Post* and *New York Times* as an insult to the United Nations, under whose aegis the Allies were fighting. The Allies, said one editorial, were supposed to be "liberating," not "colonizing."

A year before, Patton had hit in the face a soldier in a hospital who had no apparent reason for his disability, calling him a coward. Eisenhower had saved Patton's career in that incident. Now Ike told Bradley, "I'm just about fed up. If I have to apologize publicly for Georgie once more, I'm going to have to let him go."

Ike had just about decided to dismiss Patton, but then he relayed his decision to Churchill. Churchill did not understand the fuss. His reaction was that Patton "was only stating the obvious."

Eisenhower summoned Patton to Grosvenor Square. A contrite Patton was so ardent in pleading his case that his white helmet, which no one ever wore in front of Eisenhower, fell off and rolled on the floor. A glance at the disgusted look on Ike's face signaled to Patton that he had better take his leave quickly.

The next day Eisenhower reassessed the Patton problem. He weighed the offensive brilliance and leadership talents of his friend, and then relented. Patton's talents would be needed in Europe. Like Grant, Patton would advance. Yet Patton continued to bad-mouth Eisenhower: "Ike's the best general the British have."

So did Montgomery ("Poor chappie," he said of Ike, "he's a bit over his head, you know"). But unlike Patton, Ike could not fire the British Montgomery. In an ideal world, Eisenhower would have chosen Alexander over Montgomery, Tedder over Harris. As for the chief of British naval operations, Sir Andrew Cunningham, in Ike's opinion, "was the best sea dog I ever knew."

Eisenhower dreaded meetings with Patton and Montgomery, which often turned into confrontations, but he relished his twice-weekly meals with Churchill. When it was just the two of them, Ike said, it was like a tutorial with an Oxford don.

His year in France may have been his liberal arts education; his sessions with Churchill were his master's degree. They did have some spirited arguments, but not once did any account of differences leak out to others. Never did any hearsay circulate of a Churchill complaint about Ike, nor did any witty barb or one-sided accusation against Ike come to the attention of Eisenhower. To Churchill, Eisenhower was "the man who set the unity of the Allied Armed Forces above all other thought."

Churchill may have had grievances against Stalin, de Gaulle, Montgomery, and others, but not against Eisenhower.

One part of the landing strategy that Churchill did protest strenuously was Operation Anvil. Anvil was the planned follow-up to the invasion assault in southern France. After a beachhead on Normandy was established, Patton would lead an invasion landing in Brittany to secure France's biggest Mediterranean port, Marseilles. Brooke and Montgomery sided with Churchill. Eisenhower's response was to table the Anvil question by pushing back the calendar to June for landing, instead of May. He was forced to, anyway, by the shortage of LSTs.

Churchill's argument against an invasion of southern France was that it diverted army and tank reinforcement for British general Alexander's campaign in Italy. Eisenhower countered that the French landing would weaken the German army's defense in Normandy. Churchill, however, remained adamant that Operation Anvil jeopardized the Italian campaign. Churchill was still hoping that a thrust into northern Italy would lead to the Balkans.

At a dinner at Chequers, Churchill staged a scene to press his case against Anvil. Tears ran down his face as Eisenhower remained unyielding. As Eisenhower later commented, "He painted a terrible picture if we didn't do it. He said he would have to go to His Majesty and 'lay down the mantel of my high office.'" The only thing that was changed about Anvil was its name: Dragoon. "Good choice," said Churchill, "because I was dragged into it."

On May 15 Churchill and King George attended a conference at St. Paul's School in London. There Montgomery, an "Old St. Paulie," had made part of the private school (which adjoins St. Paul's Cathedral) into a planning headquarters.

In the school's largest lecture room, armchairs were afforded on the platform for the king, the prime minister, and General Eisenhower. The others sat on hard school benches.

On the back of the platform, a map of the northern coast of France was displayed, with successive phase lines of the expected advances, day by day.

The king, who was afflicted with a habitual stammer, opened with a few stuttering remarks. Ike followed. He was just about in the middle of his briefing when a loud knocking was heard at the door in the back. Patton, as usual, was late. Eisenhower frowned and then continued, "Here we are on the eve of a great battle. . . . It is the duty of anyone who sees a flaw not to hesitate to say so." No one did.

Then Montgomery outlined his battle thrust at Normandy toward Caen. He ended with the boast, "When D-day ends, I shall be knocking at the very outskirts of Caen."

The prime minister then rose. Clad in black frock coat and striped trousers for his later attendance in the House of Commons, Churchill gestured with a huge Havana cigar as he spoke. His audience, which listened intently, was aware of his doubts about the cross-Channel invasion. He closed his remarks by grasping the lapels of his coat. "Gentlemen," he rasped, "I am now hardening to this enterprise."

Any comfort that had been drawn from Churchill's remarks evaporated a day later. Churchill was demanding to go in on the landing. For Eisenhower to deny flatly the British head of government's request was not an option.

Fortunately, Clementine Churchill knew of her husband's intentions. At tea with the queen at Buckingham Palace, they hatched a plan. A day later the king informed Churchill, "Winston, I shall go with you on the invasion." Churchill knew he had been outflanked. He withdrew his request to Ike.

On March 17 Eisenhower joined Churchill on a train trip to the north to inspect troops. For most of the trip Churchill was silent, staring gloomily out the window at the rainy landscape. Finally, Churchill muttered, "There's only one thing worse than undertaking a war with allies."

"What's that?" asked Eisenhower.

"Waging a war without allies," Churchill replied.

One other niggling complication of invasion plans was reported by British intelligence two weeks before the invasion. A crossword puzzle clue in the London *Daily Telegraph* said, "This bush is the center for the nursery and revolution." The answer was "Mulberry," the code name for the center of operations.

Then in the last days of May another clue in the same newspaper: "Britannia and he hold the same thing." The answer was "Neptune," one of the beachheads in Normandy.

Another issue of the same paper posed this clue, "A state in America." The answer was "Utah," another landing beach. Later, after the invasion, the reporting of the "clues" was discovered to be totally coincidental. The puzzle maker had just written words that he heard from schoolboys who hung around the army bases.

On June 2 Eisenhower drove to Southwick House, just north of Portsmouth, the site of British admiral Ramsay's headquarters. On June 5, after dinner, the wind and rain pounded the window frames on the French doors in the mess room where the Supreme Allied Command met. The meeting had already been postponed once because of weather. Another delay would set the invasion back to June 19.

"The question," said Eisenhower, "is how long can you allow this thing to just kind of hang there on a limb?" At 4:00 A.M,. June 5, Eisenhower rubbed his six magic coins and gave his decision: "Let's go."

The next day, Eisenhower called the press in and said the invasion was on. Afterward, he scribbled a press release to be handed out in case of failure. "Our landings have failed. I have withdrawn the troops. . . . If any blame of fault attaches to the attempt, it's mine alone." Military historians will search in vain for any precedent of a general officer beforehand assigning himself all responsibility for failure.

On June 6, 1944, the House of Commons—tense because of the eerie government silence amid rampant rumors about landings in France—awaited the arrival of the prime minister. An unusually serene and reflective Churchill walked to his place at the front bench. In an offhand manner that toyed with the anxieties of the House, he opened with an announcement that was not news:

> The House should, I think, take formal cognizance of the liberation of Rome by the Allied Armies under the Command of General Alexander, along with General Clark. . . . This is a memorable and glorious event, which rewards the intense fighting of the last five months in Italy. The original landing . . .

On Churchill droned for several minutes about the Italian situation, as the House chamber grew restless, with more than the usual coughs and rustle of paper. Then, almost casually, he shifted to a new topic:

> I have also to announce to the House that during the night and early hours of this morning, an immense armada of upwards of 4,000 ships, together with several thousand smaller craft, crossed the Channel. . . . The battle that has now begun will grow constantly in scale and in intensity for many weeks to come. . . .

After days of intense fighting—particularly on Omaha Beach—the coastal landing was finally secured. Churchill had said almost exactly four years before, at the time of Dunkirk, "The battle of France is over, the Battle of Britain is about to begin." It could now be said that on this day the battle for a beachhead was over, and the battle in France to destroy the German army was about to begin. What Churchill had correctly described as "the most difficult and complicated operation that has ever taken place" had put the Allies back on the continent.

On June 10 General Marshall, General Arnold, and Admiral King arrived in London to inspect the aftermath of the landing with Eisenhower. They crossed the Channel in a destroyer and lunched on C rations on Juno Beach.

Two days later (D-day plus six) Churchill made the crossing that the king's maneuver had prevented him from achieving on D-day itself. After lunching in a tent with a jaunty Montgomery in his parachute harness and red beret, Churchill saw Eisenhower. Churchill took a look at all the personnel, mobile carriers, and temporary equipment on the beachhead and noted that Eisenhower had done the equivalent of transporting a midsized city like Leeds and establishing it across the Channel.

Three days later 2nd Lt. John Eisenhower, who had graduated from West Point on D-day, walked into his father's office at Grosvenor Square. A little later John, who was concerned about military protocol, asked, "Dad, if we should meet an officer who ranks above me but below you, how do we handle this?"

"For God's sake, John," answered Ike, "there isn't an officer who doesn't rank above you and below me!"

Two days later father and son, both history buffs, crossed to see the battle zone. They drove to Bayeux, the British headquarters of the British Second Army and the one-time home of William the Conqueror, the only other man—except for Eisenhower and Julius Caesar—to have commanded a cross-Channel invasion.

While motoring in the beach area, John was astonished to see a phalanx of military vehicles driving bumper to bumper. That was completely in violation of the military procedure he had been taught at West Point. "You'd never get away with this if you didn't have air superiority," said the freshly minted second lieutenant.

"Hell," Ike snapped back, "if I didn't have air superiority, I wouldn't be here."

Air superiority would be the decisive edge in the rout of the German army at the coast. The Allied plan thereafter would be a three-pronged attack northward through France by Generals Montgomery, Bradley, and Patton. In Operation Dragoon, Patton had landed his troops in Brittany on August 1.

For Eisenhower, execution of strategy would become entangled in personality. Pint-sized Montgomery with his red beret and strut reminded one of a bantam rooster. Patton with his white helmet and pearl-handled revolver was the American bald eagle, complete with shiny talons. Both were obsessed with one goal: to be the first to ride atop their tanks into Berlin. They also shared the conviction that they knew more about military strategy than Eisenhower. Their approach to battle, however, could not have been more different. Patton was confrontational; Montgomery, more oblique.

At the St. Paul's School briefing on London, Montgomery had vowed to be "knocking on the outskirts of Caen" at the end of the first day. By June 20 (D-day plus fourteen) Montgomery still had not taken Caen.

Montgomery's battle style reminded Ike of a young Washington Senator pitcher in the 1930s. Although the hurler possessed a good fastball, he just nibbled at the corners of the plate instead of challenging the hitters. As Montgomery wrote later, "It was always very clear that Ike and I were poles apart when it came to the conduct of the war." Monty believed in "unbalancing the enemy while keeping completely balanced himself." The British general liked to attack on a very narrow front. In some ways Ike thought Montgomery was like George McClellan in the American Civil War, who in dread of defeat always overestimated the enemy's capability.

By July 1, when Caen, Normandy's major city, had still not been captured, a frustrated Ike went to Montgomery's headquarters. Monty's lame excuse was "insufficient supplies." Returning to London, Ike went to see Churchill, armed with the

recommendation by his friend Vice Air Marshal Tedder to sack
Monty. The plan was to have Churchill kick him upstairs to
the House of Lords. Over lunch, Churchill waxed witty, "Ah,
Monty, in defeat, indomitable; in advance, invincible." After a
puff of his Havana, he added, "and in victory, insufferable."

The problem at the moment for Eisenhower was that
Monty didn't have a victory to be insufferable about. Churchill
offered to back Eisenhower in dismissing Montgomery. But Ike
could not pull the trigger. Monty was an icon in the British
press. The strands of Anglo–U.S. unity would be sorely frayed
in the London press uproar over Monty's dumping. To support
Ike, Churchill did telephone Monty to tell him that Eisenhower
alone would direct the European strategy. He then mollified
Montgomery by making him a field marshal. But Monty got
the message. On July 7, after the RAF had pummeled Caen into
rubble, Monty's troops marched in. But because of the destruction, the seaport Caen was no longer of much strategic value.

Yet Monty now thought he would spearhead the main
thrust into Germany. When he learned that Patton's army
would be heading its tanks toward Frankfurt, he erupted and
demanded that Ike come see him, even though he knew the
U.S. supreme commander was confined to crutches by a recent
knee injury.

Monty unleashed a tirade charging that Patton, not Eisenhower, was running the war. He insisted that control of the
land campaign to enter Germany be returned to him. In the
middle of his harangue he pointed to his new fifth star of field
marshal status, which rankled Ike.

"Steady, Monty," Ike answered, putting his hand on
Monty's knee. "You can't speak to me like that. I'm your boss."

Monty then pulled out his plan, dubbed Market-Garden. It
called for crossing the lower Rhine in Arnheim into the
Netherlands. The original Allied strategy was to capture and
secure Antwerp, the biggest port on the North Sea and the

closest to the German heartland. Yet Eisenhower agreed to Monty's shift in strategy because he wanted a bridgehead across the Rhine before the thrust of the Allied offensive ebbed. Arnheim was the price of placating Montgomery, but it was precipitously steep. In September the Germans beat back Monty's British airborne paratrooper attack against Arnheim.

The successive victories in France had fanned Washington's hopes for a German surrender before the end of September. A glum Eisenhower reported to a disappointed General Marshall that the spring of 1945 would be the earliest end to the war. Although some military historians think that the Market-Garden failure aborted an early ending of the war, Eisenhower, a German by blood himself, never believed the German army would surrender without a last-ditch defense of the Fatherland.

The constant demands of Monty and Georgie Patton strained Ike's patience to the breaking point, but the French commander de Gaulle continued to gain Eisenhower's respect. Although FDR still despised the French general, Eisenhower and Churchill shared the belief that de Gaulle represented the only possible rallying figure for the French Resistance. His hauteur, however, was ruffled at any imagined affront to France or to his pride. Churchill told Ike that on those occasions he looked like "a female llama who has just been surprised in her bath." But both viewed de Gaulle as the living monument to the valor of France. Eisenhower told de Gaulle, "I was wrong about you in North Africa."

De Gaulle replied, "You are a man, General." Both developed mutual respect.[1] With Ike's endorsement, French Resis-

1. When General Eisenhower died, in February 1969, his body was brought to the White House; the casket was a simple one of the type given to any GI who served under him. There it rested on a catafalque in the East Room. The next day it was taken to the Capitol for the formal services. I was then working in the White House and observed then President de Gaulle approach the bier in a general's uniform, with the little round hat with the visor, and salute the head. When

tance troops marched with Ike's old friend "Gee" Gerow as the liberators of Paris on August 29. The Parisians mobbed the French and U.S. soldiers, throwing flowers, offering glasses of champagne, and even propositioning the entering troops.

Eisenhower did not participate. It was the conquest of armies, not the liberation of cities, that was his objective. Just as his hero U. S. Grant never had Richmond, the Confederate capital, in his strategic sights, so Eisenhower regarded Berlin as a secondary matter. Churchill—not to mention Montgomery and Patton—saw it differently. Berlin was paramount in the Churchill target of shaking hands with the Russians as far east of the Elbe River as possible.

The Berlin question and Operation Anvil/Dragoon caused the most contentious clashes between the two men. They looked at Berlin from different perspectives, Eisenhower as a soldier, Churchill as a statesman; the one as a military tactician, and the other as a political visionary. Churchill's military forte was in the grand strategy. Eisenhower's genius was his mastery of logistics.

Eisenhower's priority was always the health, condition, and lives of his men. He wanted to end the war as quickly as possible. Churchill's prime concern was what happened after the war. He had learned from World War I that the cessation of hostilities was not enough if peaceful stability was not achieved.

Churchill had opposed Anvil/Dragoon as the landing operation in southern France because it drained military troops and resources from Italy, which he wanted as a launching pad for the Balkans. Churchill was alarmed by the Soviet threat in Romania and Albania, as well as Greece. In August Churchill

---

I asked a French aide why de Gaulle was in uniform, he replied, "The President said, 'Today I am paying personal respects to my former commander. Tomorrow, as President of France I am paying respects to the former President.'"

had met with General Tito of Yugoslavia, with whom his son, Randolph, was serving as a liaison.

But to Eisenhower, Churchill's "underbelly of Europe" was one chain of German mountain strongholds that would chew up American lives. In Ike's words: "I don't see the Alps as any 'underbelly.'" Eisenhower opposed Churchill on Berlin, too. Ike was prepared to allow the Soviet armies to reach Berlin first because that could prevent a half million casualties among the forces he headed. The general viewed the situation through a military prism of saving his men.

Eisenhower had no illusions about the Soviets. It was just that any decision on Berlin trespassed on the civilian policy-making jurisdiction of the president. From the report that Eisenhower had on the Teheran Conference, Roosevelt had pledged to Stalin to launch no Allied intrusion into the Balkans and to allow Soviet entry into Berlin. Anyway, why should Ike send his armies into areas that Churchill, Stalin, and Roosevelt had already sectored off as Soviet spheres of influence?

Eisenhower was no MacArthur. As a professional soldier, he resisted making decisions his commander in chief should properly make. Eisenhower thought that Churchill was justified in his fears of Soviet domination, but if so, Churchill had to convince not Eisenhower but Roosevelt. Ike's military responsibility was to his men.

In November, 2nd Lt. John Eisenhower arrived. He had been assigned to the Seventy-first Division in France. Ike gave John advice on treating his platoon: "Go around—see every man. Make sure he has warm, dry clothing—shoes and socks are of tremendous importance and . . . wear the same kind of materials your men do in training and in combat."

The old soldier warning about warm shoes was prophetic. During a December winter blast when a fog pinned Allied aircraft to the ground, the Germans mounted a 600,000-man offensive at the weakest point of the British and U.S. line in the

Ardennes. This action, fought in snow, called the Battle of the Bulge, grew desperate. On December 17 Ike drove to an Allied command meeting at Verdun, where a million French and Germans had died in World War I. Ike began, "The present situation is to be regarded as an opportunity for us and not a disaster. There will only be cheerful faces at this table."

After briefings, he asked Patton how long it would take him to counterattack.

"Three days." Eisenhower, Bradley, and the English officers gasped. Patton, however, had predicted the German advance. His troops were already in the zone.

"Funny thing, George, every time I get a new star, I get attacked. It happened in Sivi-bou-ziv and Kasserine Pass."

And Patton retorted, "And every time you get attacked, Ike, I pull you out."

Then, over Bradley's furious objection, Eisenhower put his First Army under Montgomery.

By the end of December the Battle of the Bulge was over. In one month twenty German divisions had been destroyed.

On January 7, 1945, Montgomery, wearing his red beret and parachute harness, let the reporters know he had saved Eisenhower and the Americans from their own stupidity: "I took certain steps. . . . I employed the whole power of the British Army and bang—that was it." The next day in the House of Commons Churchill took pains to correct Monty's misrepresentation and grab for glory. The prime minister said that it was an American, not a British, battle and that few British soldiers had been involved.

What angered Eisenhower more than Montgomery's taking credit for the victory was his failure to follow up and smash the retreating German troops. It was like Meade at Gettysburg. Patton commented, "Monty is a tired little fart. War requires the taking of risks and he won't take them."

At Yalta in February an enfeebled Roosevelt was taking risks in a different way. The U.S. president, despite Churchill's fears, took Stalin at his word when the Soviet premier promised free elections in Poland. Because Soviet troops were already in that country, Churchill believed that only through a concerted action by the Americans and British could a Soviet takeover of Poland be averted. Churchill later said that Roosevelt at Yalta "maintained a slender contact with life and had no energy for disputes." The president had told his State Department aides, including Alger Hiss, that the British Empire was a greater threat to another war than the Soviets.

By one report, Churchill made this toast to Premier Joseph Stalin at Yalta. Following President Roosevelt's glowing tribute to the "peace-loving Stalin," Churchill muttered to an aide, "But they do not want peace."

Finally noting the stare of the Soviet delegation, Churchill rose and said, "To Premier Stalin, whose conduct of foreign policy manifests a desire for peace." Then, away from the translator and the microphone, he whispered, "A piece of Poland, a piece of Czechoslovakia, a piece of Romania. . . ."

A few days later in London Churchill told the exiled President Benes of Czechoslovakia, "A small lion was walking between a huge Russian bear and a great American elephant but perhaps it would prove to be the lion who knew the way."

At his villa in Yalta, after Churchill hosted a dinner for Premier Stalin and President Roosevelt, he escorted them to a map room. It showed the Soviet army thirty-eight miles east of Berlin; the British and Canadian armies were at the western end of the Rhine, and the U.S. army south of them was also nearing the Rhine.

At the first glimmerings of the dawn on March 23, the U.S. army was poised to cross the Rhine into Germany near Mainz. An ember of light was flickering. The older man who saw it advanced. "Soldier," he said to this smoker of the ciga-rette, "are you feeling a bit nervous?" The nineteen-year-old soldier nodded.

"Well, so am I," said the older one. "Let's both walk by the river together, and we'll each draw strength from each other." They did. The private did not know that the arm around his shoulders was that of Supreme Allied Commander Dwight Eisenhower.

Within hours, Patton was pushing his armies across the Rhine River. When Patton was on the opposite side, he uri-nated triumphantly into the river, which he said was what William the Conqueror had done after he crossed the Channel.

At a March 27 press conference Ike was asked, "Who do you think will be in Berlin first, the Russians or us?"

Eisenhower answered, "Well, since we are 200 or so miles away and the Russians only 33 miles, that alone ought to make them be the first to do it."

On March 31 Churchill again tried to get Eisenhower to end operations west of the Rhine and move across that river east of the Elbe, which is close to Berlin. Eisenhower was an-noyed by the pressure and told Churchill so.

To calm the waters, Churchill wrote to Roosevelt, "I wish to place on record the complete confidence felt by His Majesty's Government in General Eisenhower and our pleas-ure that our armies are serving under his command and our admiration of his great and shining quality, character and per-sonality." Churchill sent a copy to Eisenhower, saying in addi-tion that it would "be a grief to me if anything I had said pains you." The prime minister could not resist the opportunity, however, to add that he still felt the Americans and British should reach Berlin first. "I deem it highly important that we should shake hands with Russians as far to the east as possible."

The German army was collapsing in the north. Gen. William Simpson's Ninth Army under Bradley had crossed the

Elbe—only fifty miles from Berlin. Simpson felt he could get there before the Soviets. Ike, however, refused permission.

On April 17 Eisenhower flew to London to confer with Churchill on the subject. He finally convinced the prime minister of the soundness of his views. Churchill admitted that the Soviet army had immense strength on the eastern edges of Berlin, in comparison with Simpson's force (Simpson had fewer than 50,000 men over the Elbe and had gone beyond the range of fighter support). The joint decision meant it would be the Soviets who first battered their way into the ruins of Berlin.[2]

Two weeks later Hitler committed suicide in his Berlin bunker. In April Hitler's jubilation over Roosevelt's death had quickly evaporated. The sounds of Soviet gunfire on the outskirts of Berlin told him it was all over.

The new head of Germany, Adm. Karl Doenitz, was eager to surrender but not to the Soviets. The new U.S. president, Harry Truman, however, insisted on "unconditional surrender." Eisenhower agreed. On May 7 the Germans capitulated. Ike dictated the message: "The mission of this Allied Force was fulfilled at 0241 local time May 7, 1945."

Back in England, Ike attended a play at a London theater. When he was recognized during the intermission, he stood up from his box and said, "It's great to be back in a country where I can *almost* speak the language."

Churchill suggested to Ike at a lunch at 10 Downing Street that he planned to honor Eisenhower with a formal celebration. Ike wrote back,

Dear Prime Minister,

    I have been thinking over the proposal you suddenly presented to me just before I left your delightful luncheon table

2. Later General Marshall, in an interview for oral history, said, "I do not think he [Eisenhower] should have gone into Berlin. I thought he did extraordinarily well in this matter."

the other day, to the effect that I should participate in a formal celebration in London. As I told you then, I think that
some simple ceremony along this line might have a pleasing
effect at home, but I sincerely hope that the arrangements
would be such as to avoid overglorification of my own part in
the victories of this Allied force. For three years I have
earnestly attempted to stress the values of team play and have
religiously kept from the public eye those affairs and decisions
which necessarily had finally to be the responsibility of one
man, myself.

A "simple ceremony" was not in Churchill's nature. In the
historic Guildhall in London, on June 12, General Eisenhower
was feted with all possible pomp and circumstance—including
a presentation to him of the Duke of Wellington's sword by
the Lord Mayor of London.

Eisenhower spoke:

Humility must always be the portion of any man who receives
acclaim earned in blood of his followers and sacrifices of his
friends.

Conceivably a commander may have been professionally
superior. He may have given everything of his heart and mind
to meet the spiritual and physical needs of his comrades. He
may have written a chapter that will grow forever in the pages
of military history.

Still, even such a man—if he existed—would sadly face
the facts that his honors cannot hide in his memories the
crosses marking the resting places of the dead. They cannot
soothe the anguish of the widow or the orphan whose husband or father will not return. . . .

This feeling of humility cannot erase of course my great
pride in being tendered the freedom of London. I am not a

native of this land, I come from the very heart of America. In the superficial aspects by which we ordinarily recognize family relationships, the town where I was born and the one where I was reared are far separated from this great city. Abilene, Kansas, and Denison, Texas, would together equal in size, possibly one five-hundredth of a part of great London.

Hardly would it seem possible for the London Council to have gone farther afield to find a man to honor with its priceless gift of token citizenship. . . .

To preserve his freedom of worship, his equality before law, his liberty to speak and act as he sees fit, subject only to provisions that he trespass not upon similar rights of others—a Londoner will fight. So will a citizen of Abilene.

When we consider these things, then the valley of the Thames draws closer to the farms of Kansas and the plains of Texas. Many feared that those representatives could never combine together in an efficient fashion to solve the complex problems presented by modern war.

I hope you believe we proved the doubters wrong. And, moreover, I hold that we proved this point not only for war—we proved it can always be done by our two peoples, provided only that both show the same goodwill, the same forbearance, the same objective attitude that the British and Americans so amply demonstrated in the nearly three years of bitter campaigning.

No man alone could have brought about this result. Had I possessed the military skill of a Marlborough, the wisdom of Solomon, the understanding of Lincoln, I still would have been helpless without the loyalty, vision, and generosity of thousands upon thousands of British and Americans.

This speech, which Ike wrote himself, is a testament to his command of the written word. It ranks with the most eloquent addresses by American leaders. The *London Times* ranked it side by side with the Gettysburg Address.

After lunch at the Mansion House, the lord mayor's residence, Eisenhower stood with Churchill on a balcony, greeting the crowd in the square below.

Ike yelled to them, "Whether you know it or not, I've got just as much right to be yelling as you do. You see, I'm a citizen of London now, too."

CHAPTER 18

COLUMBIA UNIVERSITY

More important than bricks and mortars to me was the moral and intellectual strength of Columbia.

DWIGHT DAVID EISENHOWER

AFTER VE DAY, the British Wartime Coalition government was dissolved. An election had to be held. One morning Churchill awoke from a nightmare. He told an aide, "There in my dream I was on a hospital gurney and white coated attendants pulled the sheet over my head. I knew it was an omen of my pending defeat."

At that time, Churchill was attending the Potsdam meeting with the new U.S. president, Harry Truman, and Premier Joseph Stalin when he heard the word of the final election count. (The tallying of the military votes had delayed the results.) At his headquarters at Grosvenor Square, General Eisenhower read the news of the massive defeat with astonishment. After all, the Gallup Poll had rated Churchill's personal popularity almost as high as that of King George VI. The explanation by the British press was that Churchill's very fame as a world statesman had toppled him from office. The war leader, said the pundits, was not perceived by voters to be absorbed by the homely problems of a job for the returning veteran, a better pension for Dad, or relief for Mum's mounting hospital bills.

A decade later Eisenhower better understood the Churchill defeat, when Eisenhower himself won a landslide re-election in 1956, but the Democrats took control of Congress. The British voter in 1945 liked Churchill but not his Conservative Party.

To Churchill, the defeat was more than a surprise—it was a shock. Not since Gallipoli had he sustained such a crippling blow. His wife, Clementine, thinking of his advancing age and his health, tried to console him.

"Winston," she said, "it may well be a blessing in disguise."

"At the moment," replied Churchill, "it seems quite effectively disguised."

King George VI wanted to appoint him a peer of the realm. The Duke of London would be his title. Churchill, however, would not retire from the House of Commons. His Majesty then suggested the conferral on Churchill of the palace's highest honor—that of Knight of the Garter. Churchill refused: "I could not accept the Order of the Garter from my Sovereign when I had received the 'Order of the Boot' from his people."

The kings and queens of Norway, Denmark, Belgium, and the Netherlands invited him to their courts to confer medals on him, but he spurned the honors. Conservative Party leaders tried to map for him a global speaking tour of the British Empire, as well as Europe. More than a few cities in Canada and Australia, as well as in Britain, were ready to offer him their ceremonial gold keys with the accompanying appropriate civic celebrations to honor the war's most dominating hero. Churchill saw these tributes, though, as another not-so-subtle hint that he resign his leadership of the Conservative Party. "I refuse," said Churchill, "to be exhibited like a prize bull whose chief attraction is his past prowess."

Clement Attlee, whom Churchill once described as "a modest man with much to be modest about," had moved into

10 Downing Street. Chartwell had been sold during the war because, as prime minister, Churchill had the use of Chequers. Although some inquiries were made to buy back Chartwell, Churchill, at this point, had no home.

He moved into Claridge's. The chairman, Hugh Watner, gave him his own suite. Churchill, however, was uneasy with the balcony, which had an eighty-foot drop. After a few days he told Watner, "I don't like sleeping near a precipice. I've no desire to quit the world, but thoughts desperate, come into the head." Churchill's "black dog" had returned, blacker than ever.

General Eisenhower, mindful of Churchill's situation, wrote to him, offering a villa.

> Dear Mr. Churchill:
>
> It is difficult for me to use any form of address to you other than "Prime Minister." Though I live to be a hundred I shall always think of you in that capacity and with that title.
>
> I learned through Colonel Gault that you would find a visit to the Riviera most acceptable . . . The only house that I know of on the Riviera that I would consider suitable for you and a part of your family is a villa named "Sous les Vents," rented by the American forces and held for use by me and the other senior officers of this command. The house is quite large and a number of people could be easily accommodated in it. You know so well of my deep and lasting appreciation for the staunch and unwavering support you accorded me all during the war. . . .
>
> There is no one living to whom I have a greater desire to show, in some way, the depth of my admiration and affection.

Churchill thanked Eisenhower but opted for a more secluded vacation spot, farther away from London in Lake Como, that General Sir Harold Alexander made available.

If the recent election had made Churchill's popularity suspect, Eisenhower was unquestionably the man of the hour. No man in the world now generated more affection and esteem than Ike.

President Truman recognized Eisenhower's popularity. When Truman arrived in Europe for the Potsdam Conference, he was greeted by General Eisenhower in Antwerp. Truman, who hailed from Kansas's neighboring state of Missouri, had long been an admirer of Eisenhower. Truman's brother Vivien had once lived in the same Kansas City boarding house with Arthur Eisenhower, Ike's brother. In addition, Truman as senator had always been supportive of the War Department. Truman often said that the beginning of his political life was his election as captain by his Missouri National Guard unit and that his World War I service in that unit in France was his most cherished memory.

One afternoon while Truman was driving in the presidential limousine with Eisenhower on a sightseeing tour around Potsdam, the president said, "There is nothing you want that I won't help you try to get, Ike, and that definitely and specifically includes the Presidency."

Eisenhower dismissed the idea with a laugh but then added, "Mr. President, I don't know who your opponent will be in 1948 but it will not be I." The phrasing invites scrutiny. Eisenhower was obliquely saying to Truman that he was a Republican.

At Potsdam, Truman's primary objective was Stalin's commitment to enter the war with Japan. When Truman asked for Eisenhower's approval, the general was opposed. The Soviets, Ike argued, had done nothing to defeat the Japanese, but now Truman would be putting the Kremlin in a position to seize Japanese territory and attempt to carve out a Soviet zone of occupation. (The Soviet Union did seize and annex the Kurile Islands.) Truman dismissed the warning, and Stalin declared war on Japan.

At the time, the Soviets were pushing the boundaries of the Soviet empire eastward and consolidating their domination. On August 1, 1945, Eisenhower flew to Moscow to be honored by the Kremlin. Stalin, all of five feet tall and with a pitted face, was dressed in a white uniform and looked to Eisenhower more like a headwaiter than a head of state. Stalin smiled as he toasted Eisenhower. Eisenhower had this comment afterward on the Soviet dictator: "One may smile and smile and be a villain."

Eisenhower was now head of the occupation in Germany, with headquarters in Frankfurt. Hating the Nazis, he strictly banned any fraternization with the Germans. Patton infuriated Ike by blurting out in a press conference that "the Nazis were just like a political party in America—Republican or Democrat."

Eisenhower told Patton, "I demand you get off your bloody ass and carry out the de-Nazification as you are told instead of mollycoddling the goddamn Nazis."

From Frankfurt, Eisenhower hopped by military plane to the European capitals of Copenhagen, Prague, and Oslo to attend ceremonies honoring him. He was pinned with medals and papered with honorary degrees. His feelings in attending them can better be described as duty than delight. He truly prized only one honor, he told his son John, and that was the Order of Merit presented by King George VI. John, who wanted to be sent to the Pacific to fight the Japanese, had been assigned to Frankfurt. Though it frustrated the son, it was a great comfort to his father, however, since General Marshall would not give permission for Eisenhower's wife, Mamie, to join him because other servicemen were not permitted to have their wives with them.

Eisenhower wanted to return home. John's accounts made him worry about Mamie's health. Now that the bomb had been dropped on Hiroshima, forcing Japanese surrender, World War II was over.

On November 11 Eisenhower flew back to Washington to testify to the Senate Armed Services Committee. Two days later Ike and Mamie took a train to see Doud relatives in Boone, Iowa. There Mamie came down with an attack of bronchial pneumonia.

When she recovered, the Eisenhowers returned to Washington. They were greeted with the news that General Marshall had resigned as Army Chief of Staff. Ike was to be his successor. Marshall told him, "You're going to have an awful job. Everybody is going to want to get out right away."

The highest position a West Point graduate could ever aspire to was a job Ike now did not want. Eisenhower had witnessed the results of rapid demobilization in World War I, and he did not want to preside over another meltdown of the army—particularly during a time of unchecked Soviet advances. Furthermore, the massive military bureaucracy and the colossus of the new Pentagon building it was centered in were not to his taste. The functionally built Pentagon had none of the architectural romance of the old War Department. On his second day in the Pentagon he lost his way in the maze of corridors back to his office. He finally had to ask a secretary for help.

At the same time, in England, Churchill was adjusting better to his role as Leader of the Opposition. He said, "If I could not be conductor of the orchestra, I'd like to be the kettle drum." In opposition, Churchill was now more free to pound out his own opinions.

In February 1946 Churchill sailed to the United States. He had accepted an invitation to speak at Westminster College in Fulton, Missouri, on March 5. President Truman had scrawled a postscript on the official invitation by the college president: "Come and I'll introduce you."

Now out of government, Churchill wanted to seize this opportunity to warn the free world and particularly the United

States of the mounting Soviet threat to any postwar structure of peace. He viewed an introduction by President Truman as a world forum.

Churchill and Clementine arrived in New York in January. They took the train to Miami and stayed with a Canadian friend, Frank Clark. Churchill took advantage of the subtropical sun to paint pictures, while his own portrait was being painted by Douglas Chandor.

General Eisenhower wrote him in Miami,

My hope of seeing you, therefore, springs not only from an earnest desire to renew the warmest and most satisfying contact I had in all Europe.

My own schedule for the next few weeks will apparently offer me little opportunity to seek you out but if I do not have a chance to see you any other place I do hope that your own itinerary contemplates some little time in Washington. I suppose it is too much to hope that you would stay for a period in my house. Within a few days my wife and I are moving into a very commodious set of quarters at Fort Myers, and if it would be possible at all for you and Mrs. Churchill to stay with us we would not only be overjoyed personally, but the mere fact that you would consent to be my guest would do much to impress upon everybody in America the true nature of an association (from my viewpoint a treasured friendship) that characterized our common effort throughout my service in Europe.

In Washington, by early March, Churchill had holed himself up in a British Embassy bedroom revising his Fulton speech, which he had entitled "Sinews of Peace." The title was a play on Cicero's phrase "sinews of war." Churchill was striking his familiar theme that only preparedness could ensure peace: the Soviet political and military encroachments could be stopped only by a united West under the resolute leadership of the United States. He wanted to jerk the United States out of its cozy worship of the United Nations and its intellectual make-believe. The mask of democratic pretensions had to be ripped from the Kremlin's face and its naked imperialism revealed. Because the government in Washington, as well as his own in London, was reluctant to topple the illusion of peace that existed between the wartime allies, Churchill saw it as his duty to do so. As an out-of-office statesman, he could sound the alarm that Truman and Attlee seemed fearful of uttering.

On March 4 an impatient President Truman waited for Churchill, who arrived late at Union Station for the trip to Missouri on the *Ferdinand Magellan*, the presidential train. Atop the open rear end of the lounge car, with the press milling beneath them, Truman proudly pointed out to Churchill the presidential seal that is always carried with a traveling chief executive. "Mr. Churchill, the head of the eagle used to be turned right to face the arrows, but I had it changed to turn the other way to face the olive branches."

Churchill, whose speech the next day would cast shadows on the roseate glow of the immediate postwar peace, could not quite give the new seal his full approval. He told the U.S. president, in front of the press observers, "Why not put the eagle's neck on a swivel so that it could turn to the olive branch or the arrows as the occasion demands?"

The reporters laughed. Truman, a bit miffed at Churchill's quip at his expense, replied, "Well, let's have some whiskey."

"Capital idea," replied Churchill, and they ducked into the lounge. There, tumblers with ice and a bottle of Jack Daniels were presented.

It was a 'Daniel' come to judgment, because a dismayed Churchill exclaimed, "This isn't whiskey—it's bourbon!" Churchill then, with Truman's military aide, Harry Vaughan, went out and pulled the emergency cord. The train came to an immediate halt just outside Washington at Silver Springs, Maryland, where a case of Dewars was brought to the rescue. As the B&O train rolled through the countryside of western Maryland, Churchill regaled Truman, as he once had Roosevelt, with the twelve-stanza rendition of "Barbara Frietchie," which ends, " 'Shoot if you must this old gray head, / but spare your country's flag,' she said."

Then Churchill retired to his stateroom for a nap and more work on his speech. When he emerged from his room to rejoin the president for dinner, he offered his frequent complaint on American cocktail habits: "Why do you Americans stop your drinking at dinner?"

Truman replied with a reference to the aid to Britain that was now being debated in Congress: "The cost of supplying you with wine would mean a bigger loan."

Churchill retorted, "You Americans keep trying to twist the 'loan's' (lion's) tale."

Churchill returned to his stateroom. Although advance copies had already been distributed for the next day's speech, he was still searching for the imagery that would define the thrust of his speech. Before midnight, the train stopped for refueling. Churchill opened his curtain. The sign read "Springfield, Home of Lincoln." Whether or not it was the ghost of Lincoln who inspired him, his closing of the compartment window curtain may have suggested the phrase.

When the presidential train arrived in Jefferson City, an open limousine awaited the president and the former prime minister. The procession of the motorcade was delayed temporarily until a long Havana could be purchased at a Jefferson City tobacco store for the propless Churchill. On the arrival at Westminster College, lunch was offered at the home of the college president, Dr. F. L. ("Bullet") McCluer. (The nickname was due to the diminutive man's torpedo shape.) The speech was given in the college gym, with about 2,600 in attendance. In introducing Churchill,

President Truman was curt and almost brusque: "Mr. Churchill and I believe in freedom of speech. I understand Mr. Churchill might have something useful and constructive to say."

Typically, Churchill opened on a light note that immediately won the affection of his audience. With his hands clasping the sides of his scarlet Oxford robes, granted as an honor, he peered over his black spectacles and harrumphed in his habitual stutter style.

> I am glad to come to Westminster College . . . the name Westminster is somehow familiar to me. I seem to have heard of it before. Indeed it was at Westminster that I received a very large part of my education. . . .

Then Churchill, gesturing with palms upturned as if to show that he was not stripped of power, offered a disclaimer that was meant to anticipate his cool reception in official Washington and London quarters:

> Let me . . . make it clear that I have no official mission of any kind and that I speak only for myself.

He continued by stating that the paramount mission facing the world was the prevention of another global war.

Then, with the epic foreboding of a Milton, Churchill began his celebrated description:

> A shadow has fallen upon the scenes so lately lighted by the Allied victory. . . .
> From Stettin in the Baltic, to Trieste in the Adriatic, an iron curtain has descended across the continent.

The phrase, which made its debut in this Fulton address, had been used before. In a telegram to President Truman on May 6,

1945, Churchill had written of his profound misgivings over the withdrawal of the U.S. Army to the occupation line, "this bringing Soviet power into the heart of Western Europe and the descent of an 'iron curtain' between us and everything to the eastward." Indeed, at Potsdam Churchill had confronted Stalin with the phrase "iron fence." Stalin's reply was "All fairy tales!"

At the mention of the "iron curtain," Churchill's clenched fists shook in angered dismay. Then, one by one, with finger pointing in mute chorus, he recited the litany of occupied cities behind the curtain:

> Behind that line lie all the capitals of the ancient states of Central and Eastern Europe: Warsaw, Berlin, Prague, Vienna, Budapest, Belgrade, Bucharest, and Sofia, all of these famous cities and the populations around them lie in what I must call the Soviet sphere, and are all subject in one form or another, not only to Soviet influence but to a very high and, in many cases, increasing measure of control from Moscow.

He then followed with an insight into the Kremlin mind:

> I do not believe that Soviet Russia desires war. What they desire is the fruits of war and the indefinite expansion of powers and doctrines.

For such Soviet imperialism he offered this prescription:

> From what I have seen of our Russian friends and allies during the war, I am convinced there is nothing they admire so much as strength, and there is nothing for which they have less respect than weakness, especially military weakness.

Afterward Truman (who is now remembered as straight-talking—"Give 'em hell, Harry!") could not bring himself to comment on Churchill's address. He refused, even though he had sent Dean Acheson to look over the talk and then on the train the president had read a copy of the address given to him by Churchill. Truman had given it his approval. Indeed Truman, after the Churchill address, wired Premier Stalin, offering to send the battleship *Missouri* to bring him to America, where he could answer Churchill's charges.

In Fort Myers General Eisenhower noted with dismay the reaction to the speech. At Hyde Park Franklin Roosevelt's widow, Eleanor, called Churchill a "warmonger." Three Democratic senators held a press conference in the Capitol and described his speech as "shocking."

When General Eisenhower met Churchill at his return from Missouri, he found the former prime minister's spirits sagging at Washington's response to his address. Churchill had accepted Ike's invitation to spend a couple of days with him at the general's residence at Fort Myers outside Washington. Then they would attend festivities honoring both of them in Virginia.

To Eisenhower at Fort Myers, Churchill confided that he could not understand why President Truman felt he had to distance himself from Churchill's remarks. It distressed Churchill that Truman denied to the press that he had known in advance what Churchill was going to say, even though he had actually approved the text. Still, Eisenhower and Churchill were aware that Truman's political fortunes in 1945 were uncertain; Truman was faced with increased opposition from the Democratic Party left. Henry Wallace, FDR's former vice president, was a leader of that faction. In that situation Truman was content to allow Churchill, a heroic figure to Americans, do the heavy lifting in setting out the unwelcome facts about our former ally only six months after the war had ended. Churchill was also worried about whether President Truman was going to share the secret of the atom bomb with the Soviets. At Potsdam,

Truman told Churchill of recommendations that President Roosevelt had instructed Truman to open after his death. Churchill urged Truman not to reveal nuclear secrets to the Soviets. On the train to Missouri, Churchill, though no longer prime minister, again pressed his plea. Truman was noncommittal. (Truman, however, did decide not to share the secret of the atom bomb with the Soviets.)

Churchill felt he had failed to arouse American public opinion on Stalinism. He was puzzled by the hostility of the American press to his address. The *Nation* said that Churchill had "added a sizable bit of poison to the deteriorating relations." The *Wall Street Journal* said, "The United States wants no such alliance [against Russia]." Nobel Prize–winning author Pearl Buck said, "We are now nearer to war."

A few days after Churchill returned to Washington, he visited General Eisenhower at Fort Myers. On March 8 Churchill and Eisenhower set off in a limousine to visit Richmond. With Eisenhower at his side, Churchill spoke in Richmond, Virginia's capital, of the need for united strength in the face of challenge. To the Virginia General Assembly, Churchill said,

> Peace will not be preserved by pious sentiments expressed in terms of platitudes or by official grimaces and diplomatic correctitude, however desirable this may be from time to time. It will not be preserved by casting aside in dangerous years the panoply of warlike strength. There must be earnest thought. There must also be faithful perseverance and foresight. Greatheart must have his sword and armour to guard the pilgrims on their way. Above all, among the English-speaking peoples, there must be the union of hearts based upon conviction and common ideals. That is what I offer. That is what I seek.

From Richmond the two men motored to William and Mary College in Williamsburg, the second oldest college in the United States. To the audience of students and faculty, Churchill stressed their common heritage of the rule of law, dating from the Magna Carta.

When Churchill was later shown the college's oldest building, designed by Christopher Wren, Churchill told his college guides that he found the structure "awful," "artificial," and "amusing." He then explained to his discomfited listeners that those were the words King James II used to congratulate Wren after the dedication of the new St. Paul's Cathedral in 1686. But then, Churchill added that then, "awful" meant "awesome," "artificial" meant "artistically made," and "amusing" meant "amazing."

At the same time, Churchill was saying privately in conversation that the "socialism" that the Soviets practiced was far different from the "socialism" the British Labour Party was implementing in Britain. Soviet socialism was totalitarianism, and British socialism, however wrongheaded in its results, was democratic.

From Virginia, Churchill went to New York to visit his friend Bernard Baruch. While there, Henry Luce, the head of *Life* and *Time* and another friend and admirer of both Churchill and Eisenhower, invited Churchill to speak at the Union Club. Churchill amused his audience when he related how Hitler had attacked him in the 1930s with the same words that Stalin had just used in his response to the Fulton speech: "warmonger," "imperialist," "reactionary," "fascist," and "has-been."

Churchill's speechmaking continued after he returned to London. At The Hague in the Netherlands, Churchill made this astonishing prediction in May: "I see no reason . . . why there should not, ultimately, arise the United States of Europe." As Supreme Allied Commander of the forces in Europe, Eisenhower had come to know many of the leaders who were now at the helms of government in capitals such as The

Hague, Oslo, Copenhagen, Brussels, and Paris. Eisenhower endorsed Churchill's concept but wondered how those same leaders would react to it.

Later, when Churchill spoke in Zurich about including Germany in a new Europe, Eisenhower was certain that would not play well in Europe. Yet the more Eisenhower thought about it, he agreed. The exact words in Churchill's speech were these:

> I am now going to say something that will astonish you. The first step in the re-creation of the European family must be a partnership between France and Germany. In this way only can France recover the moral leadership of Europe. There can be no revival of Europe without a spiritually great France and a spiritually great Germany.

Eisenhower's mentor when he was at the War Office, Bernard Baruch, had already coined the phrase "cold war" to describe the deteriorating relations between the West and the Soviet Union. In this developing Cold War Eisenhower had little confidence in Truman's secretary of state, Jimmy Byrnes. Byrnes's State Department, Eisenhower felt, had put the bridle on Truman. In May Ike told the president that Byrnes was underestimating the Soviet threat.

Eisenhower, however, now had only a correct but formal relationship with Truman. Perhaps the president saw in Ike a closet Republican. It did not help that when Eisenhower joined Truman on a trip to his home state of Missouri, all the cheers were for the general.

In fact, in June 1946 Truman upbraided Eisenhower for the delay in bringing the troops home. The problem, Eisenhower explained, was not the army but the navy. There were not enough ships to transport the troops. Days later, Ike was called to testify before a Senate committee. When a senator began posturing and presenting himself as "the champion of the ordinary GI," Eisenhower nearly exploded: "Those fellows are my friends. I have commanded more soldiers than anyone else in history. You cannot possibly have anyone else with a greater interest in those men than me."

As Army Chief of Staff, Eisenhower did render one significant service to his soldiers—at least to the Negro soldiers (as they were called then). Without fanfare and press releases, he sent down the order—that on all posts at three in the morning all "Colored" signs be painted out. Moreover, although the fact is little mentioned by historians, it was Eisenhower, as president, who integrated the District of Columbia. Eisenhower also appointed the first black person to be special assistant to the president on civil rights—Fred Morrow. Eisenhower signed and introduced the first program on urban housing. In addition, Eisenhower was the first president to sign a civil rights bill and then to send troops to integrate the schools in Little Rock in 1957.

Meanwhile, across the Atlantic his former warrior-in-arms was finding that he relished his role as leader of the opposition far more than Eisenhower did being chief of staff. Churchill found that he could strike some strident chords in foreign policy that as prime minister he would have had to mute.

Furthermore, the bureaucratic bumbledum of the Labour Party was such an inviting target for the Churchillian wit. He called it, "government of the duds, by the duds and for the duds" and, paraphrasing the verse of Sir Walter Scott, predicted that they would vanish "unwept, unhonored and unsung and unhung."

In its zeal to reach "the New Jerusalem," the Labour government had nationalized the steel, coal, and rail industries, as well as instituted a national health system.

In the gentleman's lavatory in the British House of Commons is a very long urinal with a great row of appliances. One

COLUMBIA UNIVERSITY • 221

day, Clement Attlee, a leader of the Labour Party, was addressing a stanchion near the door when Winston Churchill entered
and walked all the way to the other end of the room to do his
business. Said Mr. Attlee, "Winston, I know we're political op-
ponents, but we don't have to carry our differences into the
gentlemen's lavatory."

Churchill replied, "Clement, the trouble with you Socialists is that whenever you see anything in robust and sturdy
condition you want to regulate it."

But investments had declined and productivity had stagnated.
Other European countries such as France and Belgium were recovering faster. To answer the Socialists, who bannered equality
as their goal, Churchill growled, "Equality yes, the equality of
misery, but I much prefer Capitalism's inequality of wealth."

A Labourite, Denis Palings, whose name describes the
pointed picket fence around the House of Commons or the
White House on which one can be "impaled," in debate called
Churchill a "dirty dog capitalist."

Churchill replied, "My reaction to his charge was that of
any 'dirty dog' toward any 'palings.'"

Churchill poked fun not only at pretentious Socialist ministers but also at their jargon. They referred to the poor as "the
lower income disadvantaged" or "marginal stipend maintain-
ers." Churchill also belittled their description of "house" or
"home" as "local accommodation unit." He said in the House
of Commons, "Now we will have to change that old favorite
song 'Home, Sweet Home' to say 'Local Accommodation
Unit, Sweet Local Accommodation Unit—there's no place like
Local Accommodation Unit.'"

By 1948 Eisenhower had left Washington. He had a new
home at Morningside Heights in New York City as president of
Columbia. When one of the trustees had called him, Ike had exclaimed, "You got the wrong Eisenhower. You want my brother
Milton." Ike had always entertained the notion of becoming a

college president—but a small college more on the order of Gettysburg, where he would keep an office in his last years.

If Ike got lost in the Pentagon in his first few days, he also once got locked out of Columbia. One Friday evening he tried to go to his office. The watchman barred his way, even though Ike insisted he was the president. Later Ike learned that the same guard had reported to the grounds superintendent that a man claiming to be the president of Columbia tried to enter, but he had blocked the man's entrance.

Eisenhower, however, did not easily negotiate his way through the labyrinth of academe. There was too little time for thinking and planning—too many speeches and too much presiding over feckless faculty meetings. One time he found himself at a dinner where he was the fifth speaker. He said, "Every speech, whether written or oral, needs punctuation. Tonight I am the period." And he sat down. Of one meeting, he said, "A meeting whose main item was corner windows for heads of departments took almost five hours where the decision on D-day five minutes." To encourage thinking, he established the American Assembly, a Columbia forum where businesspeople and professors could brainstorm problems. He also set up a conference center outside the city as a retreat for holding conferences and seminars.[1]

As an antidote to his frustration, Eisenhower began painting as a pastime. When he told Tom Stephens, who was painting his portrait, that Churchill had suggested his taking up painting, the artist also encouraged him to try.

Eisenhower later joked to friends that his two biggest accomplishments at Columbia were persuading Isidor Rabi, the

---

1. Those in the conference management business consider Eisenhower the father of the conference center. The concept, which has spread to Britain and elsewhere, was inaugurated by Eisenhower when he persuaded Averell Harriman to give his estate, Arden House, forty miles north of New York City on the Hudson, as an overnight or weekend retreat.

Nobel Prize–winning scientist, from going to join his friend Albert Einstein at Princeton and football coach Lou Little from going to Yale. Ike had known Little at Georgetown in Washington, having once coached an army base team against him. "Lou," he said, "you're one of the reasons I came to Columbia."

Ike characteristically underestimated his impact. At a time when President Truman was instituting loyalty oaths for government employees in Washington, Eisenhower opposed such measures. (However, he allowed that if he knew that a professional applicant was a communist, he would not hire the person.) It would be Eisenhower in 1953 who as president told Dartmouth College, "Don't join the book burners. Don't think you are going to conceal faults by concealing evidence that they ever existed."

While at Columbia, Ike and Mamie took a trip to Gettysburg, where they had lived during World War I. As a student of the Civil War, Ike had always been fascinated by the Gettysburg battlefield. In addition, while visiting in 1917, Ike had discovered that many of his Eisenhower forebears had lived in Adams County.

Just south of Gettysburg, the Eisenhowers inspected a tract of land. There they decided to build a farm for their retirement. It was the first parcel of land the Eisenhowers had ever owned. When he was asked by the Registrar of Deeds at the Adams County Court House why he wanted to build a house, since he already had one in New York, Eisenhower replied, "All my years in the Army we never owned our own home, and we wanted once in our life to say we left a piece of ground to God better than we found it."

As the election year of 1948 approached, Democrats regarded Truman's chances as hopeless. Efforts were made to draft Eisenhower as the Democratic candidate. Months earlier, Truman, despite their lack of closeness, made a bizarre offer. He would run as vice president, with Eisenhower as presidential candidate. In March Eisenhower crafted a statement to discourage Republican candidates pledged to him in New Hampshire: "Politics is a noble profession; a serious, complicated and, in its true sense, a noble one. My decision to remove myself from the political scene is definite and positive."

To the astonishment of Ike and just about everyone else, Truman beat Dewey in 1948. Shortly thereafter, Truman asked Eisenhower to take a part-time consulting job—advising on the newly merged armed services. Unification had been one of Eisenhower's recommendations to Truman in 1946, and now that Truman had implemented it, Ike felt obliged to accept. It was a tiresome task, made more tedious by the rail commuting between his Columbia duties in New York and his Pentagon consulting in Washington.

In New York he met frequently with his old mentor Bernard Baruch, who now headed a commission to consider the future of the atom bomb. The Baruch plan would put the bomb under the supervision of the United Nations. Stalin opposed it, as his scientists were already working on their own bomb.

Eisenhower told Baruch, "The existence of the bomb in our hands is a deterrent to aggression." Churchill later said that "World War III would never happen because of the mutual horrors of the bomb."

Meanwhile, the Cold War between the United States and the USSR intensified. The conviction of Alger Hiss for lying about being a Soviet agent and then the invasion of South Korea in June 1950 had stirred Truman, as leader of the free world. The president instituted the Marshall Plan for aid to Europe and established the North Atlantic Treaty Organization. In late 1950 Truman asked Eisenhower to return to duty as Supreme Commander of the NATO armed forces. Some political pundits thought that Truman was removing his most threatening obstacle in the 1952 presidential election.

Eisenhower found that a mood of pessimism pervaded NATO. At an initial NATO planning session, all the staff officers of other countries were bemoaning their shortages. Ike began to seethe at this negative thinking. Finally, he banged the podium: "I know there are shortages, but I myself can make up for part of that shortage—what I can do and what I can put into this—and the rest of it has to be made up by you people. Now get at it." With that, he walked out.

Eisenhower saw his first task to be a salesman for NATO. No other general could have been a better one. He began his tour with a January trip that took him to the eleven nations that composed NATO. He told them, "I return to Europe as a military Commander but with no miraculous plans, no display of military force. I return with an unshakable faith in Europe—this land of our ancestors—in the underlying courage of its people."

One of Eisenhower's chief goals was to nail down specific commitments to NATO as ammunition against Senator Taft and other right-wing Republicans, who argued that just because Europeans were not ready to rearm, why should Americans shoulder the burden?

In July Eisenhower journeyed to London to speak to the English Speaking Union banquet at the Savoy. He was flanked at the head table by Prime Minister Attlee and opposition leader Churchill. On this black-tie occasion, Eisenhower was eloquent. His theme was the danger of any neglect in the Western alliance and the importance of a united Europe within that alliance. "A healthy, strong, confident Europe," Ike said, would be the greatest possible boon to the functioning and objectives of the Atlantic Pact.

Two days later Churchill wrote to Eisenhower,

My Dear Ike,

As I am getting rather deaf I could not hear or follow your speech when you delivered it. I have now procured a copy for which I am arranging the widest circulation in my power.

Let me say that I am sure this is one of the greatest speeches delivered by any American in my life time,—which is a long one,—and that it carries with it on strong wings the hope of the salvation of the world from its present perils and confusions.

What a great conclave we had last night! I had not comprehended the splendour of your speech until I read the text this evening, which I procured only with some difficulty. But I feel that we were close enough together anyhow. I think we ought now to be able to see the way forward fairly clearly, and I believe that events in the next two years are going to be our servants and we their masters.

I look forward to seeing you again before many weeks have passed.

Meanwhile with all my heart believe me your comrade and friend.

Yours, Winston

On September 11 Churchill went to Paris for a lunch with the British ambassador and General Eisenhower. They agreed that the French should institute a draft of those of military age for service in the NATO army. Ike also echoed Churchill's proposal that the Germans begin to ante up some appropriations for the NATO commitment.

Churchill said, "Ike, if they won't do it with us, we'll tell them we'll do it without them." Their pilgrimage together in the defense of freedom was about to resume.

CHAPTER 19

THE WHITE HOUSE

We hold it to be the first task of statesmanship to develop the strength that will deter the forces of aggression and promote the conditions of peace.

DWIGHT DAVID EISENHOWER,
INAUGURAL ADDRESS, 1953

AS AUTUMN APPROACHED in 1951, Churchill tried one last time to return to 10 Downing Street. He wanted to play a role on the world stage again. Perhaps he would be able to ease the Cold War's tensions. The Socialists, however, attacked him as a warmonger. Their newspaper, the *Daily Mirror*, asked, "Whose finger do you want on the trigger?"

Churchill answered, "I do not hold that we should rearm to fight. I hold that we should rearm to parley."

Aneurin Bevan, the firebrand Socialist, charged, "I do not think Churchill wants war. The trouble with him is that he does not know how to avoid it."

On the eve of the election Churchill journeyed to Plymouth to campaign for his son, Randolph, who was standing for election there. Churchill said that he himself only remained in public life because he thought he could still make a lasting contribution to peace. "I pray indeed," he allowed, "that I may have this opportunity. It is the last prize I seek."

On election day, October 25, 1951, the results of the year before were reversed. Then the Socialists had barely won, even though the Conservatives received more votes. This time more voted Socialist than Conservative, but Churchill's party gained five more parliamentary seats than Attlee's. The nation was beginning to weary of Socialism. What Churchill had described as the Socialist "queuetopia" of rationing, regulations, and restrictions he would now start to dismantle.

In the United States the party on the right was also mobilizing strength. Republicans had picked up gains in the 1950 election and were confident of defeating President Truman in 1952. A bill of impeachment against him had been introduced in the House. His attorney general, Howard McGrath, had been indicted. Several White House associates and others were convicted of corruption. General MacArthur's dismissal in 1951, even if it was constitutionally correct, had also caused the president's popularity to plummet. (Truman left the White House in 1953 with the lowest approval rating of any president in the twentieth century—18 percent.)

If the Republicans did win in 1952, the next president would probably be Sen. Robert Taft of Ohio. The Republican Senate leader was de facto head of the Republican Party, and he and his congressional allies held control of the Republican National Committee and would choose most of the delegates to its Chicago convention in 1952.

This worried Eisenhower. He had met privately with the Republican senator in January 1951. He agreed with Taft that Truman's Fair Deal programs were a deficit disaster, but he was alarmed by Taft's opposition to spending that included the foreign and military assistance programs to Europe.

Governor Dewey in New York, the unexpected loser to Truman in 1948, led the anti-Taft wing of the Republican Party. Senators such as Duff of Pennsylvania and Lodge of Massachusetts joined Dewey in pressuring Eisenhower to run.

Dewey had endorsed Eisenhower for president in a *Meet the Press* interview in October 1950.

Career politicians, however, never Eisenhower's favorite people, had approached the soldier in the wrong way. They assumed that anyone with the possibility of being elected president would leap at the chance. They would have—in the same situation.

The politicians of the eastern international wing were sincere in their belief that the country needed Eisenhower, but these moderate Republicans also were moved by reasons of politics and power. They wanted the White House, and all the appointive capacity and administrative discretion the presidency represented, in their hands and not under the control of Taft and his congressional allies.

In May 1951 the newly elected Sen. Richard Nixon of California visited Eisenhower in France. Eisenhower had met Nixon the year before at the Bohemian Grove outing in California. Eisenhower asked Nixon about his work on the Herter Committee, a bipartisan House committee that had toured Europe in 1948. Nixon had written most of the report, which recommended that Republican members of Congress back President Truman's initiatives, such as the Truman Doctrine, Point Four, and aid to Greece and Turkey. To Nixon's urging that Ike stand as a candidate, Eisenhower remained noncommittal. The operative word in persuading Eisenhower to be a candidate was *duty*. His brother Milton understood that in November 1951 and reluctantly concluded that his brother would have to accede to the pressure: "The possibility that the American people must choose between Taft and Truman is so terrifying that any personal sacrifice on the part of any honest American is wholly justified."

The deficit populism of Truman, as well as the short-sighted nationalism of Taft, were both unacceptable for Eisenhower; yet he also was leery of plunging into the political world. He relished his challenge at NATO. Yet how could he keep on selling a greater military commitment on the part of European nations if Taft as president would abort the U.S. involvement?

Prime Minister Churchill found his old military friend preoccupied and tense at a December luncheon at Marnes-le-Coquette, Eisenhower's villa west of Paris. During the luncheon, Eisenhower spoke earnestly of the need for a greater British troop allotment. He dwelt on this theme well into the dessert course. Finally, Churchill, who had been eyeing an ornate credenza behind Eisenhower, on which a decanter of brandy stood, said, "Ike, that's a handsome credenza. Is it Louis Seize?"

Eisenhower—despite a nudge by his deputy, Gen. Alfred Gruenther—said, "I guess it is. It was here when I came," and went on speaking about the need to enlarge the British contingent.

Then Churchill interjected, "And that's a splendid decanter on the credenza. Is it Austrian crystal?"

Ike replied, "I suppose, but about this manpower problem—"

Whereupon Churchill again interrupted, saying, "More than manpower, it's morale—and the first thing the supreme Allied commander must do is lift the 'spirits' on that credenza."

But the state of Eisenhower's own mind was in conflict. When Churchill returned, his physician, Lord Moran, asked him whether he thought Eisenhower could be persuaded to run. Churchill replied, "Ike has not only to be wooed, but raped."

To make the deadline for the New Hampshire primary, Senator Lodge released the text of a letter to Gov. Sherman Adams, stating that Eisenhower was a Republican and would "consider a call to service by the party . . . to be the highest duty." In other words, Ike was a candidate.

Eisenhower was furious at Lodge's unauthorized action but did not repudiate it. Meanwhile, John Hay Whitney, one of the owners of the New York *Herald Tribune*, organized a massive midnight rally at Madison Square Garden. From midnight to dawn, close to 50,000 screamed, "We like Ike," until they were hoarse and exhausted.

Jacqueline Cochran, the famous aviator, flew to Paris with the film of it. Eisenhower and Mamie watched it in their living room and were deeply stirred when it was over. Cochran raised her glass in a toast: "To the President." It triggered tears in Ike's eyes. He now felt he was truly responding to a draft by the people.

A month later he swept the New Hampshire primary with over 50 percent of the vote. A week later in Minnesota, write-in votes made him second to favorite son Harold Stassen, the governor of the state, who ran ahead of Senator Taft.

In March, Eisenhower asked Herbert Brownell, a New York lawyer who had managed Dewey's campaign, to come to Paris. Brownell, who hailed from a small town in Nebraska, seemed to have bonded well with Ike two years earlier, at a luncheon with Governor Dewey at the Columbia faculty club.

Brownell arrived early in the afternoon before the next morning's meeting with the general, so Brownell decided to take in the Folies Bergere that evening. The next morning, after inquiring about his plane trip, Eisenhower asked what Brownell had done the previous night. The answer "Folies Bergere" drew no Ike grin.

"A Nebraska boy, and you like to gawk at nude women?" The chagrined Brownell stammered no. The meeting did not progress as Brownell had hoped. They talked generally about domestic issues, the Taft-Hartley Act, the minimum wage, and taxes. Not until the meeting was coming to a close did Brownell dare to deliver the bad news: Unless the general returned to campaign openly, Taft would have a lock on the delegates. It was not a message Eisenhower wanted to hear. Yet as an old soldier he did not like losing. His decision to resign

from NATO was made more easy by President Truman's decision in early April not to run in 1952. It cleared away an awkward situation. Eisenhower accepted a June 1 date to open an
Eisenhower Museum in Abilene. There he would kick off his
campaign speech.

Despite his lead in the opinion polls, as convention time in
Chicago approached, Eisenhower was a hundred or so delegates behind Taft. Part of Taft's lead came from states such as
Texas, Louisiana, and Georgia in the one-party Democratic
South, where a shell of a Republican Party was controlled by
the Taft supporters. But pro-Ike Democrats in those states
were switching to the Republican Party to challenge the delegates selected by the Taft-friendly local committees.

Brownell crafted the handle to open the door that led to
Eisenhower's nomination. He designed a rule change to the
convention proceedings that proposed a contested delegation
could not vote on its own legitimacy. Brownell called it "the
Fair Play Amendment." At a Republican governor's conference
before the convention opened, Brownell persuaded a majority
of the governors to endorse the change. It was sadly ironic for
Senator Taft, called "Mr. Integrity," to have to witness in this
first nationally televised convention Ike supporters' signs saying, "Thou shalt not steal." Once the Fair Play Amendment
was passed, Taft was doomed. Eisenhower was the nominee,
and Senator Nixon would be his running mate.

Political pundits have tried to suggest that the general had
no say whatsoever in the choice. It is true that Eisenhower
never warmed to any professional politician—Dewey, Lodge,
Stassen, Duff, as well as Nixon. Ike's choices for dinner company were usually bridge-playing business and old military
friends. Nixon, who was also of a different generation from the
general, could never have become an intimate. Yet the thirty-
nine-year-old senator from the second biggest state in the nation was the right age and offered geographical, or regional,

balance. As a former naval officer in the Pacific, Nixon also had a good war record. More important, he was one of the few pro-NATO Republican senators who could bridge the gap to the Taft wing. Nixon had ferreted out Alger Hiss, who later was convicted of perjury for denying his communist associations. Nixon's prominence in that affair made him popular to the Republican conservatives.

The first brouhaha in the fall campaign was occasioned by the left-leaning *New York Post* on a "secret" Nixon fund. They dredged up a story that had been carried by the *Los Angeles Times* months before. The fund, which had been organized by Herbert Hoover Jr., was secret only in that Nixon did not know who was on the list of donors. The fund was to be used for airplane expenses from Washington back to California, as well as for Christmas card mailings.

In a telecast paid for by the Republican National Committee, Nixon pointed out that Gov. Adlai Stevenson, the prep school– and Princeton-educated Democratic candidate, had a similar fund (although he, in fact, knew the identities of his donors).

Nixon also revealed that Sen. John Sparkman, his opposite as the Democratic candidate for vice president, kept his wife on his office payroll, although she rarely showed up. Eisenhower was impressed by the talk, although he was uncomfortable with Nixon's laying bare his financial records because it forced Eisenhower (as well as the Democratic candidates) to reveal his. The speech, however, became famous as "the Checkers speech." Nixon, imitating FDR's use of his dog Fala, closed by saying there was one gift by a donor that he would never return—a cocker spaniel puppy given to his children.

Telegrams of support overwhelmed the beleaguered vice presidential candidate. Nixon proved the first vice presidential running mate to be an asset and a draw since Gov. Theodore Roosevelt was paired with President McKinley in 1900.

It may have been Ike's pledge in the closing weeks of the campaign, however, that turned the 1952 election into an electoral college landslide. In Detroit the five-star general vowed to the crowd, "I shall go to Korea." If anyone could end the Korean War, the U.S. people figured it would be General Eisenhower. Two weeks later he was elected, with 55 percent of the vote. President Truman commented about Eisenhower as the new chief executive: "Ike will find out that it's different than being a general. You can't just give orders and expect things to be done."[1]

Four weeks after the election, Ike, as promised, flew to Korea. The inspection of the terrain confirmed his thinking. Only an all-out war from a strategically weak position in South Korea against the Red Chinese in the north would gain back the northern part of Korea. The former general had to find a way to end hostilities along the lines of a status quo. "My conclusion was," as Eisenhower later wrote, "[that] we could not stand forever on a static front and continue to accept casualties without any visible results." The old soldier did, however, enjoy eating sauerkraut with troops in the front line and seeing his son John, who was then on active duty with the Fifteenth Infantry.

At 10 Downing Street Churchill greeted the election with ambivalence. On the one hand, he was delighted that his old friend Ike was president. Yet a political party twenty years out of office would not be amenable but angry. Some of the charges hurled by Republicans who now controlled Congress disturbed him. Although he knew the London press was a prism that exaggerated and distorted news from America, nev-

---

1. Yet as former Minnesota governor Harold Stassen once told me, "Do you realize that General Eisenhower in the spring of 1944 had more people—more personnel—accountable to him than President Roosevelt in 1933? Why, as Supreme Allied Commander he was drafting concordats with the Pope, meeting with kings and Prime Ministers in exile, and working out postwar arrangements. What better training could there be to be President?"

ertheless, Churchill was upset by attacks on such sensitive issues as the Yalta Conference.

The day before the New Year, Churchill boarded the *Queen Mary* at Southampton, bound for New York, to meet President-elect Eisenhower. During the New Year's festivities he teased the captain that he liked the Italian ocean liners.

"Captain, their service is impeccable, their cuisine superb and then on an Italian ship there is none of this nonsense in time of emergency" and Churchill paused, "of women and children first."

Most of the sailing time, Churchill worked with his parliamentary secretary, John Colville, on their agenda with President-elect Eisenhower. The preparation mainly involved questions about dealing with the Soviet Union. Colville asked him, "Prime Minister, when do you think the Cold War will end and the 'Iron Curtain' come down?"

"How old are you, Jack?" Churchill asked.

"Thirty-seven," Colville answered.

"If you live to be 75 or about my age, you should see it happen." (Colville would die in November 1987, at age seventy-one, two years to the very month before the Berlin Wall was torn down.) Churchill believed that the Soviet's victorious war against Germany had reinforced the legitimacy of the Communist regime and that two more generations would have to take place before there was recognition of the false promise of Marxism.

As the ship neared New York Harbor, Churchill addressed the whole crew the morning before the afternoon disembarkation. "Why is it," he asked those assembled on the deck, "the ship beats the waves when the waves are so many and the ship is one? The reason is that the ship has a purpose." Although he was talking about the ship, his mind was on the Soviets. If the United States, Britain, and the rest of the West remained strong and steadfast in purpose, the Cold War would not turn hot.

On landing, Churchill and his wife, Clementine, went to Bernard Baruch's apartment on the Upper East Side. Eisenhower arrived in time for evening cocktails. He said, "Winston, one thing I learned in this political game of yours, you got to have a sense of humor."

At a splendid dinner Churchill and Eisenhower swapped wartime stories, shared anecdotes about the charm of the new young queen, and discussed the communist "witch hunt" trials then being staged in Prague. It was fitting that they talked about "the Cold War" in the home of Baruch, who had coined the term in 1946. Churchill and Eisenhower also agreed that the Cold War had to be waged as a war of ideas. Churchill commented, "It is not only important to discover truth but also to know how to present it."

Three days later Eisenhower, along with Secretary of State-designate John Foster Dulles, met Churchill again at Eisenhower's campaign office at the Commodore Hotel in New York. Eisenhower asked Churchill if he minded Eisenhower meeting Stalin alone. Churchill did not object but advised Eisenhower to take his time. Eisenhower agreed: "As an old general, I can afford to wait for reconnaissance reports. I have four years—Why should I be in a hurry?" On one vital matter, Churchill gave his reluctant consent for Eisenhower to threaten the use of the atom bomb to force a settlement of the Korean War.

Churchill did not find Dulles congenial. He had met the international lawyer in London two years earlier when Dulles, as a Truman emissary, had briefed Churchill on the Japanese peace settlement that Dulles had just negotiated. Churchill thought that Dulles, who served on the ruling council of the U.S. Presbyterian Church, proclaimed his views as if he were Moses reading God's commandments on slabs he had just brought down from the mountaintop. Churchill's description of Eisenhower's Secretary of State to Colville was "dull, duller, Dulles."

Dulles on his part resented the intimacy Churchill had with Eisenhower. When that closeness included foreign policy counsel, it trespassed into Dulles's territory. In front of Ike, Dulles told the prime minister to make no plans for any return visit to Washington in the near future.

Eisenhower was one of the few men who found the pontifical Dulles agreeable. Dulles, who had attended the Hague Conference in 1907 and the Versailles Peace Conference in 1919, was the nephew of Wilson's secretary of state, Edward Lansing, and had been brought up by his grandfather John Foster, who had been Benjamin Harrison's secretary of state. Of Dulles, Eisenhower commented, "There is only one person [in America] who knew more leaders and players on the world stage—and that's me." The dogmatic Dulles fit into the "good cop/bad cop" style Eisenhower had developed over the years as a military leader.

Sherman Adams, his new chief of staff, was an icy deputy first called the "Snowman" and then the "No Man." The former New England governor was in the tradition of Gen. Beedle Smith—his top deputy general in the war—brusque and even brutal in controlling access to Eisenhower.

The blunt-speaking Charles Wilson, the former General Motors CEO, was Ike's secretary of defense. George Humphrey, who was death on deficits, was his Treasury secretary.

The Mormon Ezra Taft Benson, a rigid religious and political reactionary, was Secretary of Agriculture.

Under Eisenhower's direction, Nixon became the most active and involved vice president up to that time. Nixon was "deputy chief of state," dispatched around the world to represent the president for inaugurations and funerals (as well as the president's "ears" and "eyes," reporting back on political conditions). Eisenhower also made Nixon his de facto or deputy titular leader of the Republican Party. Specifically, he was charged with doing what Eisenhower disliked—delivering "red meat" speeches against the Democrats to the Republican faithful at "chicken" dinners across the country. It was another example of Eisenhower using his lieutenants as lightning rods. (After re-election in 1956 Nixon tried to beg off the partisan hatchet-man role, which he knew would undercut his election chances in 1960, but Eisenhower, through Adams, refused to let him off the hook.)

Of all of these, only one person in the Cabinet had a close relationship with Eisenhower—namely, Secretary of State Dulles. Yet partly because he recognized he might lean on Dulles too much, Eisenhower established a National Security Council. Robert Cutler, a former Harvard academic, set it up. Cutler believed that any conference with more than twelve in attendance was counterproductive. Thus Cutler produced a table of twelve at which would sit the secretaries of State, Defense, and the Treasury, the chairman of the Joint Chiefs of Staff, and the vice president. (Dulles, who tried to prevent such a panel, was a disgruntled participant.) As an outgrowth of his talks with Churchill, the new president directed the new National Security Council to have the staff outline a game plan of three Cold War scenarios.

Broadly speaking, Task Force I would review the current strategy of "containment" and consider ways of military preparation that would not bankrupt the budget. Task Force II would develop a more expensive strategy based on nuclear weapons and deterrence. Task Force III would investigate the possibility of rolling back Soviet power in Eastern Europe. This would consist of covert operations and psychological warfare.

On the covert side, Eisenhower approved a coup in Iran. Dr. Mohammed Mossadegh was *Time* magazine's Man of the Year for 1951. Because of this ranting Islam demagogue, who increasingly turned for support to the Iranian Communist Party, the British had had to close down their oil refinery operations in Iran. Churchill had told Eisenhower that Iran might fall into the embrace of Stalin and the Soviet Union, which bordered Iran.

The British proposed a joint venture with the Americans and recommended that Kermit Roosevelt, grandson of Theodore Roosevelt, direct the coup. In August rioters in favor of the exiled young shah, backed by U.S. dollars, battled on the street with the communist-organized mobs of Mossadegh. In the struggle, Mossadegh was overthrown and the Shah returned to Teheran. Stalinism was defeated in Iran, even if Stalin was dead by that time.

Stalin had died on March 5, 1953, which, as Churchill pointed out, was the seventh anniversary of his "Iron Curtain" address at Fulton. His death again sharpened Churchill's desire to meet with the new Soviet leaders, who in the beginning formed a troika—Malenkov, Beria, and Bulganin.

Churchill telegraphed to Eisenhower,

I am sure that everyone will want to know whether you still contemplate a meeting with the Soviets. I remember our talk at Bernie's when you told me I was welcome to meet Stalin if I thought fit and that you intended to offer to do so. I understand this as meaning that you did not want us to go together, but now [that] there is no more Stalin I wonder whether this makes any difference to your view about separate approaches to the new regime or whether there is a possibility of collective action.

But Churchill's wire crossed with a letter sent by Eisenhower:

I tend to doubt the wisdom of a formal multilateral meeting since this would give our opponent the same kind of opportunity he has so often had to use such a meeting simultaneously to block every reasonable effort of ourselves and to make of the whole occurrence another propaganda mill for the Soviet.

It is ironic, if understandable, that the attitudes of Churchill and Eisenhower vis-à-vis the Soviets had become somewhat reversed, at least on the subject of a "summit" conference. (This was a term Churchill had coined in 1950 when he called for a "parley at the summit.")

In World War II it was Churchill who put no trust in Soviet assurances, whereas Eisenhower as general was more circumspect. Now President Eisenhower—perhaps influenced by Dulles—saw little use for a "summit" meeting with the Soviets. In contrast, Churchill at seventy-nine was an old man in a hurry. The venerable warrior could cap his long career by pulling off some kind of détente in the Cold War hostilities.

Eisenhower's response to the new leaders of the Soviet Union was Churchillian: to present the truth but in the right forum and right occasion to win the war of ideas. Eisenhower took the offensive in rhetoric—delivering truths in a way that got the attention of the world. He spoke on April 25 at the Statler Hilton in Washington to the Newspaper Editors of America. The president said that while he welcomed the recent Soviet statements on peace, he would believe in their sincerity when they signed a treaty for Austrian independence; released prisoners of war held since 1945; concluded an armistice in Korea, Indochina, and Malaya; agreed to help establish a free and united Germany; and ensured "the full independence of Eastern European nations."

In return, the United States would negotiate with the Soviets an arms limitation pact and would accept international control of nuclear weapons. In perhaps his finest presidential speech he said, "Every gun that is made, every warship launched, every rocket fired, signifies, in the final sense, a theft from those who hunger and are not fed, those who are cold and are not clothed."

In the middle of his address Eisenhower began sweating. An intestinal attack had wrenched him in pain. He gripped the lectern and continued,

> The cost of one modern heavy bomber is this: a modern brick school in thirty cities. It is two electric power plants, each serving a town of sixty thousand population. It is two fine, fully equipped hospitals.

Sweat was now pouring from his brow, but he read on:

> We pay for a single fighter plane with a half-million bushels of wheat. We pay for a single destroyer with new homes that could have housed more than eight thousand people.

Looking out again, he pronounced his judgment.

> This is not a way of life at all, in any true sense. Under the cloud of threatening war, it is humanity hanging from a cross of iron.

In London, Churchill as well as the British press applauded Eisenhower's address. Still, Churchill entertained hopes for a meeting with the Soviet leaders.

Any dream for an immediate meeting with the Soviets collapsed on June 26, right after the coronation of the new Queen Elizabeth II. At a 10 Downing Street dinner for Premier de Gasperi of Italy, Churchill turned to a dinner guest, Lady Clark (wife of Lord Kenneth Clark, the future author of *Civilization*), and whispered, "I want the hand of a friend. They put too much on me. Foreign affairs . . ." (He had taken over the duties of foreign secretary for hospitalized Anthony Eden.) Churchill had suffered a stroke.

The next day an announcement was issued by 10 Downing that Sir Winston (he had been knighted at the time of the coronation) was "to rest for a month." The doctors kept from the press their worries that the paralyzed Churchill would never talk again, much less walk. But Churchill bounced back: in two weeks he was holding meetings at his bedside.

As Churchill slowly recovered from his attack, Eisenhower—with the backing of the British government—pushed for the threat of the bomb on selected military targets, as a club to end the fighting in Korea. The biggest obstacle to a settlement, however, proved not to be the North Koreans but Syngman Rhee, the South Korean president. Rhee was backed in his opposition by many Republican senators. Dulles was also sympathetic to this Christian anticommunist's demands. Nevertheless, Eisenhower forced the signing of the armistice, against Rhee's wishes.

It was an acceptable solution to a problem that defied solution. Eisenhower and Churchill both believed that unlimited war in the nuclear age was unmanageable and limited war unwinnable. On August 2 Churchill wrote Eisenhower, "I have recovered full mobility." In October, at the Conservative Party Conference of Margate, Churchill delivered a stirring address that belied his age and his recent illness. He closed,

> If I stay, for the time being, bearing the burden at my age, it is not because of love for power or office. I have had an ample share of both. If I stay it is because I have the feeling that I may, through things that have happened, have an influence on what I care about above all else—the heralding of a sure and lasting peace.

The ten-minute standing ovation that followed squelched any rumors of retirement.

The old statesman was resolved to make one last try for a summit meeting. In December he journeyed to Bermuda to meet President Eisenhower and Premier Joseph Laniel of France. At the meeting Churchill said the new Soviet leadership offered a hope for better relations. More contacts and more trade, said Churchill, would in time lead to a lessening of hostilities.

But Eisenhower struck back hard at the idea of a summit meeting. The Soviet Union was "still a woman of the streets." She might have a new dress and new perfume, but there had been no change, argued Eisenhower, in the Soviet policy of destroying the capitalist free world by any means, whether by force, deceit, or lies.

Churchill was crushed. To Anthony Eden, he said that he blamed the attack on Dulles. Later in the conference, after listening to Dulles, he remarked to Colville, "Dulles is a Methodist minister, and his sermon is always the same." And later he referred to the American's bluster: "Dulles is the only bull I know who carries his own china shop around with him."

Despite the clash on the "summit" question, Churchill and Eisenhower teamed together to press the French to commit to the European Defense Community (EDC). The French were not agreeable to the Anglo-American insistence that a small contingent of German soldiers should be part of the European army.

The French were only interested in gaining support for their defense in Indochina against the forces of Ho Chi Minh. Their support of the EDC was conditional on an open-ended Anglo–U.S. military commitment to the French in Asia. Eisenhower and Churchill rejected such extortion. They also were united in their resolve to build a deterrent European military force that would include German units in the future.

The two men were at the opposite ends of the leadership cycle. Churchill, now beginning his eightieth year, was under increasing pressure to resign as prime minister. The sixty-three-year-old Eisenhower, still in very fit condition, was just beginning his presidential tenure.

Again, their contrasting disciplines made it harder on the older man and easier on the younger. Churchill rose late and worked late into the night. He relished every morsel of his three meals a day and every sip of his wine, whiskey, and brandy. Eisenhower, however, was awakened at six every morning by his son Maj. John Eisenhower for a daily briefing of breaking events. (John had been ordered back from Korea by President Truman for White House duty, a move that pleased Mrs. Eisenhower but not her husband. These daily meetings of father and son were all business, with never any talk about grandchildren or any other personal matters.)

In his drinking habits Ike was more temperate than Churchill. He limited himself to one cocktail before dinner, usually a Scotch and soda. As for eating, he took no special enjoyment in meals except for those he cooked himself. (He loved to barbecue steaks for visitors at Camp David and was particularly proud of his recipe for vegetable stew.) In addition, Eisenhower had stopped his pack-a-day smoking—cold turkey—in 1949, whereas Churchill puffed his fifteen or so cigars each day. (Yet Eisenhower later commented. "I never saw him with more than half of those big cigars smoked.")

The writing disciplines of the two leaders also differed. Churchill dictated his own speeches with many revisions. Eisenhower relied on a team of White House writers. But as a former speechwriter himself, Eisenhower could be demanding. After looking at a draft, he sometimes called a writer into the Oval Office: "What's the QED?" he asked. The first time the aide heard "QED," he might have been perplexed. The president would repeat "QED—*quod erat demonstrandum?*—What's the bottom line?" Then Eisenhower would continue, "What's the message we are trying to leave with the audience?

What is the point we want the listeners to take home with them?"

One White House speechwriter, former Congregational minister Fred Fox, told a young writer who had just received the treatment, "The General believes that if you can't put your bottom line message on the back of a match book before you begin typing, you're wasting his time and yours."

They also dealt with correspondence differently. On all matters Churchill dictated to secretaries. Eisenhower, however, allowed staff to draft letters for his signature on all but the most important matters. One friend kidded Eisenhower about the stilted language of a letter he had received from him. Eisenhower answered, "I made up my mind that I just had to sign them and not try to edit and rewrite. It was just a matter of the efficient use of my time."

In Britain the prime minister is *primus inter pares* ("first among equals") in dealing with his Cabinet. A minister is an elected member of Parliament with his own constituency, just like the prime minister, and every minister dreams of sitting at the prime minister's seat at the head of the table. In that situation one might have expected a Churchill to be more deferential to his Cabinet and an Eisenhower more dominating with a U.S. Cabinet. But it was Churchill who cowed his ministers at their meeting at 10 Downing Street. As prime minister, because he did not possess absolute power, he had to show he was in charge or he would be eaten up by them.

A president, however, does not have to brandish his power. At Cabinet meetings Eisenhower usually chose the role of a listener. He often registered his command by gestures. When Ezra Taft Benson started to fulminate on taxes—a topic out of his jurisdiction—the president would look up at the ceiling with a pained expression. If a secretary took a stance in policy opposite from where Eisenhower wanted it to go, the president might show his displeasure by stabbing his pencil into the yellow tablet in front of him.

Unlike Churchill, Eisenhower often did not reveal his mind or his decisions at those meetings but reserved his final decision until later.[2]

In contrast to Churchill, Eisenhower's style, which he had perfected in his years as a general in World War II and then at NATO, was to try to get others to propose what he wanted and then later commend them for their sound ideas. His method for steering members of his Cabinet and other visitors to the Oval Office was to advance his proposals by questioning, "Now if I understand you, what you really mean is this . . ." "Let me get this straight, what you are actually proposing is . . ."

Churchill, on the other hand, was a challenger. He often bullied those proposing policies to extract their best arguments. He liked to poke holes in their recommendations and then hear their answers. That was his way of selecting, shaping, and refining his own views. Whatever the merits of the two styles of

---

2. Some could be deceived by Eisenhower's passive presence. I acted as "a sergeant of arms" at a meeting held in the Republican National Committee headquarters at 1625 I St. in Washington in 1962. The Republican National Council developed statements and reports and then issued them under General Eisenhower's name. One report at this meeting was read by a Kansas congressman. It attacked some cutbacks in the military budget. When the congressman finished, Eisenhower asked, "Who gave you those numbers?"

The representative gave the name and added, "He's a three-star general."

"Don't count stars with me, Congressman! I put some of them there. Generals can lie—when they talk about the need for more military appropriation to Congress." He then proceeded to shave off some of the numbers of military items.

Joseph Califano once told President Johnson about being dispatched to Gettysburg in 1965 to brief General Eisenhower about developments in Vietnam. When Califano began to treat the mission as a "hand-holding" gesture to the ex-president, LBJ snapped, "Hell, Joe, you don't believe all that crap about Ike being out of it! You go up there and listen to every thing that old man says and report back to me and I want you to tell me every time that old man looks up at the ceiling, or frowns or nods. He's a very wise old man, Joe."

leadership, the confrontational approach of Churchill would probably in the long run be more physically demanding and taxing than the collegial manner of Eisenhower.

By the summer of 1954 Churchill's stamina and powers were clearly ebbing. Just about all of his Cabinet members were nudging, if not pushing, him for retirement. Churchill in June decided to make one last bid for a summit. He arrived in Washington on June 25. He was met at the airport by Vice President Nixon, and together in an open motorcade they rode to the White House.

Churchill spoke later at a luncheon that Nixon attended. Nixon said later,

> I had been told that he was not half the man he used to be, and at the luncheon it did seem he was dozing or at least inattentive as others spoke. But when he arose to address the audience, he wove the remarks of others at the head table masterfully into a powerful address. He talked about "trade not aid," and argued for a strong deterrent defense. ("Peace is our aim and strength is the only way to get it.") All was laced with wit and anecdotes.
>
> Afterwards I spent some time with him. If he was, indeed, "half the man he used to be," he was the most brilliant, insightful and commanding presence I have ever known.

At the White House Eisenhower finally agreed to Churchill's request for a high-level meeting with the Soviets in a neutral city such as Stockholm. Churchill asked if he might go to Moscow first to see if such a summit meeting was worthwhile, and Ike gave his approval. It was Eisenhower's position that the growing deterrent of NATO put the West into a commanding position of strength in dealing with the Soviets. Their joint communiqué on June 29 had stated, "The German Federal Republic should now take its place as an equal partner in the community of Western nations where it can make its proper contribution to the defense of the free world."

To sell his idea for a "summit," Churchill talked to a group of senators and members of Congress at a luncheon. "Meeting to jaw is better than war," he said waving his cigar in emphasis.

On the matter of war Churchill advised Eisenhower not to commit any troops or equipment to the French, who were battling Ho Chi Minh in Indochina. This counsel fell on willing ears. Now that the war was ended in Korea, Eisenhower was not about to involve himself in another Asian conflict by assisting the French in their stand at Dien Bien Phu.

Another sensitive matter that Churchill and Eisenhower discussed was atomic energy. In Bermuda Eisenhower had broached his idea of an international agency. Churchill had been enthusiastic. At the White House Eisenhower fleshed out his ideas for Churchill's comment and reactions. One phrase Churchill changed was the earlier language that the "United States was free to use the atom bomb" to "[was] reserving the right to use the atomic bomb."

In December 1954 Eisenhower proposed his historic "Atoms for Peace" plan to the United Nations. It was universally applauded by all nations except the Soviet bloc.

On his return to 10 Downing Street Churchill's Cabinet treated his summit proposal with scorn. The prime minister would be representing, they told him, "the fag end of a government." Still, Churchill resisted pleas from Eden, his foreign secretary and now nephew-in-law, to resign. (Eden married Clarissa Churchill in 1953.)

Most of Britain figured he would resign on his eightieth birthday on November 30. The House of Commons, in a ceremony, presented to Churchill a portrait that it had commissioned Graham Sutherland to paint. Churchill wryly commented, "It certainly seems a splendid example of modern art." (Lady Churchill later destroyed the portrait, which the family detested.)

To the House of Commons he said, "It was a nation and race dwelling all round the globe that had the lion's heart. I had the luck to be called upon to give the roar. I also hope that I sometimes suggested to the lion the right places to use his claws."

A photographer later asked Churchill, "Sir Winston, I hope I have the opportunity to take your photograph on your hundredth birthday."

Churchill looked the cameraman up and down. "I don't see why not, young man," he replied, "you look healthy enough."

In March Churchill delivered his last great speech as prime minister. To the House of Commons he said that the United States together with Britain must devise "a balanced and phased system of disarmament" with effective inspection controls. Until that was achieved, added Churchill, "there was only one sane policy for the free world, the policy of defense through deterrents. These deterrents may in time become the parents of disarmament—provided they deter." "It may well be that we shall by a process of sublime irony have reached a stage where safety will be the sturdy shield of terror and survival the twin brother of annihilation. . . . Meanwhile never flinch, never weary, never despair."

Eisenhower sent a letter to Churchill, applauding his speech. He ended,

> You and I have been through many things where our judgments have not always been as one, but, on my part at least, my admiration and affection for you were never lessened. In this long experience, my hope is rooted that the two of us may bring up some thought or idea that could help us achieve a personal concord that could, in turn, help our two governments act more effectively against Communists everywhere.

The letter was never answered. On April 5, 1955, Churchill went to Buckingham Palace to give up his seals of office. The queen offered him a dukedom. He refused, telling her he wished to die in the House of Commons.

It was Eisenhower, though, who almost died in the summer of 1955. That July featured a summit conference in Geneva with the Soviets. The delegation was headed by a goateed Marshal Bulganin and Communist Party Secretary General Nikita Kruschchev. Not attending the summit he had so yearned to attend was the retired Churchill. Anthony Eden, the new prime minister, represented Britain. The summit achieved nothing on the German question. Yet Eisenhower did launch his proposal for "an Open Sky," suggesting mutual inspections of the two Cold War powers' nuclear missile emplacements. Just as he finished, a thunderstorm caused the lights to go out. In the darkness Eisenhower laughed, "Gee, I didn't think it would have that effect."

The British and French were enthusiastic, but the Soviets' stony-faced Kruschchev vetoed the plan.

Later, after he returned to Washington, the president and Mamie took some vacation time in her old home of Colorado. After some weeks' fishing in mountain streams and painting the Rockies, he returned to Denver. On September 23 he felt pains in his chest. Eisenhower was suffering a heart attack. The news, unlike that of Churchill's seizure, was made public. The front pages of the newspapers were inundated with pictures of the aorta and medical charts. The nation's preeminent heart surgeon, Paul Dudley White, said it would be four months before they knew if the president had made a complete recovery.

In the meantime, Chief of Staff Adams kept business humming. Papers were sent for the president to sign, and Nixon presided circumspectly in Cabinet meetings, not sitting in the president's chair. Eisenhower returned to Washington on Veterans' Day, November 11, saying, "The doctors have given me a parole if not a pardon."

Churchill's absence from 10 Downing Street was felt the next year when Anglo–U.S. relations received a shock. In October 1959 Prime Minister Eden—without U.S. approval—intervened militarily against Egypt in the Suez Crisis. Publicly, Churchill supported Eden, but privately, he was critical. He wondered why Eden had never talked to President Eisenhower. When Colville asked him later why he had not spoken out about the Suez Crisis, Churchill replied, "I would never have dared, and had I dared, I would never have dared to stop." In other words, Churchill would not have mounted an invasion without U.S. approval, but if he had, he would not have aborted it halfway through.

Eisenhower wrote a letter to Churchill, relating his pain in blocking the move of America's greatest ally.

Churchill said when he left office, "To retire is not to resign." He began finishing the book he had begun before the war, *The History of the English-Speaking Peoples*. His last major oration was to the American Bar Association meeting in London in 1957. It was an address critical of the direction the United Nations was taking. In his opinion, the United Nations was ineffectual and impotent and, because of that, misleading. For one thing, totalitarian nations were beginning to outnumber the free in the Assembly.

> There are many cases where the United Nations have failed. . . . Hungary is in my mind. [The previous October the Soviets had quelled an uprising in Hungary with tanks and troops.] Justice cannot be a hit-or-miss system. We cannot be content with an arrangement where our system of international laws applies only to those who are willing to keep them.

In May 1959 Churchill, still a member of Parliament, made a visit to Washington to see President Eisenhower. The journey for the venerable statesman, now in his eighty-sixth year, was opposed by Lord Moran, his doctor. The new prime minister, Harold Macmillan, had asked him to carry a message about U.S. discrimination against British defense contractors.

On his first night Churchill wrote on White House stationery, "My dearest Clemmie, Here I am. All goes well and the President is a real friend. We had a most pleasant dinner last night. . . ."

The two soldiers traversed the historic battlefield at Gettysburg in a jeep. To reporters Churchill made some comments critical of Lee's strategy, engendering a howl of protest from historians south of the Mason-Dixon line.

Later, over Scotch and soda, the two friends shared their thoughts on the future of the two democratic nations. If Churchill and Eisenhower were the greatest leaders of the twentieth century, their roots and values, however, were in the nineteenth. Both believed that the new technology would be a mixed blessing—that it not only enhanced material benefits but also eroded individual dignity and human rights. The two leaders foresaw that the political institutions of democracy would be increasingly tested by the mass urbanization of the twentieth century. Each saw that bigness in government, industry, universities, and the military might stifle the spark of the individual genius in a free society. Out of that discussion came some of the themes for Eisenhower's "Farewell Address" a year and a half later. ("In the councils of government we must guard against the acquisition of unwarranted influence, sought or unsought, by the 'military industrial complex.'")

On May 6, in rainy cold weather more like a March day, Churchill spent his last day in the United States. Before going to Andrews Air Force Base, Churchill had his limousine take him to Walter Reed hospital to see a dying John Foster Dulles.

At Andrews Military Airport a crowd—mostly of reporters—gathered to see Churchill on what was described as his "last visit to America." Most of the journalists were veterans of the Washington scene and had witnessed many presidents, kings, prime ministers, and other visitors of world renown. Yet they crowded in front of the mesh wire fence on the apron to get a glimpse of this venerable warrior for a final time.

The old man shuffled his way slowly across the tarmac as the crowd clapped rhythmically.

As Churchill mounted the steps to the plane one at a time, the rain suddenly stopped in the late afternoon twilight. The horizon loomed pink.

Churchill, cigar in hand, intoned, "Farewell to the land [and then he paused] of my mother." He waved his hand in a V-for-victory gesture. "God bless you all—Good night!"

LONDON

Sir Winston—in times of war and peace—captured the imagination of all Americans. His indomitable courage and his indestructible belief in the society of free nations and in the dignity of free men became a symbol of our way of life.

DWIGHT DAVID EISENHOWER

IN THE SUMMER of 1964 General Eisenhower journeyed to Europe to participate in the twentieth anniversary of D-day and the liberation of Paris. His office at Gettysburg College had been flooded with invitations for ceremonies to attend and remarks to deliver in Britain, France, Belgium, the Netherlands, and elsewhere. It was convenient for Eisenhower to be away. The Republican convention was set to nominate Sen. Barry Goldwater. Eisenhower had been neutral in the preconvention primaries and maneuvering though not enthusiastic about the man or his prospects of beating Johnson.[1] Eisenhower would, however, support the Republican candidate.

---

1. In April 1964 I, as a Pennsylvania Republican legislator, was part of a delegation to visit General Eisenhower in an effort to persuade him to endorse Pennsylvania governor William Scranton for the Republican presidential nomination.

"Look," said the general, "it's obvious how I feel. My brother Milton and son John are supporting Governor Scranton. But I have to stay neutral because Goldwater already has the nomination locked up." Then he pulled out a map. "These markings show the delegates I might be able to switch if I called them. It's still far

After 1959, Churchill's visits to the House of Commons became more infrequent. On one of his rare appearances in 1961, he overheard some members talking behind him as he lolled on the bench.

"Poor fellow—he's a bit ga-ga, you know. He can't understand a thing that's going on."

Churchill turned around and, fixing them with a stare, growled, "Yes, and they say the old boy's quite deaf, too."

On July 27, 1964, as the member from Woodford, a feeble Sir Winston Churchill visited the House of Commons for the last time. He was helped to his back bench seat by his aide Anthony Montague-Browne. On that day, news of his resignation from Parliament was delivered. A resolution honoring his services was then passed, and it was carried to 28 Hyde Park Gate by the prime minister, Sir Alec Douglas-Home, and the other two party leaders of the House of Commons. After some champagne, Churchill gave a few words of thanks.

Some weeks later, in August, Churchill suffered a slight seizure, which went unreported by the press. Just about that time General Eisenhower returned from observances in Paris to London. Ike stayed at the Dorchester Hotel, where he was scheduled to see some of his old war colleagues. He also called at 28 Hyde Park Gate and was told Churchill was temporarily at King Edward VII hospital. Eisenhower inquired of Lady Churchill if it would be all right if he made a brief visit. She replied that her husband would be very appreciative.

It was the last meeting of the two men who together won the war against fascism in World War II and then laid the groundwork that led to the eventual victory over communism in the Cold War.

---

from enough. I promised to stay neutral at a time I thought a Rockefeller or Nixon would beat Goldwater. But I tell you if I thought breaking that promise would stop Goldwater, by golly, I'd think about it."

When General Eisenhower entered Churchill's hospital suite, his old friend's eyes lit up in recognition. Sir Winston said nothing but put his right hand on the bedside table next to him. Eisenhower could see that Churchill was a dying man. His sagging body was propped up against the back of the bed, and his face was flaccid with nine decades of infirmities.

On the bedside table Churchill's small pink hand reached out for Eisenhower's. No words were uttered—the two men silently relived the battles they together fought for the ideals they mutually cherished. No words could have been more eloquent and poignant than the mute handclasp between two nations, two leaders, and two friends.

After nine minutes Churchill unclasped his hand and slowly waved it in a "V" sign. Eisenhower went to the door. He said to the British aide who had accompanied him, "I just said goodbye to Winston, but you never say farewell to courage."

BIBLIOGRAPHY

Adams, Sherman. *Firsthand Report*. New York: Harper & Bros., 1961, p. 427.

Ambrose, Stephen. *Solder and President*. New York: Touchstone Books, 1991.

Arper, L. J. Interview by Walter Barbash, oral historian, Dwight D. Eisenhower Library, March 20, 1964.

Berlin, Isaiah. *Mr. Churchill in 1940*. Boston: Houghton Mifflin, 1964.

Boyle, Peter, ed. *The Churchill-Eisenhower Correspondence 1953–1955*. Chapel Hill: University of North Carolina Press.

Branigar, Thomas. "No Villains, No Heroes." *Kaiser History*, 1992.

Brownell, Herbert. *Advising Ike*. Lawrence, KS: University of Kansas, 1993.

Butcher, Harry. *My Three Years with Eisenhower*. New York: Simon and Schuster, 1946.

Carter, Violet Bonham. *Winston Churchill: An Intimate Portrait*. New York: Harcourt Brace and World, 1965.

Davis, Kenneth S. *Soldier of Democracy*. New York: Doubleday, Doren & Co., 1945.

Donovan, Robert J. *Eisenhower*. New York: Harper & Bros., 1956, p. 173.

Eisenhower, David. *Eisenhower at War*. New York: Random House, 1986, pp. 18–90.

Eisenhower, Dwight D. *At Ease: Stories I Tell to Friends*. New York: Doubleday & Co., 1967, p. 36.

———. *Crusade in Europe*. New York: Doubleday & Co., 1948, pp. 5–9.

———. *Mandate for Change*. New York: Doubleday & Co., 1962.

———. *Waging Peace, 1953–1961*. New York: Doubleday & Co., 1965, p. 83.

Eisenhower, John S. D. *Letters to Mamie*. Garden City: Doubleday & Co., 1968.

Eisenhower, John S. D. *Strictly Personal.* New York: Doubleday & Co., 1974.

Eisenhower, Julie Nixon. *Special People.* New York: Simon & Schuster, 1978.

Eisenhower, Susan. *Mrs. Ike.* New York: Farrar Straus & Giroux, 1996.

Ewald, William Bragg, Jr. *Eisenhower the President.* Englewood Cliffs, NJ: Prentice House, 1981.

Ferrell, Robert H. *The Eisenhower Diaries.* New York: Norton, 1981.

Gilbert, Martin. *Winston S. Churchill. Vol. 3, The Challenge of War, 1914–1916.* Boston: Houghton Mifflin, 1971, 1975, 1977.

———. *Winston S. Churchill.* Vol. 7. London: Houghton Mifflin, 1986, pp. 348, 607.

Gray, Robert K. *Eighteen Acres Under Glass.* New York: Doubleday & Co., 1961.

Griffith, Robert H., ed. *Ike's Letters to a Friend, 1941–1958.* Lawrence: University of Kansas Press, 1984.

Halle, Kay, ed. *Irrepressible Churchill.* Cleveland: World Publishing, 1966.

Holt, Daniel D., and James W. Leyerzapf, eds. *Eisenhower: The Prewar Diaries.* Baltimore: Johns Hopkins University Press, 1998.

James, Robert Rhodes. *Churchill: A Study in Failure.* New York: World Publishing, 1970.

Krock, Arthur. *Memoirs.* New York: McGraw-Hill, 1968, p. 321.

Larson, Arthur. *The President Nobody Knew.* New York: Charles Scribner, 1968.

Liddell, Kenneth C. *Winston Churchill and the Battle of Britain.* London: Michael Slains, 1965.

Long, Mrs. Robert J. Interview by Walter V. Barash, oral historian, Dwight D. Eisenhower Library, March 3, 1964.

Lovell, Richard. *Churchill's Doctor.* Guildford, England: Parthena Pub. Group, 1993, pp. 22–29. Moran only hints at the heart attack; Lovell describes it.

Lyon, Peter. *Eisenhower: Portrait of the Hero.* Boston: Little, Brown, 1974, p. 372.

Marsh, John. *The Young Churchill.* London: Evans, 1955.

McGurrin, James. *Bourke Cockran.* New York: Scribner's, 1948.

Miller, William J. *Henry Cabot Lodge.* New York: Heineman, 1967.

Moir, Phyllis. *I Was Winston Churchill's Secretary.* New York: Funk, 1941.

BIBLIOGRAPHY • 261

Moorehead, Alan. *Winston Churchill in Trial and Triumph.* Boston: Houghton Mifflin, 1955.

Moran, Lord. *Churchill: The Struggle for Survival.* London: Houghton Mifflin, 1968, pp. 17–75.

———. *Churchill.* Boston: Houghton Mifflin, 1966.

Morrow, E. Frederic. *Black Man in the White House.* New York: Cowerd-McCann, 1963.

Neal, Steve. *The Eisenhowers: Reluctant Dynasty.* New York: Doubleday & Co., 1967, p. 16.

Nel, Elizabeth. *Mr. Churchill's Secretary.* New York: Coward-McCann, 1958.

Nixon, Richard M. *Memoirs.* New York: Grosset and Dunlap, 1978, pp. 16–73.

Pilpel, Robert H. *Churchill in America, 1945–1961.* New York: Harcourt, Brace, Jovanovich, 1976.

Pusey, Merlo J. *Eisenhower: The President.* New York: Macmillan, 1956.

Smith, Richard Norton. *Thomas E. Dewey and His Times.* New York: Simon & Schuster, 1989, p. 555.

INDEX

Chartwell house, xii, 111,
129–142, 207
Churchill, Clementine
Hozier, 1, 64–65, 93,
189, 206, 211, 248
Churchill, Diana, 98, 130
Churchill, John, 18, 209
Churchill, Lady Randolph
birth of Winston, 17–18
choosing Winston's
schools, 24
death, 98
described, 18, 19, 20, 45
financial status, 20–21
promoting Winston,
44–45, 63
Winston neglected by,
17–18, 20, 25, 26
Churchill, Lord Randolph
birth of Winston, 17–18
career, 7, 19, 26–27, 41, 115
death, 19, 43, 98
described, 18–19
financial status, 20–21
illnesses, 27
social exile, 19, 20
Winston neglected by,
18–19, 20, 22, 25, 26
Churchill, Marigold, 7, 98
Churchill, Mary, 98
Churchill, Randolph, 18, 23,
42, 130, 197, 227
Churchill, Sarah, 83
Churchill, Winston S.
"Antwerp Circus" and,
80–81, 136
birth, 6, 17–18
birthday celebration,
ninetieth, 1–2
"black dog" depressions,
83, 207
Bourke Cockran's influ-
ence on, 63, 64, 120
on British naval power, 62,
75, 77
Cabinet members and,
245, 346
as chancellor of the Exchequer, 115, 116–117, 130
character of, 6, 8, 9, 23, 125,
129, 131, 174, 182, 255
at Chartwell house, xii,
111, 129–142
childhood, 18–21
concentration ability,
42–43, 80
conversation style, 122
Dardanelles disaster and,
7, 81–83, 91, 136, 150
David Lloyd George and,
77, 92, 95, 112

death, 1, 4, 10–16
described, 23, 45, 80, 110,
131–132, 136, 162
disarmament speech, 249
dog companion, 165
drinking habits, 116, 133,
230, 244
education, 7, 21–26, 27,
41–44, 47–48
Eisenhower, friendship
with, xi–xii, 1, 9, 13,
164, 167, 183–184,
187–188, 211, 244, 252
English skills, mastery, 10,
24
father and, 1, 7, 19–20,
62–63
as First Lord of the Admiralty, 75–84, 142,
149–160
friends, types of, 137–138
Fulton speech, 211,
214–215
history knowledge, 11, 25
House of Commons and,
57–66, 129–160, 151
illnesses, 10, 22, 23–24, 97,
176, 177, 242, 247
injuries, 46–47, 130
on the Iron curtain, ix,
215, 235
as journalist during Cuban
rebellion, 45–46
leadership style, 246
on mathematics, 115–116
military service, 44, 59–60
napping habits, 46, 111,
132
NATO supported by,
225–226
Nobel Prize for Literature,
10
"No peace till victory"
speech, 93–94
as orator, 93–94
painting pastime, xiii, 9,
83, 111, 129, 131, 211
as Parliament member,
61–62, 256
peace efforts, 93–97, 217,
227, 242, 247
as pilot, 8, 92, 93
poetry interests, 22
politics and, 44, 91, 109,
117, 196
as Prime Minister,
151–160, 205–206,
249
prophetic gift, 78, 80
as secretary of state for
Munitions, 8, 92

as secretary of state for the
colonies, 95
as secretary of state for
war, 93
sense of purpose and, 41,
42, 48
"Sinews of Peace" speech,
211–212, 213–217
"siren suit," 164
smoking cigars, 46, 109,
132, 167, 213, 244
socialism and, 64, 112,
218, 221, 227
on speaking, 14, 63
speaking tours, 61, 130
sports and, 25, 47
as strategist, 6, 196
theater studies, 22–23, 25
thinking with independ-
ence, 43, 78–79
Union Club speech, 218
on war, 161–162, 196, 242
as war correspondent, 60
as "warmonger," 216, 227
"We shall never surrender"
speech, 153
writing habits, 131–133,
244, 245
Civil rights bill, 220
Clark, Mark, 147, 176
Clausewitz, Carl von, 104
Clinton, Bill, 32–33
Cliveden Group, 141
Cochran, Jacqueline, 231
Cockran, Bourke, 63, 64, 120
Cold War, 219, 224, 227, 235,
236, 240
Collins, Michael, 96
Columbia University, 205,
221–222
Colville, John, 2, 158, 235,
251
Command and General Staff
School, 105
Communism. See also Soviet
Union; Stalin
Alger Hiss as agent of,
199, 224, 233
Churchill and, xiii, 95, 235
Eisenhower and, xiii, 223
Iranian Communist Party,
238–239
Lenin and, 95
Conference center, 222
Conner, Fox, 99, 103–105,
104–105, 120
Conservative Party, 58, 97,
112–113, 115, 117, 206,
228
Constitutionalist Party,
113–115

Torch initiative. *See* North
Africa campaign
Totalitarianism, xiii, 218, 251.
See also Communism
Transcontinental expedition,
99–101
Troop carriers (LSTs), 180,
188
Truman, Harry
on being President, 234
Churchill and, 210,
212–213, 215–216
demands Germany's un-
conditional surrender,
201
Eisenhower and, 208, 219,
223, 234
Fair Deal programs of,
228
impeachment bill against,
228
initiatives of, 229
mother's influence on,
32–33
NATO established by, 224
nuclear secrets and,
216–217
at Potsdam Conference,
205
re-election of, 224
Soviet Union and, 219
Stalin and, 208, 216

U
Union Club speech of
Churchill, 218
United Nations, 172, 186,
212, 251
United Soviet Socialist Re-
public. *See* Soviet
Union

U.S. Declaration of Indepen-
dence, 112
U.S. Economy, 119
United States of Europe,
218–219
Unknown War, The
(Churchill), 130

V
Vaughan, Harry, 212
Victoria, Queen, 4, 22, 62,
156

W
Wallace, Henry, 216
Wall Street Journal, 217
War Department
Bonus Army March dis-
persed by, 122–123
budget cuts in, 119
industrial college in, 120
public sentiment towards,
119, 123
view towards tanks, 103
War Department Building,
161
War Industries Board of
WWI, 120
Warren, Earl, 5
Washington, George, 36
Washington Post, 186
Watner, Hugh, 207
Welsh miners riot, 49
"We shall never surrender"
speech (Churchill), 153
Westminster College,
213–214
West Point, 7, 42, 49–55,
67–68
White, Paul Dudley, 250
Whitney, John Hay, 230–231

Wilhelm II, Kaiser, 77
William and Mary College,
217–218
Willkie, Wendell, 156
Wilson, Charles, 237
Wilson, Woodrow
call for a League of Na-
tions, 93
Carranza supported by,
68
Churchill's opinion of, 95
proclaiming U.S. neutral-
ity in WWI, 54
war on Germany declared
by, 73
Winant, John, 160
Women's Entertainment Protection League, 57
World Crisis (Churchill), 78,
109–110, 130, 134
World War I
armistice, 89
beginning of, 54, 73, 74
bonus stipend of, 122
Dardanelles disaster, 7,
81–83, 91, 136, 150
War Industries Board of,
120
World War II. *See also* Germany; Hitler; *specific
countries*
Armistice Day, 94
beginning of, 142,
149–150
end of, 209
predicting, 119–120, 136
U.S. enters the war, 91,
144

Y
Yalta Conference, 199, 235